SOCIAL PERSPECTIVE

The Missing Element in Mental Health Practice

RICHARD U'REN

Social Perspective

The Missing Element in Mental Health Practice

UNIVERSITY OF TORONTO PRESS
Toronto   Buffalo   London

© University of Toronto Press 2011
Toronto   Buffalo   London
www.utppublishing.com
Printed in Canada

ISBN 978-1-4426-4296-6

Printed on acid-free, 100% post-consumer recycled paper with vegetable-based inks.

Library and Archives Canada Cataloguing in Publication

U'Ren, Richard, 1939–
Social perspective : the missing element in mental health
practice / Richard U'Ren.

Includes bibliographical references and index.
ISBN 978-1-4426-4296-6

1. Social psychiatry – United States.   2. Mental illness – Social aspects – United
States.   3. Mental health – Social aspects – United States.   4. Health – social
aspects – United States.   5. Equality – Health aspects – United States.   I. Title.

RC455.U74 2011   362.2'0420973   C2011-900928-5

University of Toronto Press acknowledges the financial assistance to its
publishing program of the Canada Council for the Arts and the Ontario Arts
Council.

 Canada Council   Conseil des Arts
for the Arts   du Canada

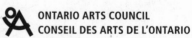 ONTARIO ARTS COUNCIL
CONSEIL DES ARTS DE L'ONTARIO

University of Toronto Press acknowledges the financial support of the
Government of Canada through the Canada Book Fund for its publishing
activities.

In memory of my parents, Harold and Cathryn U'Ren,
With infinite gratitude.
And to my wife, Annette Jolin,
The same.

Contents

Acknowledgments

A number of people read earlier drafts or parts of this book. I would like to thank Marjorie Burns, Stephen Cameron, Sydney Ey, Marc Jolin, Brenda Krishnan, Bentson McFarland, Joel Paris, Jennifer Scott, and Rick Van Rheenen for their help.

Throughout my tenure as a full-time faculty member in the Department of Psychiatry at the Oregon Health and Science University I was fortunate enough to work under three chairs who were supportive of my professional interests. My gratitude to George Saslow, Jim Shore, and Joe Bloom.

I also want to thank several sociologists who, because they write so well, made my incursion into their field easier than it might have been: Alan Horwitz, Leonard Pearlin, James House, John Mirowsky, Catherine Ross, Robert Perrucci, Earl Wysong, Carol Aneshensel, and Peggy Thoits.

Kris Henning helped me with several technical issues while I was writing this book. George Keepers provided publishing support. Terry Sullivan in Toronto helped focus my interest on social perspective by asking me and my son Matthew to contribute an article to a special issue of the *International Journal of Law and Psychiatry* that appeared in 1999. I appreciate the generosity that Joe Matarazzo extended to me early in my career. My thanks to all of them.

I am happy that the University of Toronto Press decided to publish this book, thus continuing for me a rewarding affiliation with Canada that began when I received my medical degree at McGill. Virgil Duff, the executive editor, steered the manuscript through the review process and three anonymous reviewers contributed many helpful comments.

My deepest thanks, however, go to my wife, Annette Jolin, who read the manuscript several times in spite of a very busy personal and professional life. She improved the book immeasurably. Whatever deficiencies remain are not due to her.

SOCIAL PERSPECTIVE

The Missing Element in Mental Health Practice

Introduction

My purpose in writing this book is to show what a social perspective is and how it helps to explain health and well-being, disorder and distress.[1] Clinicians, who are usually equipped with an individual rather than a social perspective on their patients, have been on my mind as I have worked on this manuscript, but I believe that anyone interested in the relationship between society and individual well-being will also learn something from what I have written here.

The perspective I present offers many clinicians an opportunity to understand patients in a way that they may not yet possess. Those who read it will come to think differently about many issues involved in clinical work. My hope is that in providing readers with a social perspective the book will give them a new perspective, one that sensitizes them to the ways that the organization of society affects individuals. The importance of economic and social resources, the power of the stratification system, and the place of social roles in explaining well-being and psychological distress are but three examples of what a social perspective offers. I think, furthermore, that social perspective makes clinical work more interesting. Most of us who read the newspapers, surf the Web, and watch television are aware of the major economic and political issues of the day. These events take on more significance when one knows how to connect them to the lives of concrete individuals by understanding who does and does not benefit from them. The failure to consider the ways that individuals' well-being is affected by the structure of society forces therapists to work with a narrow view of emotional distress and mental disorder and obscures the role that society plays in these conditions.

In spite of its low profile in psychiatry and clinical psychology, social perspective has not been entirely absent in the mental health field. Even in psychiatry, the discipline with which I am most familiar, social perspective made a brief appearance in the 1960s and 1970s in connection with the community psychiatry movement. It was sandwiched between the psychoanalytic perspective that reigned from the thirties to the sixties and the biological perspective that has dominated the field ever since. Social psychiatry in the United States still exists as a viewpoint but no longer as a discrete discipline, according to Bachrach (1993), and has disappeared from the table of contents of most American psychiatric textbooks. It is seen as the conceptual approach that informs community psychiatry, which is the application of the theory and practice of psychiatry to non-traditional settings (Group for the Advancement of Psychiatry, 1983).

Within related mental health specialties, such as clinical psychology, educational and counselling psychology, and social work, there are social perspectives that are known by such names as critical psychology (Fox & Prilleltensky, 1997; Prilleltensky, 1994; Prilleltensky & Nelson, 2002), social justice theory (Finn & Jacobson, 2003; Toporek et al., 2006), liberation psychology (Martin-Baro, 1996), feminist psychology (L. Brown, 1994; Chesler, 1973; Greenspan, 1983), and structural social work (Mullaly, 2007). These contain elements that overlap with the perspective I present here, but none focus as directly on the relationship between social class, mental disorder, and distress.

There are several reasons that, in my view, a social perspective is missing in much of clinical practice. In ascending order of importance: I think, first, that clinicians' own social class position may contribute to it. Many psychiatrists and clinical psychologists as well as physicians belong to the privileged class themselves and so see the world through the lenses of their own experience. Second, boundaries between both academic and professional disciplines are hard to cross. The information necessary to construct a social perspective has been around for years but has never been widely incorporated into clinical practice, at least in psychiatry and clinical psychology, because the information necessary for a social perspective has been generated in non-clinical fields such as sociology, economics, medical sociology, social epidemiology, and social psychology. Even the published material on social perspective that has been written by social workers, counselling and educational psychologists, and clinical psychologists has rarely crossed specialty boundaries.

As important as these two reasons may be, I do not think that either is as important for explaining the neglect of a social perspective as the two to follow. Social perspective has been neglected because it has not been presented, or defined, in a way that is sufficiently useful to clinicians. All clinicians, certainly, are aware of 'social factors' beyond the immediate social context of their patients' lives. Poverty, unemployment, unrewarding work, lack of resources for mentally ill patients, and inadequate reimbursement for mental health care are often mentioned. But any list of these factors is usually idiosyncratic, mainly because clinicians have not been given a way to think about them systematically. The second reason social perspective has been neglected is the current dominance of the biomedical model in psychiatry, a development which has turned the biopsychosocial framework for diagnosis and treatment into a bio-bio-bio model (Sharfstein, 2005). The biomedical model assumes that the cause of disorder lies primarily within the individual as a disordered genetic or neurochemical state and regards large-scale social arrangements and the conditions of living associated with them as largely irrelevant for explaining psychological states.

Any presentation that hopes to show connections between the structures of society and individual problems has to start with the fact that health is correlated with socioeconomic position. Individuals in higher positions enjoy better physical and mental health than individuals in lower positions. And this is not just a matter of rich versus poor. There is a continuum, such that the top group has better health than the one just below it, which in turn has better health than the group under it, and so on down the line. The reason for this gradient in health is the way that resources – knowledge, money, power, status, and social connections – are distributed is society. Availability of these resources shapes the life course by allowing individuals greater choice and direction. It reduces exposure to risk, particularly to the chronic stresses that mark life lower in the social hierarchy, and minimizes the consequences of stress when it occurs. A sense of being in control of one's life promotes health and well-being as do opportunities to participate in society and develop one's abilities. It may be that these psychosocial factors – a sense of control and social participation – are more responsible than material conditions (income, housing) for health and well-being at the upper end of the social scale since material conditions are adequate there for everyone. At the lower end, however, absolute and relative material deprivation contributes substantially to the health gradient, while stress operates along the entire gradient, though more powerfully in combination with other deprivations toward the bottom. Cumulative exposure to stress is the most widely accepted causal explanation for higher rates of mental disorder and distress among those lower in the social hierarchy.

Individuals are inescapably embedded in society in several ways.[2] First, through social roles learned within the institutions of society, most prominently the family and the economic system, as parents, spouses, employers, or employees. All clinicians are aware of this aspect of social perspective, though they might not always think of personal and interpersonal problems in terms of roles. Nevertheless, the stresses and strains of daily life as individuals experience them in their various roles are at the core of clinical work.

However, individuals are embedded in structures and subject to forces that go well beyond themselves, family, and work. They are subject to cultural, social, economic, and political forces mediated primarily though the stratification system, which is the second way that individuals are embedded in society. Stratification ranks people on the basis of class, gender, and race. As a system, it rests on an innate human propensity to categorize individuals on the basis of achieved and acquired traits (Massey, 2007). While the desire to categorize may be innate, the selection of traits that are favourable or unfavourable are products of society and culture. Individuals and groups at the top of the stratification system, the ones with the most power and status, are the ones who most influence the outcomes of categorization. Whites, for example, historically perpetuated stereotypes of blacks as lazy and unintelligent, just as the rich perpetrated the view of poor people as lazy and undisciplined (Massey, 2007). The important thing to know about the stratification system is its capacity to create and maintain social inequalities. The main mechanisms that stratification systems use to achieve this end are various forms of social exclusion, also called 'opportunity hoarding,' 'social closure,' or 'monopolization' (Massey, 2007; Murphy, 1985; Parkin, 1979; Tilly, 1998). These will be explained in the next chapter.

In addition to roles and the stratification system, individuals are also embedded in society as subjects of economic and political circumstances that exist in a given historical period. Economic developments and political decisions affect everyone, but not in the same way. How different individuals and groups are affected for better and for worse are the important issues.

It is an understanding of individuals with respect to their embeddedness in these three ways and how it affects their health and well-being that I call a social perspective.

Within the stratification system, class and race overlap to such a high degree (if one is black or Hispanic, one is also more likely to be in a lower socioeconomic position) that it is often difficult to distinguish between them as causes of inequality; they clearly work together in many cases. Although I do not neglect race and gender in this book, I have chosen to emphasize class. The length of the book is not the major reason for this decision, though it is a consideration. I focus on class, first, because it is a less visible category – it works more subtly and less obviously – than race or gender. It is less often appreciated as a factor in well-being and distress in spite of a large research literature which shows that it is. In a 2004 *New England Journal of Medicine* article, Isaacs and Schroeder argued that class was the 'ignored determinant of the nation's health' (p. 1137).

Also, while many people know that some inequalities between men and women and, to a lesser extent, blacks and whites have lessened over the last forty years, many are not aware that comparable progress has not been made with respect to socioeconomic inequality. Women's wages relative to men's have improved and women are much more likely to be admitted to professional schools than previously; and though blacks still lag substantially behind whites in income and wealth, a black man has been elected president of the United States. Socioeconomic inequality has diminished very little, however. In 1969, for example, the top 20% of wage earners made 43% of the money earned in the United States that year. In 2007, it was almost 50%. In 1969, the bottom 20% of earners garnered 4.1% of the income; forty years later the figure was 3.4% (Michaels, 2009). Michaels (2006, 2009) has pointed out that if we were successful in eliminating the effects of racism and sexism completely, we would still not have made any progress toward economic equality, a topic that will be discussed more thoroughly in chapter 4. Also, with respect to education, the main path to upward social mobility in American society, inequalities are more apparent along socioeconomic lines than along gender and ethnic lines. In one study, for example, 26% of eighth graders who were interviewed in 1988 had earned a bachelor's degree by 2000. Looking at gender, the difference in rates of graduation was small, only four percentage points in favour of females. With ethnicity, the differences were larger. Whites graduated more often than blacks or Hispanics, the difference being fifteen percentage points. But with respect to socioeconomic status, the difference was huge. Fifty percent of students with one parent who had a BA, a proxy for socioeconomic position, had graduated by 2000, while the rate among students who had no parent with a BA was 11%, a difference of thirty-nine percentage points. And in comparing the rates of graduation of students from the highest socioeconomic bracket with the rates of students from the lowest, the gap was even wider – forty-four percentage points (U.S. Department of Education, 2002).

The first chapter of this book contains my definition of what constitutes a social perspective, emphasizing the three elements I have mentioned. All of these elements presume that individuals are parts of larger systems, a point I discuss at some length. The chapter also introduces the concepts that underlie the rest of the book. The second chapter describes the consistent inverse relationship between social class, mental disorders, and psychological distress. In chapter 3, I address the issue of class in America, what it is, and how it works. The extent of the widening income and wealth gap during the past thirty years, its causes, and its consequences related to health and well-being are the topics of chapter 4. Chapter 5 reviews the evidence which shows that psychosocial factors in the workplace, such as control, social support, and a sense of fairness are important for health and well-being. These factors are linked to working conditions and position in the occupational hierarchy, a proxy for social class. The links that connect larger macroeconomic factors to concrete conditions in the workplace, which in turn directly affect health and well-being, are also shown.

In chapter 6, I discuss specifically how elements of socioeconomic position, class, and factors related to them are responsible for health and well-being. This chapter also ties together the preceding chapters. Chapter 7 focuses on the part that mental health professionals and physicians play in converting social issues into individual personal problems and how class differences between therapists and patients can interfere with treatment. Horwitz's and Wakefield's (Horwitz, 2002; Horwitz and Wakefield, 2005; Wakefield, 1992) important work, discussed at length in chapter 8, shows how the symptom-based psychiatric diagnostic system used by all mental health professionals biases them toward regarding most symptoms as evidence of individual psychiatric disorder. This model may be appropriate for serious mental disorders, but these are relatively few and many symptoms, particularly anxiety and depression, might more accurately be regarded as non-specific symptoms of distress often caused by difficult social conditions. A too single-minded focus on symptoms as indicators of disorder sacrifices validity for reliability and contributes to the neglect of social perspective. Chapter 9 shows how a social perspective can be incorporated in the clinical interview and an extended case example illustrates how social perspective can be applied to an individual patient. In chapter 10, I summarize the book and its aims, discuss briefly the role of social perspective in individual treatment, and argue that social action is necessary to address the social inequalities that underlie inequalities of health and well-being.

Chapters 3, 4, and 5 are most likely to be the least familiar to most clinicians since these chapters are taken from the economic and sociological literature. I hope my readers will be patient with them, however, since an appreciation of how society works is crucial for understanding how it affects individuals. Large-scale issues such as how classes maintain themselves, how resources are distributed by economic class, and the role that occupational position plays in explaining the health gradient are rarely part of mental health discourse, but they are important constituents of a social perspective. Over twenty years ago Arthur Kleinman (1986) said, 'Clinicians need models that take the social world as seriously as the biological and psychological worlds' (p. 9).

I have tried to provide such a model in the first part of this book. The literature in various disciplines that links society and health is huge. The sources I have used and referenced here are the ones that I, as a practising clinician, have found most useful for understanding the relationships between society and health.

As if designed to supplement the argument of this book – that larger social arrangements affect health and well-being – the economic recession, which began in December 2007, presents a particularly clear illustration of how damage to a major institution of society, the economy, directly affects people's lives. Foreclosures, tight credit, bankruptcies, lack of jobs, stagnant wages, and – most worrisome of all – high and sustained unemployment rates are the order of the day. All segments of the population are affected by this crisis, but there is no question that those lower in the social hierarchy suffer more than those who are higher. Misery also is distributed by class.

The structural links that connect society with the individual are stable features of our society. Even when the present economic climate improves, the analysis contained in this book will be relevant in showing how our positions in society affect our resources and influence our health.

Few books can be everything to everyone. Some readers, I know, will wish I had given them more specific instructions about when, how, and whether to bring up social perspective in the clinical interview, while others will wish I had offered more guidance to the kinds of social action that a social perspective points toward. I touch briefly on these topics in the last chapter, but my intention in writing this book is different and more focused. I want to provide clinicians with access to information that is relevant to their work but is usually dispersed over different fields. By gathering this information in one place and presenting it as my formulation of a social perspective, I hope to show that this perspective is useful for understanding the connections between society and the individual and that this understanding helps explain health and well-being. If these goals are met, I will consider this effort successful.

1 Social Perspective

Roles, social stratification, and the political-economic structure are three constructs that social scientists use to explore the relationship between individuals and society. They represent the contexts of society that pattern individuals' experiences – and lives – in complex interacting ways. Within this triad, I view the stratification system as the central component of a social perspective and social class as the dominant constituent of the stratification system. Roles are the daily expressions of the stratification system while economic and political circumstances have consequences for groups and individuals depending on their positions in the system of stratification.

Roles

The different roles we play in life are largely a function of our place in the stratification system in terms of class, race, and gender. This is especially true of our occupational roles, but all roles are affected. Our roles structure our interpersonal relationships and are always reciprocal; the role of husband makes no sense without the role of wife, for example. Roles are scripts we learn to follow; they represent social imperatives that embody expectations, privileges, and obligations. Occupants of roles are expected to act in ways consistent with their roles and not others (Sarbin & Allen, 1968). Roles promote predictability and stability. In fact, they make social life possible. Violation of role norms renders interactions unreliable, creating uncertainty, anxiety, and other negative emotions.

Socialization, a large part of which is learning role scripts, begins in the family and continues thereafter. What we call development involves taking on some roles and shedding others in response to the stages and demands of life. The constellation of roles that individuals accumulate at various stages of their lives is the basis of self-identity (Gerth & Mills, 1953).

I emphasize roles because our daily lives are organized around them – as parents, spouses, workers, and friends. Since they are so important for ordering social life, we cannot avoid being heavily invested in them. They are the source of much satisfaction and also much distress. Social roles are enduring, and when there are problems connected with them, these will be enduring also. The major role domains, in which 'the vast bulk of all life events and ongoing difficulties occur' (Thoits, 2006, p. 312), are those that involve school, marriage, parenting, work, friendship, and social participation of various kinds.

The availability of many roles is closely tied to individuals' family class background. The path to a desirable occupational role is highly correlated with educational credentials, and these cost money. Those without credentials usually occupy occupational roles that pay less, have less favourable working conditions, and are more stressful. Frequently these work roles entail manual work which may be appreciated by the privileged class, but these are not the roles they choose for themselves.

I also want to emphasize roles and the chronic strain that can be associated with them because stress research was so dominated by the life event model of stress (Holmes & Rahe, 1967) for much of the last third of the twentieth century. This model highlights one kind of stressor – an acute life event, such as divorce, death, or job loss, enshrined in the clinical interview as the 'precipitating event' – in the onset of distress and disorder. In its original formulation particular attention was paid to acute negative events, but even usually positive events such as marriage were implicated as major sources of stress.

There is no question that acute life events can be stressful, but it is those that are undesired and unexpected that cause distress, not events that are positive and desired (Eckenrode, 1984; Pearlin, 1989). Also, as Aneshensel (1992) notes, 'Life-event change illuminates only one tiny corner of the universe of social stressors' (p. 20). Strain caused by persistent problems of ordinary social life has been neglected. We now have a wider understanding of the causes of stress and know that what look like acute events have often arisen from more chronic role strains, such as divorce that occurs after years of marital problems or job loss after chronic friction at work. Acute events often exert their most disruptive consequences by altering long-lasting and valued roles, such as wife, mother, husband, boss, or breadwinner. Also, the meaning of any acute life change event for individuals is conditioned by the amount and type of chronic role strain already present in their lives (Pearlin, 1989).

The evidence that connects persistent and/or recurrent stressors, arising in the context of 'ordinary people doing ordinary things,' to negative mental and physical health outcomes is substantial (Aneshensel, 1992). Pearlin (1982) has argued that, 'If one were interested only in the more potent sources of stress, one would devote more attention to chronic stress and far less to life events' (p. 377). Chronic stress is not an event but a state or condition that wears on a person emotionally and physiologically (S. Cohen, Janicki-Deverts, & Miller, 2007). Allen Barbour (1995) also cautions:

We make a great mistake . . . if we think exclusively in terms of acute situations. The cause of depression or any kind of emotional illness is often a steady or slowly progressive state unchanged for years: doubts about one's capabilities, a limited sense of self-esteem, guilt about one's past conduct, an unhappy marriage in which one can foresee no possibility of change or escape, [or] a mundane job. (p. 142)

Not all chronic strains are role related. Serious chronic illness has been cited as a strain that cuts across roles (Eckenrode, 1984), and not being able to occupy desirable roles (parent, marital partner) can also be stressful (Wheaton & Montazer, 2010). Nevertheless, in the universe of stress, role-related strains are prominent. Enduring interpersonal difficulties have been found to be a particularly potent source of stress for most people (Avison & Turner, 1988), and it is hard to imagine many of these occurring outside role relationships within the family or at work.[1]

Types of role strain, as set out by Pearlin (1989), include (a) role overload, which results when demands on energy and stamina exceed an individual's capacity; (b) interpersonal conflicts within sets of roles, the most common type of chronic strain, in which conflicts arise between people who interact in complementary roles such as wife–husband or worker–supervisor; (c) inter-role conflict, which involves competing demands among different roles, such as those on a mother and wife; (d) role captivity, which occurs when an individual is forced to play a role such as housewife or retiree unwillingly, without the choice to leave it; (e) role restructuring, in which habitual roles are altered by age or other circumstances. Adult children who reverse roles with their aging parents is an example (Pearlin, 1983, 1989). Strain may also result from (f) role incompatibility, which exists when occupational, educational, or income attainments are inconsistent with each other, for example, a thirty-five-year-old man with a PhD without the prospect of a job in his field who drives a taxi to support his family (Gallagher, 1995) and (g) loss of a major role in any area of life.[2]

Social Stratification and Social Class

Stratification, a phenomenon that occurs in all human societies, refers to the process of ranking individuals and groups in a hierarchical fashion from top to bottom along a continuum of different attributes. In the United States, class, race, and gender are the most widely used stratification categories. Age and marital status are sometimes included in discussions of stratification but will not be the focus of attention here.[3]

Stratification by class, race, and gender results in the unequal distribution of valuable resources. Those at the top of these three stratification categories – upper classes, whites, and males – accrue the greatest benefits via different variants of exclusion (Massey, 2007). Exclusion refers to 'the monopolization by in-group members of access to a resource so as to keep it to themselves' (Massey, 2007, p. 244). In terms of exclusion by gender, admission to Ivy League colleges was until forty years ago limited to males. Medical school admissions committees also discriminated against women before 1970, and even today women are underrepresented among CEOs of large corporations and in the upper ranks of academics. As an example of exclusion by race, slavery is historically the most egregious example, and the process still operates against blacks in the real estate, credit, and labour markets in the United States (Massey, 2006, 2007; Shapiro, Meschede, & Sullivan, 2010).

In terms of class, the privileged are able to hoard educational opportunities (which means excluding others) because they are able to afford the cost of education, particularly at elite colleges and universities. This is not true of families lower on the social hierarchy, for whom admission procedures and fees, tuition, and the burden of borrowing money all serve as obstacles (Massey, 2007).[4] Legacy admissions, in which children of alumni of elite colleges and universities are given preference in the admission process, also represents a form of exclusion for non-legacy applicants. Practically, excluding some allows others to obtain the credentials necessary for the most desirable jobs. Once these jobs have been obtained, their value is protected by credentialing and licensing requirements put in place to obtain them, creating a monopoly or sinecure (Murphy, 1985; Wright, 2009). Credentialing and licensing are also forms of exclusion that perpetuate inequalities.

Another variant of exclusion stems from the ownership of property, meaning capital. In the labour market, the rights that owners and managers of property possess mean that they have exclusive authority, guaranteed by law, to determine how resources – including employees – are used in the production of goods and services. This allows exploitation to take place. In its commonly understood form, exploitation occurs when managers force employees to work overtime or when they withhold their employees' pay. In the economic sense of the word, however, exploitation refers to the practice of employers, backed by the force of law, to appropriate the regularly recurring surplus that results from the costs of production being less than what the products and services can be sold for.

Defining what social class means in the United States has always been, as Perrucci and Wysong (2003) acknowledge, 'a slippery and difficult task' (p. 6). In fact, there are different ways to define and think about class. The differences between them are important, because they each contribute something unique to the concept of social class formation. One of the approaches to thinking about social class stresses individual attributes (Wright, 2009). Individuals are ranked on the basis of different attributes: income, occupation, and education are the usual ones. These attributes are then combined to yield the individual's socioeconomic status (SES) or socioeconomic position (SEP) (Krieger, Williams, & Moss, 1997). Research in this area looks at how individuals acquire the attributes that place them in one class or another, with an emphasis on family background and education. When individuals cluster together on the basis of attributes, these clusters are called classes, the principal ones being upper class, middle class, lower class, and underclass (Wright, 2009).

While the attributes model of class is the one that most Americans are familiar with, it says nothing about the relationship between the classes it creates. Nothing suggests that the interests and aims of one class might differ from those of another class with the result that some people are better off because other people are worse off, that one group benefits at the expense of the other, or that one group has more power because the other has less. In other words, the attributes model (also referred to as the 'stratification model') is not relational. It designates 'distinction without conflict' (Aronowitz, 2003, p. 1).

This deficit is corrected in the social class model (Muntaner, Borrell, & Chung, 2006; Muntaner, Eaton, & Diala, 2000; Wright, 2009). Here, class is defined as a social relationship based on individuals' positions in the economy as either owners/managers or as workers, the two classes in this model. The first group owns and/or controls the labour power of the other group. Conflict between the groups is inherent because the dominance of one class comes at the expense of the other: whenever one class gets more, the other gets less. I will refer to this model from now on as the 'social class proper' model.[5]

A third approach to class focuses on the central role of exclusion. In this model classes are defined by their 'access to and exclusion from certain economic opportunities' (Wright, 2009. p. 104). There are three main classes in this model: capitalists who possess private property rights as owners and managers of the means of production, the middle (or upper middle) class, who owe their positions to mechanisms of exclusion (of others) in the acquisition of education and skills, and the working class, which consists of those who have been excluded from property rights and professional credentials.

Going one step further, Perrucci and Wysong (2003) propose a model of class analysis that they refer to as the 'distributional model' (pp. 8–9). This model builds on certain features of the previous models but is also different from them in that it emphasizes that, these days, the class system is organized around large organizational structures. It is through an affiliation with these structures that the most significant economic and social resources are distributed. Classes in this model are defined as groups of individuals and families who have similar levels of, and similar access to, total resources over time. The secure possession (or lack) of specific resources divides society into two main classes: the privileged class and the new working class. The details of this model will be discussed in chapter 3.[6]

Economic and Political Factors

Further upstream from the individual but no less important in shaping individuals' lives is the third component of social perspective. This consists of the economic and political factors that pertain at any given period of time. These consist of a country's (a) economy, which includes both its *nature*, capitalism in the case of the United States, and its *current state*, as measured by whether it is expanding or contracting, what kinds of jobs it generates, how productive it is, and how the productivity gains are distributed; and (b) its government – democratic in form – but, more important, its specific *social policies* that are relevant to issues such as equality of opportunity, taxes, minimum wage, unions, occupational safety, health, the environment, and education. Political and economic factors interact with social class to determine how and whether an individual is affected by the economic and political circumstances of the day, for better or for worse. When layoffs occur in a contracting economy, for example, those in the privileged class are less likely to be laid off than working-class individuals; and if they are laid off, there is a good chance that they will fare better, at least economically, than those less privileged. A fundamental question in sociology is 'Who benefits?' Asking this question in response to economic and political decisions that shape social policies is part of the social perspective.

Social Perspective

Social perspective confers an understanding of how the stratification system – class in particular – shapes lives and affects health and well-being. It shows how the roles that are determined by the stratification system, in conjunction with the institutions of society (family, schooling, the economy, and so on), shape our daily lives and are responsible for the satisfactions and chronic strains that affect health. It shows how the stratification system confers advantage or disadvantage in the face of economic policies and political decisions. Thinking of individuals' health and well-being in terms of their social class, their roles, and how they are affected by existing economic and political circumstances are the hallmarks of thinking in terms of a social perspective. A depiction of the ways that the individual (IND) is embedded in society is shown in figure 1.1 below.

A social perspective allows us to draw on a range of theoretical and empirical knowledge from other fields, thus enlarging our understanding of situations that a predominantly individual perspective cannot. Putting a common but difficult situation into social perspective terms helps make this point: A young single mother of a small child works as a nurse's aid in a nursing home. She reports depressive symptoms to her primary care physician. Having a low-paying job with difficult working conditions, such as little autonomy and high demands, and being young during a period of high unemployment

Figure 1.1. Ways an individual is embedded in society

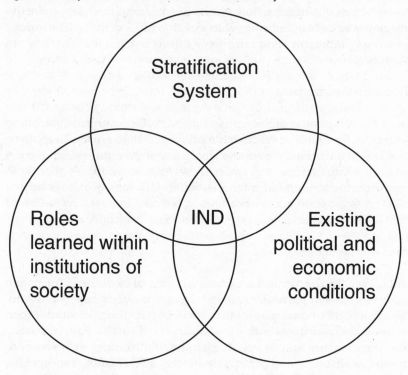

represent conditions of stress linked directly to roles (mother, parent, employee with working conditions known to be associated with depression), the stratification system (particularly lower socioeconomic position but also female gender), and the economic climate (recession, which means that a wage increase is unlikely and another job would be hard to find).

Understanding how society and the individual are connected enlarges our awareness of the causes, complexities, and contexts of health, illness, and distress. It provides a more complete and thus more valid picture of the reasons for individuals' difficulties and the problems they face. Structural contexts such as roles and the stratification system are lasting features of the social landscape that promote order and predictability but also hold people in their places. Understanding this, clinicians may well feel increased empathy for the efforts people make to cope with and improve their circumstances in the face of sometimes formidable structural barriers. Social perspective inevitably points to the importance of social and political action beyond the confines of the consulting room in improving people's lives, but that is not the topic of this book.

Psychological Distress

In the psychiatric diagnostic manual – the *Diagnostic and Statistical Manual of the American Psychiatric Association (DSM)* (2000) – there is no diagnosis of 'distress.' Emotional distress is given more specific names, such as major depressive disorder, dysthymia, panic disorder, generalized anxiety disorder. Although it is true that the same social factors that cause distress also predict the onset of mental illness (George, 2006), I have chosen the terms 'psychological distress,' 'emotional distress,' or just 'distress' in addition, and sometimes in preference, to the discrete categories of mental disorder familiar to clinicians who use the psychiatric diagnostic system. This is not meant to imply that this system is not useful. It is, of course, for purposes of case identification, treatment, and research. But the term 'distress' captures the wide range of psychological and emotional responses to social strains more sensitively than do mental illness diagnoses.[7]

Distress is a broader category than mental disorder. It is also conceptually distinct from it in that anxiety, depression, and somatic symptoms are considered to be non-specific psychobiological forms of distress and not specific disorders (Horwitz, 2002; Kleinman, 1988). Horwitz (2002) observes, 'The psychological consequences of stressful social arrangements are not specific disease entities' (p. 220). When a marriage is not going well, a job is not working out, money is short, or the house is in foreclosure, we feel anxious and depressed; most of us do not come down with what would be considered a psychiatric disorder. In Mirowsky and Ross's (2003b) view, only the more extreme levels of distress, as measured by intensity, frequency, or disability, would be considered mental illness. Mental disorders are categorical names for the extremes of graded traits or symptoms.

Distress is measured by indices, or scales, that characterize symptoms by type, frequency, and severity. It is a continuous measure, meaning that there are degrees of it, from mild to severe, and there is no sharp distinction between those who are under stress and those who are not (Horwitz, 2002). Psychiatric diagnoses, in contrast, are categorical; either one has the condition or one does not. Major depression, for example, is diagnosed when five specific symptoms are present. If only four symptoms are present, the patient does not have major depression. As we shall see in chapter 8, there are probably only a few psychiatric conditions that qualify as genuine disorders, or diseases. Among them are schizophrenia, bipolar disorder, and melancholic or delusional depression. Many of the conditions listed in the *DSM* may well represent forms of distress that have been culturally shaped into socially acceptable styles of expression (Horwitz, 2002), as will be discussed in chapter 8.

Distress is an unpleasant state of mind that is manifested by anxiety, depressive, and somatic symptoms. These symptoms are often combined (Mirowsky & Ross, 2003b). Anxiety is characterized by a feeling of being keyed up, by worry or fearfulness, and can be accompanied by physical symptoms such as sweating, palpitations, or shortness of breath. Depression in its milder forms – perhaps 'demoralization' is a better term – is characterized by insecurity, self-doubt, lack of confidence, a sense of futility, and lack of energy. In its more intense forms, depression is marked by sadness, an inability to enjoy life, pessimism, a feeling that everything is an effort, trouble concentrating and making decisions, and physical symptoms such as poor appetite, weight loss, or trouble sleeping. The opposite of distress is a feeling of well-being. Most people, when questioned, fall somewhere between the extremes (Mirowsky et al., 2000)

An extensive literature documents the relationship between social factors and emotional distress. In order to show what percentage of symptoms can be attributed to socioeconomic advantage or disadvantage, for example, Mirowsky and Ross (2003b) looked at rates of distress, measured by symptoms of depression, in a large group of individuals divided into ten different groups. These groups were ranked from more to less privileged on the basis of several measures of stratification (class, race, gender, and so forth) in addition to measures of social support, trust in other people, and a sense of personal control. Even in the top group the measured level of distress was high. This occurred as a result of more than, strictly speaking, social factors. It happens because 'even in the best of social circumstances people get sick, loved ones die, accidents happen, relationships break, ventures fail, and there are bad weeks' (pp. 257–8). They considered the symptoms in the top 10% as the baseline for symptoms for all the other groups, the number of symptoms each group would have if they were as privileged as the top group. Results showed that the other nine groups had more and more symptoms of distress as the scale of privilege was descended. The authors figured that, of the total number of symptoms in the group as a whole, 37% could be attributed to the normal vicissitudes of life (as experienced by the top tenth percentile), 63% to social factors associated with increasing disadvantage. In the lowest tenth percentile, 85% of symptoms were socially related.

As we shall see in chapter 2, there are well-established patterns of distress related to all elements of the stratification system.

The major components of distress, anxiety and depression, are negative emotions, emotions themselves being defined as 'strong feelings deriving from one's circumstances, mood, or relationships with others' (*New Oxford Dictionary of English*, 1998, p. 604). 'Distress' is a state, albeit unpleasant, that captures an intimate, normal relationship between feelings and difficult circumstances. In contrast, psychiatrists tend to view anxiety and depression as symptoms of one sort of psychiatric disorder or another.

About Aetiology

In emphasizing the value of a social perspective for a more well-rounded view of patients and their problems, I am not implying that biological or psychological factors in the causation of mental disorder (illness) are in any way unimportant. Understanding of disorder has to include consideration of biological predispositions and processes as well as individual psychological and behavioural factors. But thinking in individual terms has rarely been ignored in clinical work. Understanding disorder and distress also involves an awareness of the patient's immediate environment as well as the economic, political, and social factors that structure this environment. We do not know enough about mental illness to confidently leave out any factor. Cooper (1992) comments:

> Neither sociogenetic nor biological theories alone can provide a satisfactory explanation for the observed incidence and distribution of different mental disorders in the population, or for that matter for the forms of their clinical expression. To begin with, it is a truism that the disorders in question comprise a heterogeneous mix of organic, developmental, and psychoreactive conditions, whose causes are complex and interwoven. (p. 596)

I *am* arguing, however, that social factors should be given more attention than they have been. We have a very clear idea of the social causes of non-specific emotional distress and the 'common mental disorders,' mainly anxiety and depression or a combination of both (Fryers et al., 2003). The role of stress in these conditions is well established (Aneshensel, 1999). The place of social factors in the aetiology of serious mental illness is less clear. Horwitz (2002) concludes that social factors do not equally affect all types of mental disorders. The psychotic disorders' lack of variability across time (historically) and space (different countries) is an argument against a primary causative role for social factors in these disorders, he argues. Genetic inheritance and a variety of other factors are thought to play larger aetiological roles in severe mental disorders (Tsuang, Faraone, & Green, 1999), but social factors are widely acknowledged to affect their course and prognosis (George, 2006; Gift et al., 1986; Leff, 2001; Warner, 2004).

Broadly speaking, the two most familiar models of aetiology in clinical work at the moment are the predisposition-stress model and the biopsychosocial model. Advocates of the predisposition-stress model, which is most applicable to the more serious kinds of mental disorder, argue that it results from a combination of genetic and environmental risk factors (Paris, 1999). Complex interactions between these factors result in overt psychopathology, but a certain threshold has to be exceeded before the disorder declares itself. In this view, people do not fall ill from environmental stress unless they are vulnerable, and those who are vulnerable will not fall ill unless they are stressed. If vulnerability to disorder is high, only minimal stress will be required to cause it. If vulnerability is low, high amounts of stress will be necessary. Predispositions, measured as traits, are necessary but not sufficient causes of disorder. Environmental factors, mainly in the form of stressors, that contribute to disorder are usually multiple and cumulative. As Paris (2008) observes, 'Complex genetic dispositions subject to environmental influences' (p. 15) lead to particular traits and disorders. Three different studies by Caspi and colleagues (Caspi et al., 2002; Caspi et al. 2003; Caspi et al., 2007) in which different variants of particular genes interacting with stress, childhood maltreatment, and breastfeeding resulted, respectively, in depression, antisocial behaviour, and increased intelligence have been received enthusiastically by the psychiatric community and have increased support for the predisposition-stress model.[8]

Hawley (1992) stresses the importance of seeing individuals within systems, which he refers to as organizations:

> All evidence points to the fact that there is no individual life – whether it be cell, organ, or organism – apart from an organization. The seemingly intangible character of organization and the obvious substantial quality of the human individual are both misleading. *The separate individual is an analytical fiction* [emphasis added] . . . To view individuals simply as biological organism is to lose sight of the accumulation of behavior patterns they have acquired; to regard persons as independent actors is to reckon without the manifold organizational involvement in which their behavior patterns are embedded. (pp. 4–5)

Hawley's point would not need to be italicized were it not for clinicians' propensity to regard problems in others as individual or interpersonal problems to the relative neglect of the larger social systems to which they belong – to favour explanations that emphasize individual dispositions, traits, and deficits at the expense of contexts and circumstances. The tendency to attribute another person's behaviour to personal traits and predispositions rather than to environmental influences and circumstances was originally described by L. Ross (1977) as the 'fundamental attribution error.'

The biopsychosocial model is not really an aetiologic model. It says nothing specific about how its components interact to produce either well-being or disorder. It is more of an approach to clinical practice and treatment that is meant to remind us that individuals are always parts of different systems: biological, psychological, social (see figure 1.2). In the biopsychosocial model, the biological sphere is represented at levels at or below the person. The psychological dimension is represented at the level of the person, and the social element at levels above the person (excluding the biosphere).

In his discussion of systems theory that underlies his approach, Engel (1980) pointed out that (a) each level of the hierarchy possesses its own distinctive qualities and relationships that require study and explanation specific to it, (b) each system is a component of higher systems; every unit is at the same time both a whole and a part, (c) every system is influenced by the systems of which it is part. This means that no part of the hierarchy can be fully described as a dynamic system without describing the larger systems of which it is an element. Thus, for example,

Figure 1.2. Continuum of natural systems

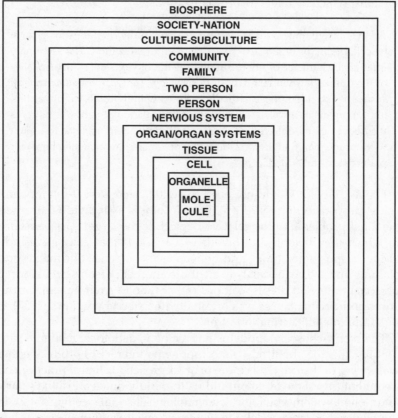

Source: G.L. Engel. (1980, May). The clinical application of the biopsychosocial model. *American Journal of Psychiatry, 137*, p. 537. Reprinted with permission from the *American Journal of Psychiatry* (Copyright 1980). American Psychiatric Association.

The term 'patient' characterizes an individual in terms of a larger social system. Identification of the patient by name, age, sex, marital status, occupation, and residence identifies other *systems* [emphasis added] of which the patient is a component and which in turn are part of his environment. (Engel, 1980, p. 537)

Figure 1.3 shows schematically that different levels of systems, from the biologic to the political and economic, combine over the life course of an individual to affect health and well-being. Factors closer to the

Figure 1.3. The layered, multi-level, longitudinal dimensions of health.

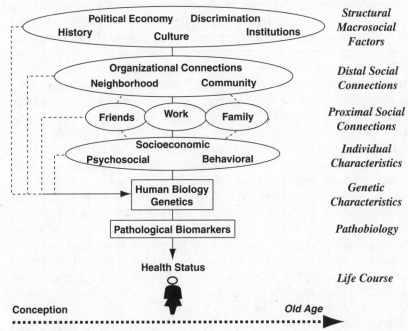

Source: G.A. Kaplan. (2004). What's wrong with social epidemiology, and how can we make it better? *Epidemiologic Reviews, 26*(1), p.127. Reprinted with permission of Oxford University Press.

individual are downstream; political-economic factors are upstream. The figure also suggests that chains of causal factors, rather than just single factors, are implicated in health and well-being. Different levels of organization are sometimes referred to as micro, meso, and macro. In figure 1.3, for example, the micro level would include all levels at and below the level of the individual. The meso level would include proximal and distal social connections, while the macro level would be represented by the structural factors at the top of the diagram.

Physical and Mental Health

The majority of studies looking at the connections between social class and health have concentrated on physical, not mental, health (Isaacs & Schroeder, 2004). This persistent distinction between the physical and mental realms, an inheritance of Cartesianism, is misleading since it treats them as separate. It is virtually impossible, however, to imagine the existence of any serious acute or chronic medical disorder without some degree of mental distress in the form of anxiety and/or depression. There is a high correlation between poor physical health and emotional distress, even for minor physical symptoms (Eckenrode, 1984). Indeed, the list of medical conditions associated with various anxiety disorders is so large as to resemble the table of contents of an internal medicine textbook (Rosenbaum et al., 1997). In addition to distress, even categorical psychiatric diagnoses such as major depression occur in 20%–40% of medically ill patients (Cohen-Cole et al., 1993).

Physical and mental states are tightly linked in several ways (Mirowsky et al., 2000). Circumstances that promote physical well-being promote emotional well-being and vice-versa. Physical and emotional problems interact with each other. Poor physical health is distressing, for example, and chronic distress can foster neglect of health and poor health habits. Good health, by contrast, raises morale. Many symptoms such as fatigue, palpitations, or low mood can occur because of either physical problems or mental strain because the body's central nervous and endocrine systems bridge the physical and mental realms. Thoughts and feelings have physiological links to a wide range of bodily processes. 'Our language distinguishes between physical and mental, but our bodies do not,' Mirowsky and colleagues note (p. 48). Because the physical and mental realms are so intimately connected, perhaps indivisible, I will make reference to both of them throughout the book though the emphasis will be on emotional distress and mental disorder.

In Summary

Class, social roles, and the economic-political milieu are the components of a social perspective. Social class is a main constituent of the stratification system, has a strong reciprocal relationship with roles, and is a major determinant of whether one benefits or suffers from particular economic policies and political decisions. Identifying these contexts helps clinicians understand how health and well-being are related to a person's place in the social hierarchy. Several complementary models of social class are presented, and the mechanisms that perpetuate inequalities in conjunction with the stratification system – variants of exclusion – are described. The decision to use psychological distress instead of mental disorder as an indicator of strain is explained. The vulnerability/stress model of aetiology, as well as the limitations and strengths of the biopsychosocial approach to practice, is discussed; the importance of understanding people not only as individuals but also as parts of systems, especially of the social system, is stressed; and the close link between mental and physical realms is emphasized.

2 Socioeconomic Status, Psychiatric Disorder, and Psychological Distress

Social classes are groups of people who have access to similar resources over time. Inequality is a concept that describes differences in these resources at different levels of the social hierarchy, most commonly in terms of income and wealth. Lower socioeconomic status is correlated with a higher prevalence of almost all medical diseases and conditions (Antonovsky, 1967; Ilsley & Baker, 1991). This link between social status and morbidity and mortality is one of the strongest and most enduring findings in medicine and social science. That there is an association between socioeconomic status and health at every level of the socioeconomic hierarchy – a social gradient for health – is a more recent addition to our knowledge (Adler et al., 1994; Adler & Ostrove, 1999).

Psychiatric Illness and Social Class in New Haven

Just as medical illness is strongly and enduringly related to class position, so is psychological distress and psychiatric disorder. Historically, an influential epidemiologic study of social class and mental illness was Hollingshead and Redlich's *Social Class and Mental Illness*, published in 1958. Hollingshead, a sociologist at Yale, and Redlich, the chair of psychiatry there, introduced their study by observing that their book was about two topics that Americans preferred to avoid: social class and mental illness. Even then, fifty years ago, they noted that the emphasis in psychiatric theory was on biological and psychological mechanisms. They were determined to broaden this perspective (Hollingshead & Redlich, 1958).

With this in mind, they studied *treated* psychiatric patients in the New Haven area. This limited the generalizability of their study but their findings were still revealing. Patients were divided into five socio-economic categories (I the highest, V the lowest) based on their education, occupation, and place of residence. The main findings were (a) an inverse relationship between social class and mental illness, (b) rates of psychotic conditions rose sharply as one went down the social class ladder, (c) prevalence rates for neurotic conditions (principally anxiety and milder forms of depression) were highest in the upper social classes (this finding did not subsequently hold up and represents a shortcoming of Hollingshead and Redlich's methodology), (d) the length and kind of treatment patients received was strongly related to their social class: most of the class I-II patients were treated by private practitioners, who treated very few (10%) of class V patients. Twenty per cent of lowest class patients were treated in state hospitals, while none in the top two classes were. The types of therapy the different classes received was striking also. Almost 50% of class I-II patients received analytic or analytically oriented treatment, while only 5% of class V patients did. Neurotic patients treated by private practitioners received significantly longer therapy sessions than did class V patients. Total length of treatment was also longer for upper-class patients.

Hollingshead and Redlich (1958) ruled out the drift hypothesis (see following) as the explanation for the higher prevalence of psychoses in the lower classes. They showed that many more class V patients were born and raised in New Haven than patients in classes I and II, thus refuting the idea that class V patients were largely transients who had drifted in from elsewhere or were New Haven natives who had drifted into the slums. Also, examining social class of the parents of patients, they found that over 90% of schizophrenic patients remained in the same social class as their parents. They concluded that the excess of psychosis in the lower social classes was the result of life conditions prevalent there, and not because psychotic patients had drifted into a lower social class because of their illness.

Hollingshead and Redlich assumed that social conditions led to mental illness but did not present a theory of how this worked. Whatever the limitations of the study, their achievement was to show that treated mental illness was not distributed randomly in New Haven. It was distributed – and treated – by socioeconomic status. In discussing their study, Hollingshead and Redlich noted that psychiatrists tended to consider only psychological and somatic factors in their evaluations of patients and did not see them as individuals who were part of a larger social system. They believed that psychiatrists needed to understand at least their own local community's social structure in order to diagnose and treat patients effectively (pp. 370–1).

Socioeconomic Status and Psychiatric Illness

Epidemiologic studies show that the commonest mental disorders are drug abuse and dependence (predominantly of and on alcohol), anxiety disorders (mainly phobias), affective disorders (chiefly major depression) and personality disorders (Eaton et al., 2008; Kessler et al., 1994; Regier et al., 1988). Less common are schizophrenia and bipolar disorder. Twenty per cent of Americans report having suffered from one or more of these conditions during 2009 (Substance Abuse and Mental Health Services Administration, 2010).

Many studies have shown that lower socioeconomic status is associated with higher rates of most of these disorders (Bruce, Takeuchi, & Leaf, 1991; Fryers, Melzer, & Jenkins, 2003; Holzer et al., 1986; Kessler et al., 1994; D.C. Leighton et al., 1963).[1] In a review of sixty studies published between 1972 and 1989 that examined the relationship between social class and mental disorder, over 75% of them confirmed an inverse relationship (Ortega & Corzine, 1990). As Eaton (2001) comments, 'The strength and consistency of the relationship is impressive' (p. 179). Higher prevalence – sometimes of all psychiatric disorders together, at other times specific disorders – is found in lower socioeconomic classes, particularly among the poorest (Dohrenwend & Dohrenwend, 1969).

A major review (Fryers et al., 2003) examined the relationship between social class and common mental disorders (CMDs). These disorders represent a higher burden of illness for society than more severe mental illnesses simply because they are much more common than schizophrenia or bipolar disorder, which are more disabling but also rarer. The authors selected nine major large-scale international studies, including the National Comorbidity Survey (NCS) and the Epidemiologic Catchment Area (ECA) programs in the United States, for inclusion in their meta-analysis. The minimum number of individuals included in any of the studies was 3,000, and the total number of subjects in all of the studies combined was close to 100,000. The markers of class position that were used in the review were four: education, income or standard of living (as measured by car or home ownership), employment status, and occupation.

Fryers and his colleagues (2003) found that in eight of the nine studies there was a positive correlation between less privileged class position and a higher prevalence of common mental disorder on at least one marker of social class position. No study contradicted this finding. The most consistent associations between common mental disorder and social class were explained by (a) employment status, with unemployment being consistently associated with common mental disorder, (b) less education, and (c) low income or a low material standard of living. Occupational social class, a category used much more often to identify class position in Great Britain than in the United States, was least consistently associated with a higher rate of common mental disorder. The consistency of the relationship between social class indicators and common mental disorders among large and varied studies that were reviewed argued for a 'considerable robustness for the findings' (p. 236), but the authors cautioned that their review established only strong correlations and not causal direction, that is, common mental disorder may also lead to unemployment or low income.

This same group of investigators (Melzer, Fryers, & Jenkins, 2004) also found that the excess of psychiatric symptoms and common mental disorders inversely related to social class was not confined to a subset of severely disadvantaged people. Just as a social gradient for most medical conditions exists, so does a gradient for mental disorders and psychological distress:

> There is clear evidence that the prevalence of symptoms and disorders increases progressively with [lower] socio-economic status even in the absence of overt poverty or obvious deprivation. Inequality itself, not only deprivation, appears to be important, and this has given rise to explanations in terms of reduced social capital [relative to others], sense of belonging, and control over one's life. The extent of inequality in society may be as important in this context as the existence of a distinctly impoverished sub-group, although the latter should be the first priority for action. (p. 102)

Holzer et al. (1986) showed that alcohol abuse, major depression, and schizophrenia, in particular, were more common among those at the bottom of the social scale – the poor – and that, over the course of the year after the study was begun, individuals below the poverty level were at increased risk for most psychiatric disorders (Bruce et al., 1991). Also individuals with a college education, a common marker of social class, were significantly less likely to have had any psychiatric disorder, compared to those with less education, at any of the three sites examined in the ECA study (Robins et al., 1984). Exceptions to the usual inverse relationship between social class and psychiatric disorders have in the past been thought to be bipolar illness and the eating disorders. This may be true for bipolar disorder. Muntaner et al. (2004) concluded that there was no evidence that lower social class status increased the risk of bipolar disorder. Goodwin and Jamison (2007) reported that most recent epidemiologic data show that bipolar disorder is distributed equally among all social classes and educational levels. Though it is widely assumed that anorexia nervosa is an illness of middle- and upper-class young women, surveys leave the question of class relationship unanswered. Clinical studies show a higher prevalence in upper-class young women, but case register studies, with much larger samples, do not (Russell, 2000).

Higher rates of drug abuse are associated with lower-class status in most studies (Dohrenwend et al., 1992). With respect to alcohol use and abuse, those in higher socioeconomic brackets drink more regularly but those in lower brackets have more bouts of heavy drinking, more episodes of acute intoxication, more hospital admissions, and higher rates of cirrhosis of the liver (Negrete, 2000). Most studies support the inverse relationship between social class and alcoholism, particularly for men (Kohn, Dohrenwend, & Mirotznik, 1998).

Socioeconomic Status and Anxiety Disorders

Many (but not all) studies show an inverse relationship between anxiety and markers of social class. The aforementioned Fryers et al. (2003) meta-analysis found that higher rates of anxiety were associated with markers of lower socioeconomic status, but the specific types of anxiety were not identified in their review.

Panic disorder, agoraphobia, and social phobia each show an association with lower social class with respect to incidence (Eaton, 2001). Prevalence data from the ECA study consistently show that panic disorder, all types of phobias, and generalized anxiety disorder are more common in the lower socioeconomic strata, findings confirmed by the NCS (Muntaner et al., 2004). The evidence is less clear for obsessive-compulsive disorder.

Generalized anxiety disorder is strongly associated with higher numbers of stressful events (Blazer et al., 1988), and since more stressful events occur in lower socioeconomic positions (Eaton, 2001), it would not be surprising to learn that there are higher rates of generalized anxiety among the more disadvantaged. Wittchen et al. (1994) found that all groups with an income of less than $70,000[2] had higher rates of any kind of anxiety disorder, as did all groups with less than a college degree. Eaton (2001) found that 'receiving income from properties, royalties, trusts, and estates was strongly associated with low rates of anxiety disorders' (p. 206), which suggests either that financial security protects against various forms of anxiety or that trusts and estates are markers of other kinds of advantage that also protect. Overall, anxiety disorders as a group are inversely related to socioeconomic position, with the rate being over twice as high for those in the bottom quartile of the socioeconomic ladder as compared to the top quartile.

Depression

Depression occurs in all socioeconomic groups, but here too there is evidence of higher prevalence rates among the lower groups (see Gallo & Matthews, 1999; O'Connell & Mayo, 1988) as well as a social gradient (Stansfeld, Head, Fuhrer, Wardle, & Cattell, 2003). In a report connected with the original Stirling County study, in which the sample population was divided into low, average, and high socioeconomic groups, the prevalence of major depression in each group, using the same order, was 12.4%, 4.5%, and 1.9% (Murphy et al. 1991). In general, individuals with lower education and income levels, both indicators of socioeconomic position, show a higher prevalence of depressive symptoms. Lorant et al. (2003) found that the odds of individuals from lower social strata reporting major depression were 1.8 times that of individuals from higher socioeconomic positions. Most longitudinal studies, Lorant et al. also noted, support a causal direction from socioeconomic position to depression rather than the reverse.

Eaton (2001) reported that individuals whose household income[3] was less than $17,500 (in 1993–4) were sixteen times more likely to meet the criteria for major depressive disorder than those making over $35,000. In the NCS replication survey (Kessler et al., 2003), the most significant demographic factor among subjects with both a history of major depressive disorder and a major depressive episode in the past twelve months was earning an income below the poverty level. This study also showed that higher levels of income above the poverty line were progressively related to lower rates of depression, again illustrating the gradient.

Much of the work implicating social factors, particularly stressful life events, in the causation of depression has been carried out by George Brown and Terrill Harris (1978) at the University of London. In a study of working-class women in south London, Brown and Harris divided the factors predisposing to depression into (a) prolonged stressful circumstances that can cause depression directly and (b) vulnerability (or risk) factors that do not cause depression by themselves but increase the (depressive) effect of other events. Risk factors were caring for young children, having no one to confide in, not working outside the home, and loss of a mother through separation or divorce before the age of eleven. Subsequent work looking at these same variables has been mixed – some studies support the original findings, others not – but lack of a confiding relationship seems to be the risk factor that has held up most consistently (Joyce, 2000). Brown and Harris also found that there were strong associations between stressful life events and depression, between social class and depression, and between stressors and social class.

It has long been noted that adverse life events precede the onset of depression. G.W. Brown (2000) refined the conceptualization of these events and looked at them in terms of whether they caused humiliation, entrapment (being trapped in a punishing situation for a substantial length of time), loss, or danger (threat of future loss). He found that episodes of humiliation and entrapment were more likely to be associated with the onset of depressive symptoms than just loss alone. If events characterized by entrapment were combined with humiliating events, the risk of depression was increased threefold. A similar finding was reported by Kendler et al. (2003) in the United States. Humiliating events are more common in lower socioeconomic strata.

In an important study that simultaneously looked at outcomes both continuously (as depressive symptoms) and categorically (as major depressive disorder), Turner and Lloyd (1999) studied 1,400 residents between the ages of eighteen and fifty-five in metropolitan Toronto. They found that depressive symptoms and major depressive disorder were distributed in the community according to elements of the stratification system – specifically, by age, gender, marital status, and socioeconomic status. The highest levels of depression occurred in the youngest group, aged eighteen to twenty-five. Women reported more depressive symptoms and major depression than men, while unmarried or previously married individuals had more depression than married individuals.

Both depressive symptoms and major depression increased with declining socioeconomic position.

Seeking to understand in more detail what might account for these familiar patterns, the authors looked at six different measures of the stress process that might account for these findings. The measures they selected reflected exposure to acute and chronic stress in addition to social and personal factors that would either buffer or exacerbate it. The six measures were (1) stress exposure to both acute adverse life events and chronic life conditions; (2) perceived levels of social support. The other four measures were personal characteristics, including: (3) sense of personal control or mastery; (4) self-esteem; (5) emotional reliance (dependency); and (6) ability to assert one's autonomy. The goal was to see how much of the variation in depressive symptoms and major depressive disorder could be explained by the stress process operating through the stratification systems (as defined in this study) of age, gender, social class and marital status.

Whether or not stress was important for explaining both depressive symptoms and major depression depended on the stratification system under examination. Stressful events explained only a small amount of the association between *age*, depressive symptoms, and major depressive disorder, for example. Exposure to acute and chronic stress accounted for more of the association between depression and *gender*, with both higher emotional dependence and lower self-esteem also making substantial contributions to the level of depressive symptoms and major depression. Exposure to stress and lack of social support was the combination that differentiated the previously married from the currently married and accounted for almost all of the relationship between *marital status* and depressive symptoms.

It was with respect to socioeconomic status that the stress process was especially important. All of the six measures, both individually and combined, were significantly related to depressive symptoms. For major depression, greater stress exposure and lack of personal control (mastery) were the important factors. For depressive symptoms, lower sense of personal control was the most important component of the stress process. In fact, when only one element of the six included in the stress process was excluded from the analysis (autonomy, an outlier in the sense that increasing levels of autonomy were reported for decreasing levels of social status) and the others combined with socioeconomic status, 100% of those with depressive symptoms and 61% of those with major depression were accounted for.

This study confirmed that society distributes exposure to stressful events and the resources available to cope with them along familiar social stratification lines. Socioeconomic status is the stratification category in which the stress process plays the most prominent role, however. The highest levels of stress and the lowest levels of resources to cope with them are found in the lower socioeconomic strata, which results in the highest levels of depressive symptoms and major depression. In contrast, lower levels of stress and the resources to cope with them (social support, personal control, and better self-esteem) are strongly correlated with higher socioeconomic status and less depression.

Most studies affirm the relationship between lower socioeconomic position and both depressive symptoms and major depression, though the relationship may be gender-specific or depend on the marker of social class used. One study, for example, found that education is related to depressive symptoms only among women, another that lack of income was related only to depressive symptoms in men (Ortega & Corzine, 1990), while other studies have found that lower socioeconomic status is more strongly related to the *persistence* of depressive symptoms and major depression than to their onset (Craig & Van Natta, 1979; Lorant et al., (2003).

Whatever the nuances – and there are many – that exist in the relationship between socioeconomic position and depression, the evidence is very strong that both the core elements of SES (education, income, occupation) and many conditions closely associated with those elements are implicated in depressive states. The associated conditions, to mention just a few, are as varied as parental social position, the work environment, job insecurity, financial dependence, a poor social network, and individual values and beliefs that shape the meaning of stress. This is also true for many other psychiatric conditions.

Suicide

Suicide is not formally classified as a psychiatric disorder, but it is of great concern to all clinicians. It is the leading cause of death among psychiatric patients because of its association with mental disorder. It is widely believed that, among mental disorders, depressive disorders are the strongest predictors of suicidal attempts and deaths. It turns out, however, that depression is the best predictor of suicidal *ideation*, not attempts or completion. Once ideation is established, disorders characterized by anxiety/agitation (anxiety disorder, PTSD) and poor impulse control (conduct and substance abuse disorders) are more predictive of suicide than depression (Nock et al., 2009). Indicators of lower class position such as unemployment, social isolation, and poverty are recognized as risk factors for suicide (Maris, 2002). Suicide is more common among low-income individuals whose lower-status jobs are least secure (Warner, 2004). However, the association between class and completed suicide is not as strong as it is for disorders such as schizophrenia or major depression. It is also a more complicated one, since higher than average suicide rates are seen in at least one high status group, physicians (Lindeman et al., 1996).

Suicide rates for physicians are elevated, anywhere from 1.1 to 2 times the general population. However, suicide is a relatively rare event – 10.7 per 100,000 in the United States per year (Maris, 2002) – and the elevated suicide rate in physicians, themselves a relatively small though privileged group in society, is not large enough to reverse the overall relationship between lower socioeconomic status and suicide. Even though the majority of suicide attempters do not go on to commit suicide, a strong predictor of suicide is a previous history of a suicide attempt. There is substantial evidence that most individuals who attempt suicide are from lower social strata (Lonnqvist, 2000). Some of the best data come from Europe. In Holland and Britain those who attempt suicide have less education, higher levels of unemployment, and more poverty than individuals who have never made an attempt (Kerkhof & Arensman, 2000). 'Suicide attempts seem to reflect the degree of powerlessness and hopelessness of young people with low education, low income, low employment, and difficulties in coping with life stress,' the authors comment (Kerkhof & Arensman, 2000, p. 1043).

Schizophrenia

The literature has consistently documented the inverse relationship between socioeconomic status and schizophrenia (Kohn et al., 1998). Indeed, schizophrenia is so predominantly a lower-class disorder (Hollingshead & Redlich, 1958; Kleinman, 1988) that the gradient for it is steeper than it is for several other mental disorders. The ECA study showed that the prevalence of schizophrenia is almost eight times greater in the lower socioeconomic quartile than in the upper quartile (Holzer et al., 1986).

The controversy has long centred on why. Causation and drift/selection hypotheses have been proposed. The social causation hypothesis maintains that the higher prevalence of schizophrenia in lower social classes is the result of adverse lower-class living conditions acting on vulnerable individuals. The drift/selection hypothesis has two parts. The drift hypothesis holds that the onset of mental disorder affects an individual's ability to hold a job and earn an income so that they drift down the social ladder. The selection hypothesis proposes that premorbid characteristics of individuals with mental disorder prevent them from achieving as high a social class position as do individuals in the general population (Ortega & Corzine, 1990). One of the most widely cited studies of this issue concluded that drift and selection are more important than social causation in the genesis of schizophrenia (Dohrenwend et al., 1992). There is little relationship between schizophrenia and parental SES but 'a gradual onset of subtle educational and occupational disabilities associated with an eventual diagnosis of schizophrenia' (Muntaner et al., 2004, p. 54) causes individuals with this condition to drift down the social hierarchy.[4]

Personality Disorders

Ortega and Corzine (1990), on the basis of their review, concluded that the inverse relationship between social class and psychiatric disorders appears to be strong and consistent for personality disorders. This is true for personality disorder in general (Dohrenwend et al., 1980) and for antisocial personality disorder in particular (Kohn et al., 1998), but the findings are more mixed for other personality disorders. Two studies, using subjects from the Baltimore ECA site, found that histrionic personality was unrelated to education and that compulsive personality was more prevalent in the highest, not the lowest, social stratum (Nestadt et al., 1990; Nestadt et al., 1991). Nestadt et al. (1990) found a trend in the association of borderline personality disorder with less education, but another study showed no relationship between either education by itself or socioeconomic status and borderline personality disorder (Swartz et al., 1990). It would seem that personality disorders that begin early in life would support the drift hypothesis since troublesome traits interfere with educational attainment (Miech et al., 1999).

Socioeconomic Position and the Course of Psychiatric Disorders

Socioeconomic class has a strong effect on the outcome of mental disorder, including schizophrenia. Myers and Bean (1968) followed up the same patient population that Hollingshead and Redlich (1958) had studied over ten years before. They found that social class was related to the outcome of psychiatric treatment as well as to adjustment in the community. Comparing clinic patients (most of whom had neurotic problems) and hospital patients (most of whom had psychoses) by social class, Myers and Bean found that higher social class was related to higher rates of outpatient treatment, lower rates of hospitalization, higher rates of discharge if hospitalized, and fewer readmissions. It was also related to the types of therapy the patients received: psychotherapy versus drug treatment or custodial care. Higher status patients also made significantly better adjustments to the community after hospitalization even when type of disorder was controlled for.

Gift and his co-workers (1986) at the University of Rochester found that three different ratings – by parents' socioeconomic position, by patients' socioeconomic position, and by neighbourhood residence – were significantly associated with improvement among hospitalized psychiatric patients at two-year follow-up. Higher individual social class was related to greater improvement in neurotic (anxiety and depression) symptoms, fewer socially disruptive behaviours, and greater improvement in ratings of illness severity. Higher parental socioeconomic position was associated with greater improvement in psychotic symptoms, while higher residential status was tied to greater improvement in quality of life ratings. Higher socioeconomic position among patients was associated with more improvement regardless of the type of the psychiatric disorder.

Socioeconomic Status and Distress

Emotional distress is strongly correlated with lower socioeconomic status. In their 1990 review, Ortega and Corzine concluded that distress is overwhelmingly more prevalent in lower positions. They also noted that some aspects of socioeconomic status are more closely related to distress than others. For example, lower levels of education predicted distress better than occupational status or income in women, but lack of income was more important for predicting distress in men.

Evidence for the part that roles and elements of the stratification system play in distress comes from the work of Mirowsky and Ross (1989,
2003b). Reviewing a number of community mental health surveys that
looked at emotional distress, they identified six basic patterns of distress in the population of the United States. The first two are directly
related to social class, the remaining four to other aspects of the stratification system.

1 Higher socioeconomic status is consistently associated with lower
   levels of distress. Higher class position, compared to a lower one,
   affords many advantages in terms of education, occupation, income,
   and quality of life. The contribution of the individual components
   (education, occupation, etcetera) that comprise social class make
   to well-being (or distress) is the subject of chapter 6. Overall, the
   resources that individuals in higher social positions command tend
   to protect them against many kinds of chronic strain, particularly
   financial.
2 The greater the number of undesirable changes in a person's life,
   the higher the level of distress. Lower socioeconomic position is
   associated with more acute and chronic stressors (G.W. Brown et al.,
   1975; Eaton & Muntaner, 1999; Warner, 2004). Events over which or
   in which individuals have some control or responsibility are less
   distressing than those over which they have none. Ongoing stressors, however, are more important than discrete negative life events
   as overall causes of distress. Many of the problems that people
   report as discrete events are actually ongoing problems, such as
   serious physical illness, unemployment, trouble with a supervisor,
   or financial problems.
3 Women are more distressed than men. Women are more likely than
   men to have several simultaneously demanding roles as home-
   makers, wives, workers, and caregivers. They experience more
   constraints on employment and advancement, and receive less
   pay, authority, and recognition when they work. The tension they
   feel between family responsibility and employment can be severe.
   A woman's lower earning power is often used as the reason that
   she should assume more of the housework and child care than her
   husband. If one partner or another has to give up employment, it
   is usually the woman's lower-paying job that goes. Mirowsky and
   Ross (2003b) make the telling point that these differences between
   men and women amount to economic and status inequality within

the family. Women experience more distress than men because of these inequalities.

Powerlessness within marriage is an especially potent cause of distress for women. Employment outside the home is the best indicator of the distribution of power in a marital relationship. If the wife has a job, she is more likely to be in a stronger position than a housewife since she has potential resources – economic, social – that equalize the relationship. The greater the amount of income she has relative to her husband, the better is her mental health.

4 Married people are less distressed than unmarried individuals. Those who are widowed, divorced, or separated have higher levels of distress (measured by depressive symptoms) than those who are living with someone. The explanation for less distress among married people lies not in just living with someone. Unmarried individuals, even when they live with someone, have higher levels of distress than married people. Social support may be the explanation. It has been found, generally, that those who are married give each other more support than those who are not (Mirowsky & Ross, 2003b). The quality of the marriage also matters, however, and it is obviously not always the case that marriage is better than living alone. Lack of consideration, caring, and esteem on the part of a marital partner are associated with more distress than living alone. Both married men and women experience the least distress when they share major decisions, but the one who dominates feels less distressed than the one who is subordinate. Shared decision making increases a sense of mutual support and can represent a major benefit of marriage. Married individuals also have higher household incomes than unmarried people. Marriage reduces economic hardship for both men and women. Higher household incomes and lower levels of economic stress among couples partially explain their lower levels of distress. Overall, more emotional support and better economic circumstances account for the fact that married people, when they are getting along, are less distressed than unmarried individuals.

5 Parents with children at home are more distressed than adults not raising children. Children increase distress in a marriage by increasing financial need, by reducing support from one's spouse, by making household inequality worse, and by raising tension between work and family responsibilities. When these strains are not present, however, children can improve the psychological well-being of

parents. Single and divorced mothers are most likely to be distressed by children. It has been estimated that two parents raising a child require over twice the income of a childless couple in order to maintain their standard of living. Many studies have shown that satisfaction with marriage decreases after the birth of the first child and does not return to pre-child levels until the children have left the home (Mirowsky & Ross, 2003b, p. 94). Marital partners spend less time together after the birth of a child, and the time that is spent together is focused on the child. Husbands can feel neglected, as can wives, particularly when husbands distance themselves from the care of the child. Good marriages, characterized by support, care, and equality reduce the strain that children create, but even in good marriages with children the distress levels are greater than they are for childless couples.

6 Distress is associated with age: middle-aged people in the United States are the least distressed of all age groups. The elderly are the least anxious. Reviewing four large-scale surveys between 1990 and 2000 that included over 18,000 randomly selected individuals between the ages of eighteen and ninety-nine, Mirowsky and Ross (2003b) found that the relationship between depressive symptoms and age is curvilinear: depressive symptoms are high in the youngest groups, level off in middle age (ages forty to sixty), and increase again after about sixty years old. Anxiety shows even higher levels in younger people and steadily drops across the age range, so that adults in their seventies report 40% less anxiety than do individuals under thirty. Mirowsky and Ross note that this is one of the rare examples in which patterns of depression and anxiety differ.

It is not hard to explain why depressive symptoms are at their lowest in middle age. People are typically at the height of their powers. Their earnings are as high as they will ever be, they are more likely to be married, their children have left or are about to leave home, their physical health has not declined noticeably, and their sense of personal control over their lives is still high. Beginning about sixty or shortly thereafter, this begins to change. Physical and mental abilities begin to erode at a gradually accelerating rate that results in increasing disability by the seventies. Loss of a spouse becomes more common. Friends die. Social isolation increases. Income declines with retirement, particularly in the case of single women. A sense of control also declines with age so that individuals over eighty feel half the sense of personal control that people in their early forties do (Mirowsky & Ross, 2003b, p. 127). This may well contribute to the rise in depressive symptoms.

In the case of anxiety, different processes are at work. As a group, young adults experience the greatest number of financial problems, a potent cause of anxiety. Though most older individuals see their income shrink after retirement, this does not usually cause distress because they are less likely to have dependent children at home than younger people. Also, savings, home ownership, Medicare, and Social Security offset the reduction in earnings of older people. It may well be that, over the life course, depression is related to factors that reduce levels of control, while anxiety is related to financial stress.

Further Evidence for the Role of Social Factors in Distress

In a paper titled *Social Sources of Emotional Distress* that was published in 1979 and is still relevant, Pearlin and Lieberman selected three roles: occupational (representing socioeconomic status), marital, and parental. They looked at these in conjunction with three kinds of life strain to see what contributions they made to emotional distress, measured by a scale emphasizing symptoms of anxiety and depression. They classified types of life strain according to whether they were (a) unexpected or 'non-normative' events, (b) normative or expected life-cycle transitions, and (c) persistent problems associated with a particular role. An unexpected event under occupation, for example, was being fired or laid off. A normative event associated with occupation was retirement, while a persistent problem associated with occupational role was lack of reward or pressure to work overtime. For marriage, a non-normative event was divorce, a normative event was a remarriage, and persistent problems were disappointment of expectations or non-acceptance on the part of a spouse.

Of twenty-nine different possible stressors that Pearlin and Lieberman (1979) found were connected with the three roles and the three types of strain, ten were particularly important in causing distress. Of the ten, half were occupational. Being fired and being demoted were first and second, followed by feeling dehumanized at work, having to leave a job in order to take up homemaking (for women), and experiencing persistent job pressures, including work overload. Three were related to persistent marital problems: disappointed expectations, lack of reciprocity, and lack of acceptance by a spouse. Two pertained to parenting: the death of a child in particular and the failure of a child to work toward expected life goals. These conditions that resulted in distress were distributed in familiar ways by gender, age, and socioeconomic position. Eight out of the ten stressors were disproportionately concentrated among women. All ten were concentrated by age in the younger population, and those of lower (as opposed to higher) occupational status – a proxy for lower socioeconomic position – reported the highest levels of distress.

Stratification and Mental Disorder

In discussing mental disorders in this chapter, I have emphasized their relationship to socioeconomic position. With regard to distress, I have broadened the discussion to include other elements also, including gender, marital status, and age. *DSM* mental disorders are also distributed by age and gender. In the ECA study, for example, the highest lifetime prevalence of mental disorders occurred by age: younger groups (ages twenty-five to forty-four) had higher rates than older groups. Diagnoses were distributed by gender also: antisocial personality and alcohol abuse and dependence occurred significantly more often among men, while major depression, agoraphobia, and simple phobia were more common among women. There were no gender differences with respect to manic episodes and cognitive impairment. Education was inversely associated with lifetime prevalence of mental disorder. With respect to race, there were few differences in mental disorders between blacks and whites (Robins et al., 1984).

The National Comorbidity Survey (NCS) (Kessler et al., 1994), the second of four major psychiatric epidemiologic investigations in the United States in the last thirty years, showed that rates of almost all mental disorders declined with increasing levels of two markers of socioeconomic position, education and income. Mental disorders were more common in the youngest age group in this study, similar to findings in the ECA. In terms of gender, women did not have a higher rates of psychiatric disorder than men, but they showed higher rates of affective disorders (with the exception of mania, for which there was no sex difference), anxiety disorders, and non-affective psychotic disorders (schizophrenia, delusional disorder, et cetera) while men had higher rates of substance abuse and anti-social personality disorders (Kessler et al., 1994). Obsessive-compulsive disorder and schizophrenia have no particular gender affiliations (Kohn et al., 1998).

In terms of major depressive disorder (MDD), the National Epidemiologic Survey on Alcoholism and Related Conditions (NESARC) study (Hasin et al., 2005) showed that the highest prevalence rates of MDD over both a lifetime and a twelve-month period were distributed by gender (women), ethnicity (higher for Native Americans than for whites, lower in Asians, Hispanics, and blacks as compared to whites), age (strongest risk for ages forty-five to sixty-four, lowest in individuals over sixty-five), marital status (risk significantly increased among widowed, separated, or divorced individuals, risk lower among those married or cohabiting), and income level (lower income associated with greater risk). This structure of major depression is similar to the structure of distress as described earlier. The exception is age, which was higher in the NESARC study. This disparity may represent a cohort effect. The NESARC study was carried out several years after the last study included in Mirowsky and Ross's (2003b) work on distress. Earlier epidemiologic studies of mental disorder showed that major depression was more prevalent in the younger groups (Hasin et al., 2005). As these groups have aged, their depression may have accompanied them, thus accounting for the higher rates of major depression in middle-aged subjects in the NESARC study.

Social Class, Disorder, and Distress

I pointed out in the last chapter that socioeconomic status and social class proper are different ways of looking at class. Socioeconomic status refers to the ranking of an individual from higher to lower on a number of attributes such as education or income whereas social class proper refers to the relationship of power and control between employers and employees in the workplace. Social class proper is associated with psychiatric disorder and distress over and above socioeconomic class indicators (Muntaner, Borrell, & Chung, 2010; Muntaner et al., 1998). Using class (not socioeconomic) indicators such as the power to influence company policy and to supervise employees (characteristic of managers of a company), the power to supervise employees only (called 'non-managerial supervisors'), and no power to do either ('non-managerial workers'), Muntaner and his colleagues

(2003) found that high level managers and supervisors reported the best health, but that low level supervisors had higher rates of anxiety and depression than either upper-level managers, upper-level supervisors, or non-managerial employees. This was explained by the fact that management expected lower-level supervisors to supervise and discipline workers, which then aroused antagonism among employees toward the supervisors, a stressful condition. At the same time, these same supervisors had no say in, and no control over, company policy. As we shall see in chapter 5, this combination of high demands and low control is often implicated in stress at work. A further point is that the socioeconomic model would not have predicted what the social class model showed. The SES model would have predicted that the supervisors would have had less stress than the employees because they had higher incomes. Muntaner et al. (2010) point out the need for other models of how class works besides socioeconomic position if we are to understand better the relationships that exist between the structures of society and the individual. Since most studies that look at the relationship between health and social standing use socioeconomic indicators rather than social class proper, however, those will be my focus when talking about this relationship in the rest of the book.

In Summary

Lower socioeconomic position is related to psychiatric disorder in general, and to overall psychopathology. Specific psychiatric diagnoses vary in the strength of their inverse relationship to class, the link being strongest for schizophrenia and antisocial personality. Socioeconomic position also affects the course of mental disorders.

Distress, a broader measure of emotional suffering than psychiatric disorder, is strongly and directly related to lower socioeconomic position. Distress, like mental disorder, is structured by the social stratification system – not only by social class, but also by sex and age. There is a gradient for distress and for mental disorder, such that the prevalence of each diminishes as SEP improves. The individual constituents of SEP that help explain the relationship between class, disorder, and distress will be left to chapter 6.

Although SEP is the most widely used marker of social position in most studies, it is not the only one. Social class proper is a different concept, and when markers of social-class relations are used in studies of health and well-being, they reveal different patterns of distress than do markers of SEP.

***

In the meantime, there is the matter of society. The two chapters that follow describe the structure and dynamics of American society. They also document the widening inequalities that these dynamics are generating, the reasons why, and some of the consequences for health and well-being.

3 Social Class

Class, however defined, embodies inequalities. This book argues that inequalities of health and well-being are largely reflections of social inequalities. This being the case, it is important to know what our system of inequalities – the class system – looks like, how it works, how it is maintained, who benefits from it, and who does not.

The concept of class has never had much currency in the United States. Historically, class awareness in America has had to struggle against the conviction that, as the Declaration of Independence puts it, 'All men are created equal.' This has been misinterpreted to mean that individuals have the same chances in life. This being so, it follows that what becomes of individuals is largely determined by their own efforts. Those who do best are considered to have something special about them. If everyone begins at the same place, what else can explain differences in outcome? The problem with this notion is that it confuses legal equality with social and economic equality. We are, in principle, equal before the law. But that is all. Socially and economically individuals begin their lives from very different positions (Packer, 2003).

The idea of class and class conflict also did not catch on in the United States because the capitalist system in this country has been successful in delivering the goods and raising the standard of living for most people most of the time. In addition, Americans have been able to tolerate class differences and inequality because they believe that individual effort by the ambitious and motivated can overcome class boundaries (Emmott, 2003).

Whatever the reasons, class is rarely discussed. Sociologists Robert Perrucci and Earl Wysong (2003) point out that the topic suffers from a virtual blackout in the mainstream newspapers and television stations in America. Almost no public forum exists for discussing the nature and consequences of social class (Perrucci & Wysong, 2003, p. 44). Politicians avoid class-based rhetoric because they fear that openly acknowledging differences in interests between the working class and the privileged class would be too divisive. When a mainstream politician does in fact mention class issues, especially when he or she is sympathetic to workers, 'the responses of politicians, pundits, and the mass media tend to be swift, dismissive, and derogatory' (Perrucci & Wysong, 1999, p. 38). Such was the response to Patrick Buchanan in the 1996 Republican presidential primary when he pointed out the huge discrepancies in pay between CEOs and employees and argued that corporations, not workers, were the ones who stood to gain from international trade agreements. Ralph Nader endured similar opprobrium in 2000 when he declared that no substantial differences existed between Democrats and Republicans and that both were in thrall to corporate class interests (Perrucci & Wysong, 1999; 2003).

Nevertheless, the concept of class is important. Class is shorthand for the patterned and unequal distribution of resources in society. This distribution has real consequences for people's lives. It helps explain why some people live in penthouses while others live in basements – or on the streets.

The position an individual occupies in the social hierarchy as an adult is not a random event. The social class of an individual's parents, for example, exercises a strong influence on the child's later class position since it plays a large part in how a child is raised, socialized, and educated. More education generally leads to a better job, more income, and better physical and mental health in adulthood. Virtually all advantages and disadvantages in life are distributed by social class, with those ranking higher having more advantage, those ranking lower having less.

Class influences the amount of respect one gets from others, the quality of one's relationships, the sense of control one exerts over one's life, the amount of security one feels, how likely one is to stay married or not, and the kinds of stressors one is exposed to. Class position is related to the material, social, and emotional resources one possesses when problems do occur. It is associated with the opportunities one has in life, as well as the means to pursue them. It affects how one feels about oneself, how one's children will do in school, what their health will be like, whether or not they will enjoy job security, and what social class they will end up in. No wonder that one's position in the class hierarchy has such an influence on well-being or distress. Alfred Lubrano (2004), a reporter for the *Philadelphia Inquirer*, puts it this way:

> Class is script, map, and guide. It tells us how to talk, how to dress, how to hold ourselves, how to eat, and how to socialize. It affects whom we marry; where we live; the friends we choose; the jobs we have; the vacations we take; the books we read; the movies we see; the restaurants we pick; how we decide to buy houses, carpets, furniture, and cars; where our kids are educated; what we tell our children at the dinner table; whether we even have a dinner table, or a suppertime. In short, class is nearly everything about you. And it dictates what to expect out of life and what the future should be. (p. 5)

Definition of Social Class

Social classes are collections of individuals and families who have similar levels of, and similar access to, scarce and valued resources over time (Perrucci & Wysong, 2003). Barondess (2007) and Carpiano, Link, and Phelan (2008) list money, knowledge, power, prestige, and social connections as the essential resources. Perrucci and Wysong's (2003) list of resources is slightly different. They group resources into four categories which they collectively call 'generative[1] capital': consumption capital (income), investment capital (wealth), skill capital (education and training), and social capital (social connections and networks).

Capital represents the resources individuals use in exchange for what they need and want. Consumption capital is income – wages and salaries, dividends, interest, rent, unemployment compensation, Social Security benefits, or welfare cheques.[2] Investment (or wealth) capital is the capital individuals use to create more capital. With a surplus of consumption capital, one can buy a house, purchase stocks and bonds, earn dividends, and realize capital gains. Wealth represents the total value of financial assets plus durable assets (houses, cars, refrigerators) minus all liabilities such as mortgages and consumer debt. This is known as total net worth. Wealth is a more significant category than income because it tends to be more stable over time and serves to transmit privilege across generations. As one commentator said, 'Lack of income means you don't get by; lack of assets [wealth] means you don't get ahead' (Boshara, 2002, p. 13). Wealth inequality is also much greater than income inequality in the United States. And it is primarily wealth that lies behind power in society.

Skill capital is the knowledge that people accrue through education, training, or work experience, knowledge that is exchanged for money in the labour market. Access to the highest paid jobs associated with high levels of skill is facilitated through credentials awarded by colleges and universities, particularly the elite ones.

Social capital is the fourth form of generative capital in Perrucci and Wysong's model. This is the network of ties that people have to family, friends, and acquaintances, ties that can provide useful information, opportunities, emotional support, and financial assistance. Social capital also refers to the current memberships that individuals hold in social networks that are connected to different levels of organizational power, prestige, and opportunities, ties that can be converted into financial and social advantage. Social capital is connections.

Structure of Class

When and if we think about class in America, we usually think of it as layered like a cake, with each layer representing a different class. There is no universally agreed on number of classes, but most concepts of class include an upper class, a middle class, a working class, and a class composed of the poor. In contrast to the layer cake image, however, Perrucci and Wysong (2003) propose a double diamond diagram of class structure (see figure 3.1). The smaller diamond on top represents the privileged class – the 20% at the top of the hierarchy. The much larger bottom diamond stands for the new working class, the largest part of which the authors call the contingent class, composed of wage earners and the self-employed (Perrucci & Wysong, 2003, pp. 29–30).

The largest segment of the new working class, the contingent class, representing the majority of the working population, is largely composed of wage earners who have modest skills and little job security, mainly because they are vulnerable to being displaced by new production technology and outsourcing. In Perrucci and Wysong's (2003) model, it is not occupation, education, or social status alone that determines class position but *access* to the four kinds of generative capital that represent secure, stable resources over time. Members of the super, managerial, and professional classes have a stable income flow, stable employment, savings, pensions, and insurance. Their resources enable them to further increase their resources and stability over time. The same is not true for the new working class.

Figure 3.1. Class structure in the United States

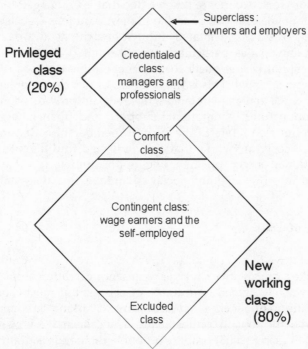

Source: R. Perrucci & E. Wysong. (2003). *The new class society: Goodbye American dream?* (2nd ed.). Lanham, MD: Rowman & Littlefield, p. 29.

Perruci and Wysong (2003) contend that there is no middle class. The double diamond model of class structure, joined by only a small comfort class, is intended to make the point that American society is highly polarized in its distribution of resources. The separation is between the two groups is stark: 'Either you have stable, secure resources over time, or you do not. Either you have a stable job and income, or you do not. Either you have secure health insurance and a pension or you do not' (p. 37). I will return to a discussion of the privileged class later in this chapter.

Table 3.1 shows in detail the class characteristics of each segment within the Perrucci and Wysong's (2003) figure (figure 3.1), including the approximate range of incomes for each. Perrucci and Wysong's double diamond diagram is a graphic way of depicting the shape of

Table 3.1
Characteristics of classes in America

Class	Characteristics	% of population
Superclass	Owners and employers; make living from investments of business ownership; incomes at 6 to 7 figure level lead to substantial consumption and investment capital	1–2
Managers	Mid- and upper-level managers and CEOs of corporations and public organizations; incomes for upper-level CEOs in 7 figure range, rest in 6 figures	13–15
Professionals	Credentialed skill in form of college and professional degrees; use of social capital and organizational ties to advance; incomes from $100K to upper 6 figures	4–5
Comfort class	Nurses, teachers, civil servants, very small business owners, and skilled and union carpenters, machinists, or electricians. Incomes in $35–$50K range but little investment capital	10
Wage earners	Work for wages in clerical and sales jobs, personal services, and transportation; also skilled craft workers, machine operators, and assemblers; often college graduates; incomes $30K and lower	50
Self-employed	Self-employed with no employees; very modest incomes with high risk of failure	3–4
Excluded class	In and out of labour force in variety of unskilled temporary jobs	10–15

Source: R. Perrucci & E. Wysong. (2003). *The new class society: Goodbye American dream?* (2nd ed.). Lanham, MD: Rowman & Littlefield.

the class structure in the United States today, but information about the distribution of income and wealth is usually presented in more tabular form, by percentiles. Perrucci and Wysong acknowledge that 'total annual income of individuals and families provides useful and approximate empirical reference points for identifying class membership' (p. 227).

Table 3.2 shows the distribution of mean household income (in 2009 dollars) across the five quintiles of the population. Note that almost half of all household income goes to the top fifth. The median household income in the United States in 2009 was $49,777 (U.S. Census Bureau, n.d.a.).

Looking at wealth rather than income, table 3.3 shows its distribution in the United States. The distribution of wealth is much more unequal

Table 3.2
Mean household income by quintiles, 2007

Quintile	Dollar amount	Share of aggregate income (%)
Bottom fifth	11,551	3.4
Second fifth	29,442	8.7
Middle fifth	49,968	14.8
Fourth fifth	79,111	23.4
Top fifth	167,971	49.7

Source: U.S. Census Bureau (n.d.b.). *Historical income tables; Households*, Table H-3. Retrieved from http://www.census.gov/hhes/www/income/data/historical/household/index.html.

Table 3.3
Average wealth by household quintile (2004 U.S. dollars)

Segment	Average wealth	Share (%)
Bottom fifth	−11,400	−0.5
Second fifth	14,400	0.7
Middle fifth	81,900	3.8
Fourth fifth	243,600	11.3
Top fifth	1,822,600	84.7

Source: Wolff as cited in L. Mishel, J. Bernstein, & H. Shierholz. (2009). *The state of working America 2008/2009*. Ithaca, NY: ILR Press (of Cornell University Press), 267–68.

than income. The top fifth owns 85% of it, the bottom fifth owes more than it owns. The top 1% owns 33% of the wealth (Mishel, et al., 2005). The figures to remember from the two preceding tables, however, are that the top 20% earns 50% of the income and owns 85% of the wealth.

Basis and Dynamics of Wealth and Power

The top segment of the privileged class is the superclass. These are the owners,[3] executives, employers, and managers who have seven figure salaries, receive even more in stock options, and make substantial income from their investments. They run the manufacturing, financial, and commercial firms and corporations that dominate the American economic landscape. Estimates of the exact size of this group vary from 0.5% to 2% of the population (Domhoff, 1983; Lind, 1995; Perrucci & Wysong, 2003).

Affiliations with large organizations, both financial and non-financial corporations, generally lead to the best jobs in terms of remuneration and benefits. Perrucci and Wysong (2003) emphasize that the considerable resources that these organizations command– disbursed through formal distributional procedures shaped by laws, policies and corporate practices – are the basis for individual and family wealth. What gets distributed through these policies and practices are wages, salaries, interest income, dividends, pension, benefits, tax breaks, educational credentials, and organizational affiliations.

The privileged class's domination of the distributional order insures that the largest share of economic and social resources are transferred to itself. It is the unequal distribution of these resources that is reflected in the American class system.[4]

The larger part of the privileged class – the credentialed segment – consists of executives, supervisors, and managers in mid- and upper-level positions in corporations and public organizations whose education, skills, and organizational ties provide access to the secure resources over time that typify this class. They are joined by credentialed professionals who command low to high six figure earnings. The credentialed class constitutes about 18% of the population.

The superclass, along with help from their credentialed class allies, direct and coordinate the corporate-based power networks that operate in the economic, political, and cultural spheres. They exert control through their dominance of the national economy, government and politics, media and popular culture, and the educational system.[5] Within the economic arena, for example, corporations use globalization and downsizing to maintain their market position and extend its reach. Politics are influenced by corporate lobbyists, think tanks, research groups, and trade associations that advance privileged class interests. These associations employ thousands of credentialed professionals 'to form a dense, reciprocal web, weaving together corporate interests, credentialed class professional skills, and political contacts' (Perrucci & Wysong, 2003, p. 124). Lind (1995) contends that the privileged class (whom he calls the 'white overclass') controls both political parties through its near monopoly of campaign financing: 80% of donations to congressional campaigns come from 1% of the population (Editorial, 2010). Through their control of these power networks, the privileged class agenda is maintained and legitimated, its power, wealth, and security maintained and enhanced. There is no reason to assume that a privileged or white superclass conspiracy exists in order to maintain the status quo of the social structure. The coordinated, mutual interest-supporting activities of this class are integrated in a complex organizational base that is relatively homogenous. Members tend to share similar elite cultural backgrounds, to be high level managers or CEOs of large, interlocked firms, and to be members of a small number of social and cultural organizations. These shared experiences lead to common worldviews, common interests, and common values (Domhoff, 1983; Perrucci & Wysong, 2003), what C. Wright Mills (2000) called 'a coincidence of interest' (p. 276). The system works in their favour, and incentives to change it in significant ways are weak. That they have been successful in maintaining their grip on wealth is indisputable. In 2004, the top 1% owned about the same amount of wealth that they did in 1962, the top 20% slightly more (Mishel et al., 2005; Mishel et al., 2007).

The cultural sphere consists of the media – newspapers, the Web, television, magazines – and the educational system. They influence the distribution of information and education. The media controls how society is perceived by most people. Critiques of corporate power and policies are rare and are unlikely to be found in mainstream media outlets, since they themselves are usually owned by large corporations. In fact, large corporations now own most of the conventional news media they wish to influence and tend to deliver news and information that reinforces privileged class interests (Perrucci & Wysong, 2003). Examples of such messages have included the inevitability of globalization, the advantages of free markets, the importance of labour flexibility. Education, at the primary but especially at the high school levels, reinforces the status quo primarily by excluding any critique of it. In high school, students are rarely exposed to the concept of class, stratification, or the existence of inequality, though (once again) this varies by social class. Some years ago a study by Edgar Litt (1963) found that, compared to students in a working-class school, students in an upper-middle-class school had much more exposure to information in civics education classes that emphasized the role of power, influence, and conflict in the political process. In contrast, students in a working-class school were exposed to textbook material that was considered bland, descriptive (rather than analytic), and that presented politics as essentially harmonious rather than conflictual. More recently, Peter Sacks (2007) has documented, in an indispensable book, the specific ways that high schools reflect and reinforce class differences.

Countervailing forces exist that correspond to, and oppose, the dominant power networks. 'With varying degrees of vigor and with limited resources' (Perrucci & Wysong, 2003, p. 78), the labour unions and other progressive organizations challenge the strategies, policies, and messages of the power networks within the government, the economy, the media, and the schools. Labour unions, even in the face of their decline in recent years, remain key organizations in the alternative class-power network because they possess 'the greatest concentration of human and economic resources available to challenge corporate privileged class interests' (p. 79).[6]

The overall goal of the superclass and its credential allies is to promote the capitalist agenda, to which its fortunes are tied. This agenda is laissez-faire liberalism, which extols individualism, equality of opportunity, free enterprise, competition, and minimal governmental interference with the economy (Domhoff, 1983). When looking after their own interests, however, the privileged class tilts the process by financing causes and individuals it favours, ensures that its own children obtain the kinds of education that will lead to high-status jobs, and argues that differences in educational and occupational achievement are differences in individual abilities rather than differences associated with class advantage.

Class Mobility and Education

Generational privilege is passed along by encouragement, by wealth, and by education. It is no secret that the children of the privileged class go to college at the highest rates and attend the most elite schools, just as their fathers and mothers often did. Almost 75% of Harvard undergraduates come from families in the top quarter of the income distribution; a mere 7% come from those in the bottom quartile (Arenson, 2004). Among the entering class of the 250 most selective colleges and universities in the United States in 2000, 55% came from families in the top quarter of income distribution. Thirty-three per cent came from the middle 50% and 9% from the lowest quarter. In 1985 the comparable figures were 46%, 41%, and 13% (Leonhardt, 2004), a trend that shows that students from the upper end of the social hierarchy are increasingly attending the more prestigious colleges compared to those from the middle and lower ranges. Leonhardt (2004) points out that at the most selective private universities in the country more fathers of freshman are doctors than hourly workers, clergy, farmers, or members of the military combined.

Elite schools facilitate the transmission and guarantee the stability of privilege with their admission policies. Table 3.4 shows the advantage in admission rates at several selective universities that children of alumni enjoy. This educational transmission of privilege enables upper-class children to acquire the social and skill capital that in turn allows them to fill positions of power and influence in American society (Perrucci & Wysong, 2003). It also hinders social mobility for those not so privileged.[7] While higher education can be the route to upward mobility for the working class, it more often works to stabilize it between generations (Zweig, 2000). The sheer size of the privileged class – twenty million households or close to sixty million individuals (out of a population of three hundred million) – means that it has the numbers to fill the top positions in society. Michael Lind (1995) has pointed out that legacy preference in college admissions amounts to the biggest affirmative action program that currently exists in the United States. This disparity in access to elite education represents a powerful opportunity advantage that the privileged class possesses since education has traditionally been the main route to better jobs, higher income, and more wealth.

This educational hegemony on the part of the privileged class is one reason the class structure in America is much more generationally

Table 3.4
University legacy preferences

University	Overall acceptance rate (%)	Legacy acceptance rate (%)
Harvard	11	40
Princeton	11	35
Stanford	13	25
Pennsylvania	21	41
Notre Dame	31	23

Source: D. Golden. (2003a, January 15). Admissions preferences given to alumni children draws fire. *Wall Street Journal*, pp. A1, A2; and (2003b, May 14). For Supreme Court, affirmative action isn't just academics. *Wall Street Journal*, pp. A1, A11.

stable than generally thought. Americans have traditionally believed that social mobility is high, that children will usually do better than parents. A growing awareness that this may no longer be so is realistic. Even before the recession, the dominant tendency was one of inter- and intra-generational stability. Intergenerationally, blue collar fathers tend to have sons who work in blue collar occupations, just as white collar fathers have white collar sons. The United States has a reputation for high social mobility, but compared to other developed nations, Germany and the Scandinavian countries among them, rates of social mobility in the United States are either no different or worse than they are in those countries (Hutton, 2004). The recession and its aftermath are likely to slow mobility even further. Layoffs and a poor job market have either interrupted careers or delayed entry into the labour market for those starting out. These interruptions and delays are very hard to make up for later.

Also, those who are upwardly mobile do not usually penetrate very far into the next level above them (Berger, 1986). Children of poorly educated parents make up just 2% of the managerial and professional classes (Kahlenberg, 2003). Krueger (2002) reported that a child born in the top 20% has a 42% chance of staying there as an adult, and only a 6% chance of falling into the bottom quintile. By contrast, those born in the bottom 20% of families by income have close to a 40% chance of staying there as adults but only a 7% chance of ending up in the top quintile (Krueger, 2002; 'Upper Bound,' 2010).

Class Conflict

As the middle class has continued to shrink even while financial institutions have been bailed out of their bad investments with tax dollars and corporations have posted record profits (Di Leo and Sparshott, 2010), ordinary Americans are aware as never before of the widening gap between the privileged class and themselves. Whether they think of these disparities in terms of class and class conflict is less clear, however.

Class conflict is a result of the unequal distribution of resources. One group accumulates them, the other believes that this is unfair and wants a greater share. Generating profit to accumulate capital is the key dynamic, the prime mover, the raison d'etre of capitalism, which in its simplest definition is the investment of money with the expectation of profit. Profit is used not only to create wealth for the owners, managers, and executives of capital. It is also used for reinvestment purposes to strengthen the company or corporation, thus making it more competitive and more profitable. Unlike any other precapitalist economic system, where wealth is an end in itself, capitalism treats wealth as a means to create more wealth (Heilbroner, 1985).

In the pursuit of profit, owners and managers of capital attempt to achieve a maximum level of production for a minimum outlay of wages and other costs. In their search for ways to reduce the costs of production and increase capital accumulation, they introduce new technology or outsource[8] manufacturing and service work to low-wage countries or to low-wage states without labour unions within the United States. Also, they replace costlier full-time workers with temporary hires, who work for low pay without benefits.

In addition to the control of their employees, the owners and directors of companies and corporations also have control of their own rewards. They are able to allot to themselves a favourable share of wages, pensions, fringe benefits, and share options and consider them necessary costs of production whereas their employees' wages and benefits are viewed as expenses that must be tightly controlled. It is this control over profits that pressures and antagonizes labour and is responsible for the enduring conflict between capital and labour.

Conflict Intensified

The corporate privileged class has waged what amounts to a class war on the new working class during the last thirty years with the goal of increasing the rate of capital accumulation – profit (Altman, 2004). Lind (1995) calls this 'the revolution of the rich.' This revolution is responsible for all of the other causes of inequality – outsourcing, failure to raise the minimum wage, preferential taxation, and so on – that will be discussed in the next chapter.

The revolution occurred because of declining corporate profits in the late sixties, resurgent competition from Japan and Western Europe, and the civil rights acts of the 1960s that fractured the Democratic coalition in the South. In time, after the Republican Party attained power with the help of southerners who had left the Democratic Party because of its anti-racist position, conditions were right for corporate interests to pursue policies designed to reduce or eliminate restrictions on capital accumulation.

A particular target of business interests has always been the social insurance programs that were created during the Depression and extended in the sixties: Social Security, Medicare, Medicaid. Business originally accepted governmental programs when it was in crisis in the thirties. Massey (2007) details the actions that capital has successfully carried out in the past three decades to skew the market in its favour, actions that have widened the gap between the privileged and everyone else and undermined the economic security of most Americans. These actions include lack of enforcement of the rules that prohibit corporate interference with union organizing, failure to raise the minimum wage significantly, reduction of welfare and income transfers, diminished federal employment opportunities (which are a significant source of jobs for poor minorities), making debt more difficult to get out of by tightening of bankruptcy laws that favour business and the credit card industry, and major reductions of taxes on the wealthy and on corporations combined with modest to small reductions for everyone else.

In Summary

Classes exist in America. The main class division is between the privileged class and the new working class. The corporate superclass, the 1% to 2% at the top of the hierarchy, is recruited from the managerial and professional segments of the credentialed class. The class system in the United States is organized around large organizational structures – the economy, politics, the media, and the elite universities – through which four forms of generative capital are distributed.

The two principal classes differ greatly in income, wealth, social ties, educational attainments, and opportunities. The function of credentialed class members in the production process is one of direction and control in their pursuit of capital accumulation. They have control, by law, of what their employees produce. They possess relatively secure incomes, benefits, and pensions. Indeed, secure possession of resources over time is the criterion that distinguishes the two major segments of the class structure in the United States.

The new working class is composed of non-supervisory employees whose incomes, benefits, and pensions are increasingly insecure. Since their functions in the production process are circumscribed by management, their sense of control is often limited. Intergenerational and class mobility exists in the United States but is more limited than many are aware. Both the legacy tradition that prevails in most of the elite universities and the rising costs of education hamper mobility for those who would most benefit from it. Exclusion in its various forms is the mechanism by which the privileged class maintains its advantage over the working class.

In the last thirty years, the privileged class has extended its advantages in significant ways. The next chapter will show to what extent. Explanations for widening inequalities will also be discussed. Since health and well-being reflect the distribution of resources in society, the developments described here would be expected to have implications for health. These are described at the end of chapter 4.

4 Growing Inequality: Causes and Consequences

For almost thirty years after the Second World War, economic inequality in the United States declined, largely as a result of legislation enacted during the New Deal of the 1930s. During the war and particularly after it, all segments of the population experienced roughly equivalent gains in income, which were substantial. In the period between 1947 and 1973 family income rose 104% (Mishel et al., 2003). During this period America looked as if it were on its way to truly becoming a middle-class society. This changed in the 1970s, however, and America became much more polarized, economically and socially. Large corporations, which drive the economy, have been criticized for this turn, and a great deal of it is warranted. But not all. The years after World War II were, as Scheiber (2008) points out, a historical anomaly. American corporations had no competition from overseas. They were able to meet the demands of labour with wage and benefit increases. But with the resurgence of competition from overseas in the 1970s, profit margins in the United States declined and workers' wages were squeezed. Demands from Wall Street to show a steady growth of profit further pressured corporations to curtail labour costs and benefits.

In any case, the trend toward greater income equality that was so prominent after the war began to wane in the seventies. With it, for the majority of workers, came the age of insecurity (Elliot & Atkinson, 1999).

During the last quarter century a number of significant changes have affected the American working class for the worse. Wages have risen much more slowly than they did in the years after the war and, for many, wages have stagnated, benefits have been cut back, concessions by labour have risen, Americans are working harder and longer

(Schor, 1991) under more stressful conditions (Head, 2003; Linsky, Bachman, & Straus,1995; Northwestern National, 1991; O'Toole & Lawler, 2006),[1] job insecurity has increased and the unemployment rate more than doubled between January 2007 and October 2010 (U.S. Department of Labor, 2010). Wage stagnation, particularly for men, has been a prominent feature of the economic scene during this period. A male worker at the fiftieth percentile in income actually made a few cents less per hour in 2007 than he did in 1973. In contrast, women saw their wages increase by almost a quarter during that same period, but they started from a much lower baseline (Mishel et al., 2009).

Workers with less education, who cluster in the lower economic rungs, suffered disproportionate wage losses during this time. Between 1973 and 2007, for example, high school dropouts saw their hourly wage drop by over two dollars. High school graduates watched their wages fall forty cents during the same period while college graduates experienced a four dollar hourly increase (Mishel et al., 2009). This period also witnessed a substantial decline in benefits. Employer-provided pensions were replaced by pension plans without employer contribution ('The End of the Company Pension,' 1999). Health care costs were steadily shifted from employers to employees. Unemployment insurance now covers only a third of American workers (Reich, 1998). Paid sick and vacation leave provisions have also been reduced (Greenhouse, 2008; 'Work Rises,' 1992).

The Wealthy

While all this occurred, the upper tiers of wage earners did very well. Between 1979 and 2007, wages for workers in the eightieth percentile increased 17%. From 1979 to 2006, wages and salaries for the top 1% rose 144%, for the top one tenth of a per cent, 324% (Mishel et al., 2009). In 2007 the top 1% of households controlled over 23% of the income (the figure was less than 10% in the 1970s) (Reich, 2010) and owned almost 35% of the wealth, wealth being a better indicator of economic strength and opportunity than yearly income (Domhoff, 2010). This increasing concentration of wealth at the top end has led several commentators (Hacker and Pierson, 2010; Krugman, 2007; Phillips, 2002) to argue that the real class divide in America is not between the top 20% and the rest, as Perrucci and Wysong (2003) argue, but between the top 1% (and up) and the bottom 99%.[2]

These income figures for top earners are impressive enough, but they gain significance when compared with statistics that show how modestly most Americans live. Between 1979 and 2007, workers at the fiftieth percentile of earnings saw their wages increase by only 8% (Mishel et al., 2009). The median hourly wage among full-time workers in the U.S. in 2009 was $15.95 (U.S. Department of Labor, 2009). Median net worth of all households in the United States in 2004, the most recent figure available according to the Economic Policy Institute (Mishel et al., 2009) was $77,900, including home equity. The bottom 30% of Americans in income, a total of 100 million people, have a total net worth of $10,000 or less (Kuttner, 2007). Slightly over a quarter of the total workforce earns poverty-level wages, which in 2007 dollars was $8.04 per hour and below (Mishel et al., 2009). In 2008, the average amount an individual held in a 401(k) account was $12,655 (Hacker and Pierson, 2010). These discrepancies in income and wealth, which are of course much greater if the rich are compared to the poor instead of just those in the middle, have made America the most economically unequal of all industrial nations, well ahead of the runner-up, Great Britain (Bradsher, 1995a; Phillips, 2002).

The Poor

Looking at the opposite end of the income scale, at poverty, the statistics here are as startling as the statistics about the rich. Many of them are summarized in Mark Rank's (2004) important *One Nation, Underprivileged*. The current poverty rate is 13.2%, or 39.8 million people out of a total population of 300 million. For a family of four, the poverty line in 2008–9 was $22,050 and below; for a single individual it was $10,830 and below (DeNavas-Walt et al., 2009; U.S. Department of Health, 2009). Another 6% of Americans live in near-poverty, defined as 1.5 times the poverty rate, which amounted to an annual gross income of $33,075 for a family of four in 2008. Thus the total of Americans living in poverty or near-poverty is around 57 million. However, the situation is more dire than it sounds, since 40% of people living below the poverty level live in households where the annual income is less than *half* of the official poverty level (Rank, 2004). More than a third of the poor are children, which is alarming since it means that rapid physical and mental development takes place under conditions of deprivation. Women who are heads of households with children under 18 are particularly likely to live in poverty (Rank, 2004, p. 32).

Poverty rates in the United States are significantly higher than in many developed countries. Defining poverty relatively, as the percentage of people living below half the median income in each country, the poverty rate earlier in the decade in the United States was 17.8%, with Italy next at 13.9%. The average of all seventeen countries was close to 9%. If poverty is defined absolutely, in terms of U.S. income criteria, America ranks third in poverty, behind Australia and the United Kingdom. As Rank (2004) emphasizes, the United States is the wealthiest nation in the world, with the exception of Luxembourg, as measured by per capita GNP, yet it has the highest relative rates of poverty and close to the highest rates of absolute poverty among developed countries. Poverty is also the most persistent in the United States, meaning that it contains a higher share of people who are in poverty for a three-year period (Mishel et al. 2005). It has the highest rates of permanent poverty, 15%, compared to other OECD countries, and the lowest rates of movement out of poverty.

Poverty rates in the United States are lower now than they were in the past, however. In 1880, for example, the poverty rate was 47%. In 1935, during the depression, it was 45%. As recently as 1955 the poverty rate was 26%, and it was only in 1973 that it dropped down to a level – 11% – comparable to rates today (Beeghley, 2005). Much of this improvement occurred because of policy decisions that improved the economic situation of those over the age of sixty-five. Social Security payments were increased and indexed to inflation in the 1960s and 1970s. Medicare was introduced in 1965 and the Supplementary Security Income program in 1974. These measures had the effect of reducing poverty rates among the elderly from 35% in 1959 to 10% today. Without Social Security, the poverty rate today among older people would be over 33% (Kuttner, 2007). Other facts about poverty in America (Rank, 2004) include:

- average amount of time a household is below the poverty line: one to two years
- chance that a household that has fallen below the poverty level once will do so again: 80%
- percentage of the poor who will spend five or more years below the poverty line: 51%
- percentage of Americans who will spend at least five years in poverty: 30%
- most common immediate causes of poverty: reduction in or loss of work, divorce/separation, ill-health

The cumulative chance of an individual spending at least one year in poverty in the United States increases with age so that the rate reaches an amazing 58.5% at age seventy-five (Rank, 2004). This figure at first seems high. Typically, one learns that closer to a third of Americans will be in poverty at some time in their lives, but the study that reported that figure followed individuals only over a thirteen-year period (Blank, 1997). Rank's figure, by the way, does not include poor college students. He has said that even excluding everyone under the age of twenty-five, the chance of experiencing poverty by age seventy-five is still close to 50% (Hacker, 2006).

Education, race, and gender affect the long-term course of poverty. Lack of education (education being a proxy for socioeconomic position) plays an increasingly large role as a risk factor for poverty over time. By age thirty, a third of those with less than twelve years of education will have experienced at least a year of poverty compared with a quarter of those with more than twelve years of schooling. At age seventy-five, three-quarters of those with less than twelve years of education will have been in poverty for at least a year during their lives. By the same age, 48% of those with more than twelve years of education will have dropped below the poverty line (Rank, 2004).

The relationship between race and poverty is the most striking. At the age of twenty, 30% of black Americans have experienced at least a year of poverty and by age seventy-five, the figure is 91%. The comparable figure for white Americans at the same age is 53%.

The effect of gender on poverty, in contrast to race and education, is small. By age forty, slightly more than a third of women and about the same number of men will have experienced poverty. At age seventy-five, the percentages for women and men are 59% and 55.5% respectively. The reason for this is that both men and women spend 70% of their time married between the ages of twenty and fifty-nine. Marriage blunts the impact that female gender alone exerts on financial vulnerability. Other risk factors for poverty include age (younger, particularly with children), marital status (single female head of a household with children under eighteen), place of residence (the South, in central cities, and in rural areas), physical or mental disability, and other demographic characteristics such as having a child outside of marriage at an early age and coming from a family with many children.

These factors represent the individual and family dimensions to poverty and, as Rank says, are important in identifying the attributes of those who have lost the economic race. What this fails to explain, however, is why there have to be economic losers in the first place. For that, a consideration of socioeconomic factors is required.

Rank (2004) illustrates his point with the analogy of the game of musical chairs. Imagine there are eight chairs and ten players. If you focus on individual winners and losers, it is apparent that luck (where you are when the music stops) and individual characteristics (speed, agility, even the strength to bump someone out) are important. This is analogous to the way we usually view poverty. In looking at why people are impoverished, we emphasize the deficits that increase their risks of becoming poor: their lack of education, training, and skills. What this perspective ignores is that no matter what characteristics an individual possesses, there will always be two losers no matter what. The game is organized to ensure that outcome.

The American economy is organized like musical chairs, Rank argues. The labour market does not provide enough decent-paying jobs to support the number of families who need them. And with the advent of the Great Recession, it is not providing enough jobs, period. In May 2010, for example, there were 4.7 job seekers for every job. Before the recession began, in 2007, the ratio was 1.5 to one (Shierholz, 2010). The long-term increase of low paying jobs and the shorter term loss of jobs in general means that there are fewer jobs available, even while the workforce is growing. Thus, there will be losers no matter what.

Low wages would have less impact in the United States if social benefits were more generous. In most western European countries and Canada unemployment benefits are more liberal. In addition, health care is state sponsored and child care is more widely available. As a result of these provisions, these countries have managed to reduce poverty (defined as less than 50% of the median household income) by anywhere from 66% (the United Kingdom and Canada) to 92% (Sweden). The comparable figure for the United States is 38%. In Rank's view, this is a failure that has nothing to do with the individual. In fact, by focusing on the individual characteristics of the poor we overlook the fact that government can do a great deal to reduce levels of poverty in society.

Robert Sapolsky (2004) points out that the best example of chronic stress is poverty. It is often physically stressful, since most low-end, low-paying jobs involve manual labour and a higher risk of work-related accidents. Low wages also entail a need to work more than one job with resulting chronic sleep deprivation. Psychological stress is high, too, with lack of control on the job, lack of predictability about employment and income, and tedious work (when it can be obtained), characteristic of jobs that the poor are forced to accept. Coping with life's problems is also diminished because of lack of resources. 'Growing strong from adversity is mostly a luxury for those who are better off' (p. 365), Sapolsky comments. Chronic activation of the stress-response system, a risk factor for many illnesses, is consistently associated with lower socioeconomic status, which is perhaps the reason that 'poverty itself is the biggest health risk in all of medicine' (p. 366).

Poverty has mental health consequences. J.W. Lynch, Kaplan, and Shema (1997) showed that individuals who saw their yearly income fall to below twice the poverty level anywhere from once to three times between 1965 and 1983 (and were followed up in 1994) had a significantly higher prevalence of major depression and depressive symptoms than a group that had experienced no such decline. The study demonstrated a strong and consistent graded association between economic hardship and depression such that groups with the longest periods of economic hardship had the highest level of depressive symptoms. These declines were by no means uncommon. About a third of people between the ages of forty-five and sixty-five years experienced income reductions of at least 50% or more at least once in an eleven-year period. This volatility in income is a reflection of less stable jobs, which cluster at the lower end of the socioeconomic ladder.

The Middle Class

Income growth for the middle quintile of families in the United States rose 12% between 1973 and 2000. This extremely modest improvement is dwarfed by the earnings of the top 20%, whose earnings increased 70% during that time and the top 1%, who watched theirs rise by over 140% (Mishel et al, 2007, 2009). If the middle class is defined more broadly, not just by the middle quintile but by all those who earn between half and twice the median family income per year ($61,355), it is shrinking. This segment represented 71% of the population in 1979 but only 61% in 2002. (Mishel et al., 2005). Income that previously belonged to the middle class has been redistributed upward. Furthermore, the increase in income for the middle quintile was a result of wives entering the workforce and people working longer hours, not because of a significant increase in wages (Ip, 2004). Close to 60% of families now have two wage earners (R. H. Frank, 2007), as compared to 45% in 1973 (Mishel et al., 2007). Both men and women are working longer hours than in the mid-1970s: women two hundred hours more each year, men one hundred hours more.

These modest income gains for all but the top 20% present a problem because the cost of living for so many goods and services has risen in recent years. The price of being middle class has outpaced wages. The costs of both education and health care have consistently been higher each year since 1975 than the rate of growth in median family income (Madrick, 2003).[3] In their book, *The Two Income Trap*, Warren and Tyagi (2003) argue that families increasingly feel pressured to spend more of their income on houses in safe neighbourhoods with good schools. The growth of demand relative to supply in the housing market created a bidding war that drove prices of housing to unprecedented levels until the housing bubble burst, even while other costs continued to rise. For example, the costs of a mortgage are up 76% from a generation ago; health insurance has increased 74%; transportation costs have risen 52%; child care, which was negligible thirty years ago, now costs the average family with two children over one thousand dollars a month; and taxes are 25% higher than they were in 1972, largely because two family incomes (instead of one) are now taxable (Warren, 2007).

Besides sending more women into the work force and working more, American families have managed to keep up their standard of living by borrowing. Families reduced their savings to the point that aggregate savings rates were actually negative in 2005, and the number of bankruptcies soared after 1980 (Warren, 2007). R.H. Frank (2007) points out that commuting time to work, itself a risk factor for poor health, has increased dramatically because of rising house prices in many communities, which requires people to move further from their workplace. There is also more sleep deprivation because of longer work hours and commutes. Finally, middle-class families are less willing to pay for public services when they feel strapped themselves. Public school teachers earn relatively less now than they did in 1962, while half the roads and a third of the bridges in the country urgently need repair. As Madrick (2003) says, 'Typical families cannot afford the high-quality education, health care, and neighborhoods required to be middle-class today' (p. C2). This is a source of strain for middle-class families, not only because it engenders feelings of failure at not being able to live up to the American Dream. It also engenders anxiety in them about their children's ability to remain in the middle class (Ehrenreich, 1989).

Causes of Inequality

Capitalism

In the Marxist view, the capitalist economic system itself is responsible for creating inequality through exploitation. Owners and executives of all profit-making companies claim the entire output of production, both products and profits, for themselves. Employees receive wages, of course, but it is understood, by tradition and practice, that employers pocket the profits, that is, the net gain between production costs and the market value of the product, creating inequality in its wake. As a rationale for this arrangement, a small business owner said to me, 'My employees don't share in profits because they haven't invested anything except their time and labor.' Unlike him, his employees did not invest, and risk, their money.

The extent of inequality that results is a function of how high or low labour costs and prices are. The lower the labour costs and the higher the prices, the greater the profit and the greater the inequality. But as Murphy (1985) and Massey (2007) point out, extra-market mechanisms are at work as well. Discrimination and exclusion on the basis of the stratification system, which, for example, lower the cost of labour, serve to exacerbate the inequalities created by the capitalist economic system itself.

Technology

Technology and trade are often cited as major causes of increasing inequality.[4] The role of technology in widening inequality is the most visible yet probably the least important cause. It has plausibility, however, because its effects are visible: telephone operators, bank clerks, and secretaries who have disappeared come immediately to mind. Technology inevitably causes inequality, the argument goes, because those with the requisite skills and education necessary to master the new machines and computers are rewarded with higher pay since they bring increased efficiency to production. Technological advances increase the productivity and pay of those who are educated enough to take advantage of them. Those without such skills watch their wages drop or their jobs disappear because they are, in effect, technologically obsolete. The fact that those with the most education have fared best in wage earnings while those with the least have fared worst in the past thirty years is used in support of this argument. Additionally, it has been shown that earnings are higher for workers who use computers, and industries that make intensive use of technology have high productivity growth and employ more highly skilled workers (Freeman, 2007).

Some thoughtful arguments have been marshalled against technology as a *major* cause of wage inequality, however. David Gordon (1996) for example, pointed out that even skilled workers' wages remained stagnant throughout much of the 1990s and that the argument that the most common form of technology, computerization, was responsible for the displacement of lower-skilled workers did not match the timing: computerization was not prevalent until the mid-1980s but the greatest number of low-skilled employees in the manufacturing sector were laid off before 1983.

Mishel et al. (2005) support Gordon's (1996) conclusion that technology has not had a significant effect on the wage structure. They point out that technological changes have demanded more workforce skill and education throughout the entire twentieth century and therefore do not explain why wage inequality began to grow so markedly only in the past thirty years. To my mind, the most convincing argument against technology as a major cause of income inequality is that other developed countries now use the same computer-based technologies that the United States does and inequality has not increased to nearly the same extent. Also, Krugman (2007) points out that, while the benefits of education have risen, even the well-educated have seen their wage gains lag behind productivity. The median college-educated man has seen his income rise by only 17% since 1973. This has occurred, Krugman says, 'because the big gains in income have gone not to a broad group of well-paid workers but to a narrow group of extremely well-paid people' (p. 136). Krugman argues that this fact – even highly educated Americans have not seen their wages rise very appreciably – undermines the case for skill-based technological change as an explanation for income inequality.

Globalization

A second cause of inequality, and perhaps the most publicized, is globalization, best defined as the increased speed, frequency, and magnitude of access to national markets by non-national competitors (C. Wolf, 2000). Although globalization is associated with such practices as deregulation, privatization, reduction of social spending (to promote fiscal responsibility), and the free flow of information and capital across national boundaries (Hodgson, 2004), it is really the spread of American-style capitalism to countries around the world that had previously isolated themselves from it (Emmott, 2003).

The goal of corporations is, of course, a profitable return on investment. A major aim in pursuit of that goal is to eliminate restrictions on private capital investment, domestically and internationally. This is the justification for the deregulation of industries and the financial market that has marked the past thirty years. Whatever increases the cost of doing business, including environmental regulations, labour laws, safety standards, and taxes, are constant targets for modification or elimination. Modern corporations plan their global operations with many considerations in mind, including the quality of the work force. They also look at where the cheapest labour costs are, where taxes are lowest, and where environmental regulations are least restrictive. They look at where financing is cheapest, where subsidies are highest, in which country or state it is most advantageous to declare profits and expenses, and which markets are the most lucrative and the easiest to penetrate.

In the context of globalization, corporations in the United States put downward pressure on wages (and thereby widen income inequality) in several ways. Trading with developing countries such as China or Indonesia keeps wages low in the United States because consumers here buy low-priced imports made in those countries instead of buying higher-priced goods made by low-wage Americans. This reduces the demand for American labour and keeps wages low. The wage gap is increased when American companies sell high-tech goods and services to other countries, thus increasing the demand (and pay) for the higher-skilled – as opposed to low-skilled – American workers who produce them. The third, and more controversial, way that businesses keep wages low is by moving operations to lower-cost regions of the United States, to Mexico, to China, Indonesia, or India. Manufacturing jobs, which have traditionally provided the most generous wages and benefits, largely because of high rates of unionization, have declined substantially since the 1980s, when competition from imports first became intense. In 1998, for example, 18.8 million individuals, out of 126 million at work, held manufacturing jobs, whereas in 1973 there were 20.2 million individuals working in manufacturing out of a much smaller workforce of 77 million people (Friedman, 1998), a decline of 11%. Between 1979 and 1993, many thousands of jobs in steel, in textile manufacturing, and in electronics were lost (Gordon, 1996), a trend that has only accelerated. From 2000 to 2005, for example, slightly over three million manufacturing jobs were lost. Corporations in all industrialized countries have moved some of their production to low-wage countries, but the United States has been foremost (Lind, 1995). Manufacturing plants situated in free-trade zones just over the U.S. border in Mexico, have been set up by General Electric, Ford, General Motors, RCA, and Westinghouse, among others. Six hundred twenty such plants, employing 120,000 workers in 1980, grew to 2,200 plants by 1992, employing 500,000 workers at a wage one tenth of the American rate (Korten, 1995). By 2001, the number of such plants had grown to 3,700, but by the summer of 2003, 500 of them had shut down in Mexico, many of them relocating to China, where labour costs are four times lower than in Mexico (Forero, 2003) and many times lower than in the United States or Europe. In automobile manufacturing, for example, labour costs in China in 2005 were ninety-five cents an hour. In the United States they were twenty-six dollars an hour (S. Power, 2005).

Sending work elsewhere in order to take advantage of lower labour costs continues to generate strong feelings, though resignation is setting in since the losses have gone on for so long and so relentlessly. And at least until the Great Recession, arguments were made that most of the several million manufacturing jobs in the United States that had been lost between 2000 and 2007 had not been due to outsourcing but to a substantial decline in business investment that accompanied the earlier recession of 2001 and a marked rise in productivity that has made it possible to make more goods with fewer workers (Andrews, 2003d). Also, many manufacturing jobs that disappeared in the late 1990s and early 2000s did not necessarily go to China or Brazil, two countries with the lowest labour costs. Many jobs simply disappeared because of increased productivity associated with the increased use of technology. Factory employment fell in twenty major economies between 1995 and 2002. Even China lost 15% of its manufacturing jobs during that period, Brazil 20% (Henwood, 2004).

But it is not only manufacturing jobs that are affected by globalization. Highly skilled white collar jobs are also increasingly being moved overseas. Mishel and his colleagues (2005) believe that the role of globalization in keeping labour demand (and therefore wages) low has been underestimated. The pace of outsourcing and offshoring may already be more advanced than we know since companies, for political reasons, are reluctant to provide information about their plans. Service offshoring has moved far up the social scale so that the work of highly paid computer programmers, engineers, scientists, lawyers, and physicians in the United States is now being done overseas. As Mishel et al. (2005) comment, 'If the jobs of such highly educated workers are now at risk in the global economy, it makes one wonder which jobs cannot be moved offshore' (p. 185). Roach (2004) cites the growth of low-end jobs in the United States as evidence that American companies are already well along in replacing high-quality high-wage service workers in the United States with high-quality low-wage workers overseas. During the fiscal year that ended in July 2004, for example, over 80% of the job growth in the United States occurred in low-end areas such as transportation, material moving, sales, repair, and maintenance services. By 2009, the Labor Department estimated that five of the ten occupations expected to add the most jobs through 2016 will pay, at the most, $22,000 a year. Another three will pay only up to $31,000 ('Where the Jobs Are,' 2009).

For individuals in low paying service jobs who do not have the skills to get another job easily ('Does Trade Help,' 2004), globalization has been a misfortune even before the recession. Periods of unemployment have increased markedly in recent years. Even for those who find another job, over two thirds earn less than they did in their previous job; a quarter of them take pay cuts of 30% or more (Hilsenrath & Freeman, 2004; Uchitelle, 2006). Similarly, communities suffer greatly in terms of revenue and employment when a major manufacturing company leaves (Blumenthal, 2003; Greenhouse, 2010).

Changing Social Norms and CEO Pay

Paul Krugman (2002, 2007) argues that it is not only economic factors that explain growing income inequality. Changing social norms also have a part. The social and economic programs of the New Deal imposed norms of relative equality in pay that lasted close to forty years and created the middle class in the United States. Over the last thirty years, these norms have changed. One example is the way corporations operate. Institutional investors are no longer willing to let CEOs choose their own successors, as was once the case. It was felt necessary to hire charismatic figures, often outsiders, who could be obtained only by the offer of immense salaries. Lee Iacocco, who rescued Chrysler from the threat of bankruptcy in the early eighties with the help of a sizeable government loan, set a pattern as the first of these corporate celebrities.

Academic economists also helped change the norms. They argued that corporations and their executives, in the interests of efficiency and profitability, had no business concerning themselves with anything but increase of shareholder value.

Growth of executive (CEO) pay and its spillover effects (raising the salaries of other managers and executives) is indeed a cause of increasing income inequality. While the median hourly pay for all workers increased 6% between 1989 and 2000, the median wage of top executives increased 79%. If bonuses, incentive awards, stock options, and stock gifts are added to salary, full compensation for CEOs grew 342% over that period. In 1965 CEOs of major companies in the United States made twenty-six times the salary of the average worker; in 2000, it was three hundred ten times, moving Mishel and his colleagues (2003) to comment that a CEO earned more in one workday than what the average worker earned in a year. In 1965 it took two weeks.

The Decline of Unions

Another reason for the rise of inequality, most economists agree, is the decline of unionization, which means the loss of the ability of employees to bargain collectively for better wages and benefits. In 1954, a time when income and wealth inequality was far less marked than now, 35% of the workforce in the United States was unionized. By 2003, only 13% of the workforce belonged to a union, and the figure was even lower in private industry (Bureau of Labor Statistics, 2004). Unions lost 2.7 million members between 1980 and 1984 alone, partly because of economic recession in those years (Folbre, 1995). Since then, increasing resistance to unionization on the part of employers – 'employer militancy' – has been prominent (Greenhouse, 2009; Kuttner, 1997).

The consequences of declining union membership for workers are significant. Unionized workers, both white and blue-collar, enjoy hourly wages that are 25% higher those received by non-union workers. Unionized workers are 18% more likely to have health benefits than their non-unionized colleagues (Mishel et al., 2009).

The number of employees covered by some form of company pension declined significantly between 1980 and 1994 (Kuttner, 1997; Uchitelle, 1993), but union members are still much more likely to be covered than their non-union colleagues. In 2001 72% of union workers had employer-provided pensions in contrast to only 44% of non-unionized workers (Mishel et al., 2005). Currently, union members are 23% more likely to have company provided pensions than non-union workers (Mishel et al., 2009). Union members enjoy more job security because their collective bargaining agreements require termination for cause instead of the at-will employment policy applicable to almost all non-union employees. Many Americans are still unaware that, unless they are covered by collective bargaining agreements in their workplace, private employers can fire them at any time for any, or no, reason.

The wage and benefit advantages of union membership diminish income inequality. The decline of unions is a blow for equality since the higher wages and benefits that unions bring puts pressure even on non-union employers to raise wages and benefits (Kuttner, 1997).[5] Wage inequality has always been highest in countries with weak labour movements (Lind, 1995).

The erosion of union power has been attributed to trade pressures, the shift to a service economy, and ongoing technological change – the same inevitable economic forces that have been implicated in widening inequalities and that no one claims to have much control over. Critics, however, have pointed to the many laws and regulations that make labour organizing difficult as well as corporate anti-union tactics such as firing union organizers, interrogating employees about their support for a union, and threatening to close plants or cut back on wages and benefits if workers unionize. Critics also point to the failure of government to enforce labour laws (Freeman, 2007; Greenhouse, 2008, 2009; Mishel et al., 2007). Krugman (2007) is blunt about why unions have declined: 'The answer is simple and brutal: Business interests went on the offensive against unions beginning in the 1970s' (p. 150).

The decline of unions and the loss of bargaining power have not been good for workers. Weakening of unions has resulted in a collective loss of control over issues such as wages, benefits, and working conditions. This exacerbates widening income inequality, insecurity, and stress on the job, all of which are implicated in health and illness. Loss of union power represents the loss of the main countervailing force to the unequal and upward distribution of wealth, to the power and practices of corporate America.

Governmental Policies as Causes of Inequality

THE MINIMUM WAGE AND TAXATION

The real value of the minimum wage, at its high point in 1970, was $7.20 (in constant 2001 dollars). In 2002 it was about five dollars, a loss of 30%. Only 29% of minimum wage workers are teenagers. Although the majority of those who earn minimum wage work part-time, less than thirty-five hours per week, 46% work full-time. Minorities are disproportionately represented among these workers, but close to two thirds of minimum wage workers are white. Women comprise 58% of the total (9.9 million). Even though the minimum wage was raised four times in the 1990s, its value in 2001 was 21% less than it was in 1979. In that year the minimum wage amounted to 55% of median hourly income; in the first half of 2003, the federal minimum wage of $5.15 an hour amounted to 38% of median hourly income ('U.S. Minimum Wage,' 2003).

The minimum wage is especially important to the poor since it helps those with the least income the most. Since the minimum wage level disproportionately affects the lowest paid workers, erosion of this income significantly increases inequality, particularly between families in the middle of the income distribution and those at the twentieth percentile and below (Mishel et al., 2003). The federal government voted to raise the minimum wage in 2007 so that, by 2009, it had risen to $7.50 an hour. An improvement, but still below the minimum wage standards of West European countries, such as France, where it is currently $8.27 an hour or the United Kingdom, where it is $7.96 (Fokken, 2007).

Changes in the tax code have also had a role in widening the income gap. The tax rate for the highest earners has been reduced by more than half since 1963 (Phillips, 2002). Between 1979 and 2000 the tax rate on the top 1% declined substantially, from 37% to 33%, and during that same period their after-tax income rose 201%. By way of contrast, the tax rate on the middle fifth decreased from 19% to 17% during the same period but their after-tax household income grew only 15%. It is true that the top 1% pay 39% of federal *income* taxes ('Their Fair Share,' 2008), but to cite this figure as representing an unfairly disproportionate tax burden is misleading. The other federal tax, the payroll (FICA) tax, which funds Social Security and Medicare, and brings almost as much money into the federal treasury as the income tax, falls heavily on the bottom 80% of wage earners because the payroll tax is capped at $106,800 a year. In 2005, for example, the middle fifth income group paid almost 10% of their income in payroll taxes whereas for the top 1% of households it was less then 2% (Mishel et al., 2009).

The result is that the overall federal tax burden is less severe for the wealthy than income tax alone would indicate (Andrews, 2003c). At the state level, a 2001 study in Oregon showed that when state and local taxes initially levied on businesses are then subsequently passed on to employees, consumers, and owners the tax rate for all income groups was about the same. The bottom 12.5% of households (in income) paid 13%, while the highest 12.5% paid 12%. Those in the middle paid 11% (Mayer, 2001). Given the much higher incomes of the top groups, this means that state and local taxes fall disproportionately on the less well-off.

The tax cuts of 2003 resulted in nearly half of the tax benefits going to the top 10% of earners. An unmarried person with no children who earned $40,000 a year saw his or her federal taxes drop by $126 while an individual in the top 1% watched his or her taxes decline by $32,000. Overall, the top 1% received 42% of the savings under the proposal and the top 5% received 67% of the savings (Andrews, 2003a, 2003b, 2003c). This comes on top of the government's 2001 tax cuts that also strongly favoured higher earners ('Rewarding,' 2000).

THE POLITICAL PARTY IN POWER

Bartels (2008) has shown that whether a Republican or Democratic president occupies the White House has a great effect on income distribution, a consequence of the different ideologies and macroeconomic policies of the two parties. Democratic administrations support policies that favour the 'have-nots,' including progressive taxation, support for public programs, and a higher minimum wage. Republicans favour the 'haves' and oppose these measures. The result is that, since 1949, income growth for families has been robust across the entire economic spectrum under Democratic presidents, while under Republican administrations the rich have benefited while the middle class and the working poor have not. Extrapolating from existing data, Bartels has estimated that if the Democrats had been in control continuously since 1949, economic inequality would not have increased through 2005. Had Republican administrations been in power continuously, income inequality would be about 30% higher than it already is. To illustrate this point, Bartels points out that under the first four years of the Bush administration, families in the ninety-fifth percentile of income watched their earnings increase 2% while middle-class families and the working poor watched their incomes decline 1% and 3%. Had Al Gore been president, Bartels shows, incomes of the working class would have risen 6% and the middle class 4.5%, while the incomes of the upper class would have remained constant. Bartels argues that the single most important influence on widening income inequality is whether the administration is Republican or Democratic.

Other Causes of Inequality

The discussion above by no means exhausts all of the factors that have been discussed as causes of income inequality in recent years. These include the growth of low-wage service jobs; the unemployment rate, which puts downward pressure on wages when high (Galbraith, 1998); the impact of immigration, which enlarges the pool of low-wage workers; and the failure of higher education to produce enough highly educated workers in the face of continuing technological demands, a situation which increases inequality because it allows those who are highly educated to command higher pay than less educated individuals (Goldin and Katz, 2008). Also mentioned has been the entry of women and baby-boomers (those born between 1946 and 1964) into the labour market; a 'winner-take-all' system in which the highest-ranked individuals in entertainment, sports, and culture get financial rewards far larger than those ranked even slightly lower because of their ability to reach a global audience (Frank, 2007; Frank & Cook, 1995); and assortative mating, which is the tendency of professionals to marry other professionals, which can greatly increase their joint income (Fernandez & Rogerson, 2001).

In Summary

The picture of American society that emerges is one of increasing income and wealth inequality. The privileged class, particularly the top levels of it, has done very well for itself. The middle class is beset by rising costs but has managed to keep up, barely, by sending its women into the workforce and by working longer hours. In what shape it will emerge as a jobless recovery continues (as of the beginning of 2011) remains to be seen. The extent and depth of poverty in the United States is surprising; the poverty rate has not significantly fallen in the last thirty years, and it will undoubtedly increase as the number of unemployed either grows or remains out of work.

The growth of technology and trade are widely cited as the causes of inequality, but institutional arrangements, including the decline of unions, failure to raise the minimum wage, and tax policies that favour those at the top of the social hierarchy in addition to changes in social norms and what political party is in power may be the more important causes (Levy & Temin, 2007).

Coda: Results of Widening Inequalities

Inequality of resources lies behind the social gradient for health in the first place; 'Growing inequalities in income and wealth portend growing socioeconomic inequalities in health,' Nancy Krieger and her colleagues predicted in 1997 (p. 343). Several studies suggest that this has come to pass. Between 1980 and 2000 all SES groups in the United States experienced gains in life expectancy, but individuals in higher groups experienced significantly larger gains than those in more deprived groups: 4.5 years versus 2.8 years. The authors (Singh & Siahpush, 2006) linked this to increasing inequality of household incomes, which they noted had widened 'dramatically' (p. 977) over the last three decades.

Between 1960 and 1988 the overall death rate in the United States decreased, yet in the latter year poor and poorly educated people died at higher rates that those with better incomes and educations. This disparity was also greater in 1986 than in 1960 and the differences were not confined to the rich and the poor but extended across the entire socioeconomic spectrum, gradient-like (Pappas et al., 1993). In 1996 Kaplan and colleagues reported that the states with the greatest increase in income inequality between 1980 and 1990 were also the states with the least decline in mortality.

Looking at the effect of education on longevity, Meara et al. (2008) found that the gap in life expectancy between groups of high (at least 13 years of education) and low (12 or fewer years) education levels increased by 30% between 1981 and 2000. Comparing 1981–8 to 1991–8, life expectancy at age twenty-five increased 1.4 years for the high education group and only 0.5 years for the lower group. In the period between 1990 and 2000 alone, the high education group added another 1.6 years while the lower group added none. The authors concluded that virtually all of the gains in life expectancy that occurred in the last twenty years of the last century went to the higher educated groups.

The Index of Social Health is a report that has been published since 1987 (M. Miringoff & Miringoff, 1999). The project provides a picture of the social dimension of American life. It consists of sixteen different indicators that assess quality of life (suicide, drug use, health care) and socioeconomic indicators of well-being, including average earnings, poverty, and income inequality. The different components are then combined into a composite score for each year.

The social health of the United States has deteriorated significantly since 1970 (M.-L. Miringoff & Opdycke, 2008). The Index was at its best in 1973, often considered the last year of the post-war economic boom, when it stood at seventy on a hundred-point scale. It reached its lowest point in 1982, a recession year, when it was forty-two. In the early nineties it hovered in the mid-forties, reached sixty toward the end of the prosperity associated with the dot-com bubble in 2000, but then declined for five straight years until it reached fifty-three in 2005. It is significant that the Index of Social Health ran parallel to measurements of gross domestic product until the mid-1970s, at which point they increasingly diverged, indicating that wealth and income gains were being distributed less equally than before. While the gross domestic product increased 158% between 1970 and 2001, the Index of Social Health declined by 38%. Not all of the sixteen indicators comprising the Index showed deterioration since the 1970s. Six of them, including the infant mortality rate, the high school drop-out rate, and homicide rates, improved. But ten of the markers got worse, including child poverty, teenage suicide, health insurance coverage rates, food-stamp coverage, and affordable housing.

The authors did not speculate about the reasons for these changes and presented their findings as descriptive, not analytic. Still, their findings unequivocally show that a number of health markers worsened in the United States between 1970 and 2005 and that overall social health has declined 20%. The parallel with this and growing material and social inequalities during this same period is hard to overlook.

5 Work and Whitehall

Our embeddedness in society is illustrated concretely by our work roles. They largely define our social class, constitute a major part of our identity, and are at the centre of our daily lives. Our jobs command our best waking hours and determine what we do during them. Work provides structure and rhythm to our lives. It furnishes income, which gives access to opportunity, and has historically been linked to the availability of health insurance in the United States. It is in our roles at work that we relate most publicly to each other. Occupations define a whole set of experiences and exposures. If work is good, it is a major source of health and happiness, if not, a major source of distress.

What makes jobs good and bad? Why do some people get good jobs, others not? What working conditions lead to health and well-being or illness and distress? How do larger considerations of social perspective help explain working conditions and health? I address these questions in the following discussion.

Good and Bad Jobs

Good jobs engage interests and abilities. They offer autonomy as well as control in carrying the work out. Good jobs make reasonable demands on time and effort, pay well, and provide good benefits. They allow for advancement, offer security, confer status, and provide a safe and supportive work environment. Good jobs, which are found in medicine, law, and other professions, in academia and research, in high-technology industries, and in finance and banking (Bartley, Ferrie, & Montgomery, 2006) usually require levels of education, skill, and credentials and allow individuals to have careers, not just a series of jobs.

Bad jobs offer simple repetitive tasks with high demand, little scope for how the work is done, poor pay, little status, no security, minimal support, sometimes dangerous working conditions, and – overall – little access to resources. They require a minimum education and training (even though many of them are quite hard). The prototype of these kinds of jobs is the 'McJob,' named after the fast-food franchise, McDonald's. This dichotomy between good and bad jobs has led some economists to regard labour markets as segmented or polarized, in which jobs in the first category compose the primary labour market and jobs in the second the secondary labour market (Piore, 1975). It is very difficult to cross over from the secondary to the primary market. Membership in the primary segment is associated with access to resources, membership in the secondary labour market with exposure to risk.

Access to Better Jobs

How does one get into the right segment of the labour market? The attributes approach to social class, described in chapter 1, partially answers this question. Those who acquire the necessary attributes are most likely to get good jobs. The key attribute is education, and the social class of one's family of origin plays a large role in whether and where one gets a higher education. Indeed, parental levels of wealth and education are far and away the most significant determinants of all life chances for their children. Individual motivation is important, but social and family connections and cultural resources help greatly (Wright, 2009). The state of the labour market, which determines whether and what kinds of jobs are available at any particular time, is also a critical factor.

Work and Health: The Whitehall Studies

Health and well-being are related to access to various resources. In addition to the generative resources discussed earlier, privileged groups have less stress, more security, better places to live, more opportunities to exercise, and better information about healthy eating habits. They also have better work, better jobs. It is not always easy to disentangle the role of work from the other two elements that traditionally comprise socioeconomic position – education and income – because they are closely related to each other. Nevertheless, there is a great deal of evidence that work factors related to position in the occupational hierarchy play an important role in health, illness, and distress.

The pioneering Whitehall studies (Marmot, 2004) – Whitehall is a street in London on which the governmental offices are located, but the name is also synonymous with the British civil service – have shown that differences in working conditions linked to social class lead to differences in physical and mental health. The studies are also known for calling attention to the existence of a social gradient for health. This means that being healthy or not is not just a matter of being rich or poor; it means that health improves incrementally as one goes up the social scale: any one social class has better health than the one beneath it and worse health than the one above it.

The first Whitehall studies, called Whitehall I (Marmot, 2004), looked at the impact of occupational status and work conditions on cardiovascular disease, not distress or mental disorder. Later studies included distress – depressive symptoms – as an outcome. Whitehall I was begun in 1967 and included almost 18,000 male civil servants. They were divided into four grades, or ranks, based on occupational characteristics and status: administrators, professionals and executives, clerical staff, and messengers and porters. Individuals in all grades had free access to health care and stable, secure jobs with benefits; none would have met criteria for poverty. Occupational or employment grade was a measure of position on the occupational hierarchy, but the authors acknowledged that it was a proxy for social class since it included more than just the experience of work; higher occupational grade was also associated with higher educational level and income, with status, self-esteem, and living conditions (Marmot & Shipley, 1996).

The outcome measure for the different groups, as just outlined, was mortality rate from cardiovascular disease. The difference in mortality rates from cardiovascular disease after seven-and-a-half years between those at the top and those at the bottom of the occupational hierarchy was dramatic. Among men aged forty to sixty-four, those in the lowest occupational grade had morality rates 3.6 times those in the highest. Equally striking was the health gradient. Those in the second highest group had significantly greater mortality than those in the first group and so on down the line, each group showing higher mortality rates as the occupational grade diminished (Marmot et al., 1978). When the usual cardiac risk factors such as high cholesterol, hypertension, and smoking were controlled for, the gradient was still strong, causing the authors to conclude that the differences in mortality from heart disease could only partially be explained by these traditional risk factors. What other risk factors might be responsible remained to be discovered.

Further follow-ups of the Whitehall I men at both ten and twenty-five years showed that the step-wise relationship between mortality and occupational grade persisted well into old age (Marmot & Shipley, 1996).

Eighteen years after Whitehall I was begun, a new cohort of over 10,000 civil servants between the ages of thirty-five and fifty-five, this time including women, was recruited. This study was called Whitehall II (Marmot, 2004). This time the investigators concentrated on cardiac morbidity, as measured by detectable ischemic changes or symptoms of angina pectoris, rather than mortality. Compared with men in the highest grade (administration), men in the lowest grade had a 50% greater risk of developing coronary heart disease. The rate was almost as high for women. Men in lower grades were also more likely to have suffered strokes and cancer.

The Whitehall II studies elucidated more clearly the factors that explained the gradient between disease and social class. Individuals in lower status jobs were less likely to have had higher education or certain material advantages, such as owning a car or their own home. They were more likely to have had fathers in manual occupations. Those in lower grades were also heavier and shorter, smoked more, exercised less, ate less healthy diets, and drank more alcohol. Their social networks, in contrast to the networks of the more privileged grades, consisted predominantly of family rather than friends. They had fewer confidantes, less practical support from people within their social circle, reported more negative reactions from people close to them, scored higher on a measure of hostility, and were more fatalistic about their health. They also reported more stressful events in the previous year and more problems paying bills. In terms of job characteristics, what distinguished the lower from the higher groups was less control, less variety in their work, and less overall satisfaction with their jobs.

With so many differences, which were most important for explaining the health gradient? This question was answered in articles by Marmot and his co-workers published in 1997 (Bosma et al., 1997; Marmot et al., 1997). Of all the factors examined, the largest contribution to the gradient – half, in fact – in terms of coronary heart disease was low control at work. Control was measured both subjectively and objectively, and though the correlation between them was low, indicating that the two measures assessed different aspects of the job, both independently predicted heart disease (Bosma et al., 1997; Marmot, 2004). However it was measured, a psychosocial variable at work, low control, was shown to be the major factor linking lower position in the occupational hierarchy with an increased risk of heart disease (Marmot et al., 1997). Height, considered a marker of nutritional status in childhood, and traditional risk factors for coronary arteriosclerosis also contributed to the gradient, but their contributions were much smaller.

Whitehall II also looked at the effects of work characteristics on depressive symptoms. Stansfeld, Head, and Marmot (1998) found that work characteristics related to control – specifically, 'decision authority,' the authority to make independent decisions about different aspects of work and 'skill discretion,' the opportunity to use one's particular skills on the job – explained most of the differences in well-being and depressive symptoms between occupational grades, especially in men. Differences in social support explained a third of the gradient in this particular study, while life events and chronic stress associated with finances or housing explained less than a third.

In a later study, Stansfeld and his colleagues (1999) found that low levels of both social support and control, in addition to high job demands and an imbalance between effort and reward, were risk factors for depressive symptoms in both men and women. In other words, higher levels of social support and control at work protected mental health while high job demands and an imbalance between effort and reward jeopardized it. The proportion of men and women with depression increased inversely and continuously with lower employment grade, but the gradient was not as dramatic for depression as it was for cardiovascular disease: the risk of depressive symptoms among those in the lowest grade was twice (rather than three or four times) that of individuals in the higher grades (Stansfeld et al., 2003). Work characteristics, material problems (inadequate income, housing problems, and neighbourhood difficulties), and less social support explained much of the gradient for depression for both men and women, with work characteristics (high demand, low control) being paramount for men and a combination of work characteristics and material problems being important for women.

Depression and cardiovascular disease have often been linked to one another. Depression, for example, significantly raises cardiovascular morbidity and mortality in a dose-related manner (Connery et al., 2001; Everson et al., 1998; Musselman, Evans, & Nemeroff, 1998; Simonsick et al., 1995). Although the Whitehall is better known for its cardiovascular rather than its depression component, these studies have shown that both outcomes share similar risk and protective factors, namely a sense of control, demands of work, social support, and balance between effort and reward. Of these, imbalances between control and demand

as well as between effort and rewards have been the factors most studied as sources of stress at work.

Stress at Work: Two Models

The first model, the demand/control model, predicts that stressful experience at work results when demands are high and control, or autonomy, is low. Karasek and Theorell (1990) were among the first to show
that the most stressful jobs are those that combine high psychological
demands with a low degree of control. Low control is characteristic of
low-status jobs. Jobs with high psychological demands require workers
to work too fast or hard within a too-short time period whereas jobs
characterized by a low degree of control do not enable workers to make
decisions on their own, do not allow for learning new skills, and are
usually repetitive. Machine-paced workers such as assemblers, cutting
operators, inspectors, and freight handlers as well as low status workers such as waiters, cooks, and nurses' aides fit into this category.

Testing their model, Karasek and Theorell (1990) reported that significantly higher rates of heart attack were associated with low-control,
high-demand jobs compared to low-demand, high-control occupations. The same work conditions of low control and high demand were
also found to predict increased rates of depression, a finding confirmed
by others (Niedhammer et al., 1998). Karasek and Theorell believe that
many of the newer jobs in the post-industrial era fall into the high-
demand, low-control category. Figure 5.1 shows where a variety of
jobs are positioned on the demand/control dimensions. 'Decision latitude,' on the ordinate represents control. Jobs in the northeast corner
of the figure, characterized by high demands but also a considerable
degree of control, are considered 'active jobs' by the authors, while jobs
in the southeast corner, where demands are high but control is low,
are considered 'high strain jobs.' It is the control dimension that has
been related most consistently to cardiovascular risk. The demand dimension has been less consistently linked to heart disease risk in some
studies (Schnall et al., 1994) but not all (Marmot, 2004). With respect to
the development of depression, however, another team of investigators
(Netterstrom et al., 2008), reviewing a large number of studies, found
that psychological demands on the job more reliably predicted the later
onset of depression than did decision latitude.

The second model used to explain work-related stress is the effort/
reward imbalance model. The idea behind this model, introduced by

Figure 5.1. How jobs rate on axes of control and demand

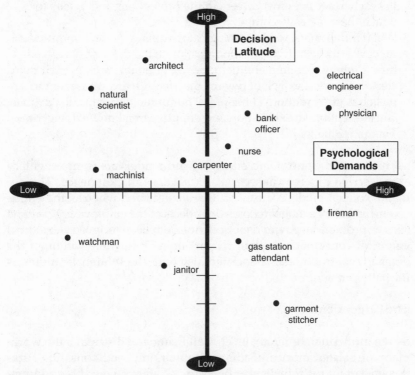

Source: R. Karasek & T. Theorell. (1990). *Healthy work: Stress, productivity, and the reconstruction of the working life*. New York, NY: Basic Books, p. 43.

Siegrist, Siegrist, and Weber (1986), is that stress, with adverse effects on psychological and physical health, results if effort is not appropriately rewarded by tangible rewards such as income, promotion, or job security (Siegrist, 1996; Siegrist & Theorell, 2006). Lack of reward is particularly likely to occur under three conditions:

1 When workers have no power and the risk that employees will protest unfair treatment is low – unionization usually protects against this, but employment contracts with unskilled and semi-skilled workers often do not

2 When individuals accept high cost/low gain conditions for a certain time voluntarily because they improve their chances of career

advancement and promotion at a later time – this pattern occurs in the early stages of most careers in the professions and in jobs for which there is heavy competition

3 When individuals, for psychological reasons, are overcommitted to work – these individuals underestimate the demands, overestimate their own coping abilities, and are often unaware of their own contribution to the lack of reward they feel. Overcommitment to the job is often reinforced for years, but in the long run such people 'are susceptible to exhaustion and adaptive breakdown' (Siegrist & Theorell, 2006, p. 77)

The demand/control and effort/reward models are complementary and describe different aspects of stressful work experience. The demand/control model focuses on work conditions whereas the effort-reward imbalance model focuses on aspects of the employment contract such as promotion, pay, and job security. Both have received substantial empirical confirmation, either in part or on the whole, although the demand/control model, associated also with the Whitehall studies, is the better known.

The Larger Context

At the individual, or micro, level, well-being and distress in the workplace are related most immediately to working conditions. Of course it is important for clinicians to be aware of what favourable and unfavourable working conditions consist of. Adverse conditions associated with occupational diseases are common knowledge, but the psychosocial factors that affect health, as revealed in studies like Whitehall, have yet to be fully appreciated in the United States

Working conditions do not, of course, exist in isolation. They are dependent on company or corporate policies and rules (the meso organizational level) that reflect the needs of these organizations. These needs are linked to macro-level structures such as the labour market, which in turn is influenced by changes in the global and national economies, institutional norms (usual pay rates, how employees should be treated), government regulations, and by the stratification system (Fenwick & Tausig, 2008).

Take the stratification system first. Fenwick and Tausig (2008) also refer to this system collectively as 'the structures of inequality' (p. 149). The segment of the labour market in which one can get a job is influenced by class, race, and gender. Educational credentials, a proxy for class, enhance the ability to compete for certain jobs in the primary segment. Individuals without educational credentials, women, and blacks are more apt to be sorted into the secondary labour market where satisfactions are fewer, pay less, chances of promotion rarer, and layoffs more likely.

Outsourcing of manufacturing jobs, a fiercely debated issue until the advent of the Great Recession, and the shift to a service-oriented economy are macro-level phenomena that affect types of jobs available. Many of the new service jobs require less skill than the old manufacturing jobs; the expanded pool of workers, swelled by the loss of manufacturing jobs, increases competition for the jobs that exist and has kept wages down. The growth of technology has enhanced economic productivity, but it has also eliminated jobs. As well, the decline of labour unions (itself linked to the loss of manufacturing jobs, which were more highly unionized than service jobs) has adversely affected pay, benefits, and job security for many workers. Although those toward the bottom of the occupational hierarchy have suffered the consequences of these changes more severely than those higher up, not even white collar workers have been immune.

The most prominent macro-level phenomenon that affects labour markets is recession, an endemic feature of capitalism (Fulcher, 2004). The Great Recession, which began in December 2007, is an example of a macro-level event that spreads systematically through the various levels of the economic system, affecting the labour market, organizational structures, and work conditions, thus creating health risk for individual workers. Losses caused by defaults on sub-prime mortgages and risky real estate loans caused banks to restrict lending. Without the necessary credit or cash, companies were forced to cut back on production of goods and services, resulting in lay-offs, which is bad for the mental health of most workers (Bartley et al., 2006). Layoffs increase the number of available workers, and wages stagnate or decline in the face of a more competitive labour market, which weakens employees' resistance to changes in job conditions that can affect them adversely. Decisions at the managerial level of firms to restructure the activities and positions of their employees, in order to make them more productive, often means increasing job demands and decreasing decision latitude. Changing the work conditions in these ways increases stress among employees (Fenwick & Tausig, 2008).

Trends

And, indeed, this has been one result of the Great Recession of 2008–9. Even before the recession, however, work conditions were getting worse – more stressful – for both white- and blue-collar workers (Brody, 1991; Fraser, 2001; Greenhouse, 2008; Kilborn, 1995; O'Toole & Lawler, 2006; Shulman, 2003). Widely reported were management demands for increased work speed and increased productivity (Glaberson, 1987; Kilborn, 1990a; Schumpeter, 2010); longer working hours and more mandatory overtime (Schor, 1991); the conversion of daytime jobs to shift work; and the use of techniques such as 'management by stress' in which assembly line work (think of automobile plants or poultry processing companies) is continually monitored so that weaknesses, such as an employee's inability to maintain a fast pace, can be identified (Holusha, 1989). Along with intense and frequent monitoring (Kilborn, 1990b) came a reduction of 'slack,' the moments when one can relax, talk with co-workers, or just take a break (Rochlin, 1997). In 1993, years before the recession, the International Labor Organization said, 'Stress has become one of the most serious health issues of the 20th century' ('Employers Recognizing,' as cited in Rifkin, 1995, pp. 189, 317). The Metropolitan Life Insurance Company has estimated that on average one million workers in the United States miss work each day because of job-related stress (Rifkin, 1995). Seventy-five per cent of American workers describe their jobs as stressful and believe that the pressures that cause stress are steadily increasing. Nationwide, in 1980, less than 5% of workers' compensation claims were stress-related. By 1989, 15% were (*World Labour Report*, 1993) and by 2002, 30% (Tangri, 2003).

Another trend, also apparent before the recession, was that job insecurity was increasing (Handel, 2005). More workers were losing or changing jobs than in the past (Gross, 2005; Hacker, 2006). The decline of paternalistic corporations, which once promised life-long jobs in manufacturing; the rise of corporate demand for labour flexibility; and the transition to service jobs, most of which offered little security, were the major reasons. The median length of time that American men between the ages of thirty-five to forty-four held a job dropped from eight to five-and-a-half years between 1963 and 2000. American workers with two years of college could expect, by 2004, to change jobs at least eleven times in the course of their working lives ('Why Business,' 2004), sometimes by choice, more often not. Hardly any stress is able to produce more of an adverse effect on health and well-being over a lifetime than economic strain (Lynch et al., 1997). Even in 1998, when the economic boom of the late 1990s was in full swing and unemployment was low, fewer workers felt that their jobs were secure than they had nine years earlier, in 1989, when the unemployment rate was in fact higher. Just the anticipation of job change or job loss, much less unemployment, leads to significant deterioration in self-reported health status, an accurate predictor of mortality (Dragano et al, 2005; Ferrie et al., 1995).

Another casualty of the altered workplace has been trust between employers and workers. A survey of 906 large and medium-sized U.S. employers revealed that almost two thirds of them, when all types of monitoring were included, admitted to spying on their employees. Technology has made monitoring easier (Fraser, 2001; Kilborn, 1990b). Police officers, truckers, garbage collectors, United Parcel Service employees, and ambulance drivers are among the groups being monitored with global positioning system tracking devices attached to their vehicles, sometimes with their knowledge, sometimes not (Forelle, 2004). Employees in call centres, finance offices, insurance claims departments, airline reservation centres, and many who work from home are routinely monitored via computer software that allows their activities to be tracked (Fraser, 2001; Richmond, 2004). A nationwide study of 745 telephone workers showed that those who were monitored had significantly higher rates of depressive symptoms than those who were not (M.J. Smith et al., 1992)

Economist David Gordon (1996) showed that the managerial and supervisory personnel of U.S. corporations have actually grown in proportion to non-supervisory employees, even in the mid-1990s, when managerial downsizing was reported to be so prevalent. Gordon's argument is that increased supervision became more necessary after the early 1970s when corporations began driving down wages and reducing benefits. This in turn undermined employees' loyalty and sense of commitment to their work, thus increasing the need for supervision. Gordon concluded that millions of workers experience intense supervision nearly every day in many different ways and that 'supervision, in short, seems to be the prevailing experience for most workers in the United States.' (Gordon, 1996, p. 71). The growth of supervision is the antithesis of the need for autonomy and control in the workplace.

In a large survey looking at stress on the job sponsored by the Northwestern National Life Insurance Company (1991) twenty years ago, 72% of a random sample of six hundred full-time workers in all types of jobs said they suffered from three or more stress- and work-related symptoms, such as anger and anxiety, headaches or insomnia, muscle pain or gastrointestinal symptoms, 'frequently' or 'fairly frequently.' Seventy per cent said that job stress interfered with their work and 20% had missed work because of it in the previous year. A third had considered quitting their jobs in order to reduce their stress in the year previously and the same number said they had quit their previous jobs because of it. The cause of stress most commonly cited in the survey was the experience of having 'little personal control' in the execution of one's job. More recent surveys confirm these conclusions (O'Toole & Lawler, 2006). The Pew Research Center (Taylor et al., 2006) found that, by an overwhelming majority, American workers thought they were worse off now than they were a generation ago. On several different dimensions of work life, including on-the-job stress, job security, and loyalty between employers and workers, employees said that conditions had deteriorated.

In Summary

There are better and worse jobs. Individuals are able to acquire better jobs by being born with resources and by acquiring certain attributes that facilitate access to the primary job market. The central attribute is education. The state of the labour market is also important.

Psychosocial factors associated with working conditions have emerged as important for health and well-being. These include a sense of control and autonomy at work, social support, and a feeling that rewards are commensurate with effort. Better working conditions are associated with higher position in the occupational hierarchy, a proxy for social class status, and one that guarantees more access to scarce resources.

It is important to understand which working conditions are related to health and illness, but it is also important to see them in light of a social perspective. Management most directly determines working conditions, but its decision and policies are influenced by such diverse macro-level factors as the state of the international and national economies, societal norms that set limits to what company can do, and a society's system of stratification.

6 Links between Socioeconomic Status, Well-Being, and Distress

We know, as discussed in chapter 2, that lower class position is tied to more distress, more mental illness, and poorer physical health, just as we know that higher social status leads to better health. But these associations, which have now been confirmed so many times, now require explanation. What are the processes or mechanisms that account for the relationship between social position and health?

Overview

Health disparities reflect socioeconomic disparities. Where an individual is positioned in the stratification system by class, race, and gender has a great effect on the possession of particular resources that promote health and well-being. Blane (1995) observes that what societies do is 'structure the life experiences of their members so that advantages and disadvantages tend to cluster cross-sectionally and accumulate longitudinally' (p. 904). It is the long-term effects of occupying either a high or low position in the social hierarchy, and the cumulative experiences of social conditions related to those positions, that lead to good or poor health. This topic defines an influential area of health research, known as the life course perspective on health (Blane, 2006).

Socioeconomic status (SES) or position (SEP) consists of 'associated conditions that individually affect health and well-being or that are correlated with other conditions that are stressful' (Baum et al., 1999). Education, income, and occupation are the 'associated conditions' that are most commonly used to define socioeconomic position. Socioeconomic status is a proxy for many life conditions that influence the health and welfare; it encapsulates complex information about individuals and groups (Blane, 1995).

SES is also associated with almost every conceivable health outcome. As Michael Marmot (2004) says, 'We see the health gradient everywhere' (p. 19). Besides cardiovascular disease (coronary artery disease, stroke), most mental disorders and distress, a gradient has been shown to exist for cancer of the oesophagus, stomach, colon, rectum, and lung; for AIDS, diabetes, chronic obstructive pulmonary disease, pneumonia and influenza, tuberculosis, kidney disease, cirrhosis, homicide, accidents, and suicide (Davey Smith et al., 1996; Marmot, 2004). Link and Phelan (1995) argue that socioeconomic status should be elevated to the status of a 'fundamental cause' of health and disease because the associations between social class and health have been so consistent historically. The reason why, Link and Phelan believe, is that the privileged use their resources – their education, their information resources, their social networks – to capitalize more quickly on the knowledge and practices that promote health and avoid risks. It is because race/ethnicity and sex/gender are also so closely tied to resources that they should also be considered fundamental causes of health and disease, according to Link and Phelan.

There are different ways of conceptualizing the factors associated with socioeconomic position or social class that lead to well-being and health – or their opposites. Here is mine, the one I will follow in the discussion below: Education, income, and occupation, in addition to the place or neighbourhood in which a person lives, are markers of adult socioeconomic status. These markers set the stage for, and are intertwined with, other factors that affect well-being and health. The degree and kinds of stress individuals are exposed to, which depends on their SEP, is a major one. How they cope with it depends heavily on their prior sense of control and the quality of their social network. Parents' socioeconomic status influences the development of their children in a multitude of ways via the material and environment they provide and the ways they interact with, and raise, their children, both of which affect later well-being and health.

Education

Education is considered by some to be the most important component of socioeconomic position for health and well-being because it structures the other constituents. It sets one on the road to employment, a satisfying job, and a decent income (Mirowsky et al., 2000; Ross & Wu, 1995). It improves health and well-being because it increases 'effective agency' – a sense of personal control – for individuals (Mirowsky & Ross, 2003a).

Education is good for health and well-being in many ways. It increases the chances of finding a job in the first place and then finding a job that is full-time, fulfilling, and remunerative. In 1991, among persons aged twenty-five to thirty-four, 87% of college graduates were employed, compared to 77% of those with a high school diploma and 56% of those with some high school. The well-educated are also more likely to work full-time when compared to the poorly educated, which insures a big advantage in wages and benefits. Unemployment is strongly associated with poor health and psychological distress for both men and women (Ross & Wu, 1995). Well-educated people are also more likely to have jobs that offer more autonomy and variety. They experience less supervision and are more likely to be supervisors themselves. They are less likely to be in jobs that are physically dangerous and are less likely to expose them to hazardous materials. They have more personal control and are more likely to be recognized for their achievements. The pay and benefits are better. All of these characteristics enhance psychological functioning, job satisfaction, and emotional well-being (Mirowsky et al., 2000).

Individuals with more education also have more information about health (Deaton, 2002). They are more apt to adopt better health habits and more likely to modify harmful ones. Education is correlated with higher levels of social support. Social support, a sense of personal control, and better health habits combine to improve health and reduce morbidity and distress.

Ross and Wu (1995) conclude that high educational attainment improves health and well-being indirectly through its effects on employment, work, and income. But even when employment status, occupation, control, health risk behaviours, and social support are controlled for, education remains associated with good health and well-being. One explanation of this, they believe, is that education fosters the development of communication, reading, writing, analyzing, synthesizing, and interpreting skills. This not only enhances a sense of confidence, mastery, and control, it also promotes an active problem-solving approach to life that is good for health. Education provides people with better equipment for living.

Many studies confirm the link between less education and higher levels of psychological distress (Mirowsky & Ross, 2003a). For serious mental illness, such as schizophrenia, it is more likely that the disease interferes with educational achievement rather than that a low level of education predisposes to schizophrenia, though it may work that way in some cases. The incidence and prevalence of the common mental disorders, however, which are much higher than those for schizophrenia, are inversely related to level of education. It is true, of course, that anxiety and depression may also lead to low levels of education, but the British birth cohort study (discussed later) suggests that class-related childhood disadvantage, which of course occurs early in life, is a more important cause of impaired educational achievement than are common mental disorders, which usually appear after childhood.

In terms of physical health also, well-educated people have better health and higher levels of well-being than the poorly educated, whether measured by self-report or more objective assessments of morbidity, mortality, or disability (Feldman et al., 1989; Ross & Wu, 1995; Snowdon et al., 1989). College graduates have lower mortality rates than high school graduates who in turn have lower rates than those who have not completed high school. The relationship between education and mortality is a direct one: life expectancy increases with more schooling (Rogot, Sorlie, & Johnson, 1992). Individuals with higher education also stay healthy longer. They show almost no functional disabilities until they reach old age (sixty-five and older). In contrast, the less educated begin to decline functionally in early middle age, some twenty years earlier than the educated group (House, 2001).

Employment and Occupation

There are three topics here that relate to health and well-being: employment status, occupational or job status, and workplace conditions. Unemployment is a major risk factor for emotional distress and depression (Bartley et al., 1999), largely because it increases financial strain. An Italian study, however, showed that laid-off workers had increased rates of psychological distress and physical illness even though they continued to receive their usual wage (Rudas et al., as cited in Bartley et al., 1999, p. 88). Unemployment often results in social isolation, inactivity, loss of daily structure, lowered self-esteem, diminished status, and weight gain, all of which affect health and well-being.

Employment status – whether one has a job or not – is also one of the strongest predictors of early mortality rate, especially for those who are classified as unable to work and are less than sixty-five years of age.

Their risk is three to eleven times higher than the risk for individuals who are employed. The reason for this is that many of the unemployed have serious medical problems that lead to early death. However, individuals who become unemployed for reasons other than illness also face an increased risk of death, even after social class, individual risk factors, and coexisting medical illness are taken into account (Morris et al., 1994).

With respect to occupational status and working conditions, the Whitehall studies discussed in the last chapter showed that jobs linked to higher occupational position and characterized by a high degree of control and social support protected against depression and cardiovascular disease (Stansfeld et al., 2003). Conversely, other studies have shown that certain other work conditions associated with lower status jobs, such as irregular schedules and supervisory harassment, also contribute to the burden of stress implicated in psychological and physical disorder (Marchant et al., 2005).

Income and Income Inequality

Many studies have confirmed a link between low individual or family income and higher rates of mental illness and distress (Bruce et al., 1991; Eaton, 2001, Mirowsky & Ross, 2003b), poor physical health, and premature death (McDonough et al., 1997; Rogot et al., 1992; Sorlie et al., 1995). Bruce et al. (1991), analyzing data from the New Haven catchment area of the ECA program, reported that those with very low income were at risk for new episodes of all psychiatric illnesses except panic disorder. Mirowsky and Ross (2003b) found that psychological distress increased in a linear fashion as household incomes decreased from over $100,000 to $5,000 per year.

Typical of studies for physical health is McDonough's, which showed that individuals living in the poorest households, earning less than $15,000 in 1993 dollars, had mortality rates almost four times those living in households earning more than $70,000, while those living in households with incomes between these extremes showed intermediate rates.

At the lowest income levels, poverty means lack of access to some necessities of life, such as shelter, clothing, food, or medicine. At these levels material deprivation accounts for much of psychological distress and poor health. Not only do poor people have to struggle to obtain the basic necessities of life, they often live in bad neighbourhoods with overcrowding, crime, and disorder. These problems constitute endemic stressors that are well-known to affect health and well-being.

For people living in poverty, more income improves health and well-being. However, there is a point past which more income does not lead to better health. Beyond a family income of $40,000 (2003 U.S. dollars) the relationship between increasing income and better health becomes negligible (Mirowsky & Ross, 2003a). Nevertheless, a social gradient for many medical conditions, depression, and distress continues to exist even when the effect of income is negligible. This is where the concept of relative income inequality comes into play. According to M. Marmot (2004), 'If you have little of it, more money would benefit health, but if you have more of it, then it is how much you have compared to other people in your society that is more important for health' (p. 73).

Feeling relatively deprived means feeling deprived in comparison with what constitutes a decent standard of living in a given society. In one European survey, for example, individuals considered themselves poor if they did not own a television set or a telephone, if they were not able to replace worn-out furniture, if they were unable to take a holiday away from home, and if they could not buy their children a bicycle (Marmot, 2004).

This may affect health and well-being by causing feelings of inadequacy. The lower an individual is on the social hierarchy, the stronger the feelings of not measuring up in terms of income and all that money provides access to (Wilkinson & Pickett, 2009; Wilkinson, 1996). *Feeling poor in relationship to others*, in other words, may be a factor that links low social status, poor health, and distress. Negative self-appraisals, associated with feelings such as shame and feelings of failure adversely affect the health of the individual by either activating the stress systems of the body or by leading to negative health-related behaviours, such as smoking. Whether negative feelings of sufficient magnitude to account for poor health are generated in this way is controversial, however. We normally compare ourselves with a reference group of people who are close to us on the social hierarchy, not the very rich. This does not exclude invidious comparisons, but it may reduce their intensity.

However, there is another way that income inequality is thought to harm health: by diminishing social capital. Social capital refers to levels of trust, cooperation, reciprocity, and mutuality that exist in societies, communities and neighbourhoods. Higher levels of income inequality are associated with lower levels of social capital (Wilkinson & Pickett, 2009). Inequality increases social distance between social classes and individuals, who often do not share values and so have little in common. This undermines trust, and without trust, social ties are fewer and social support weaker for individuals in a community (Wilkinson, 1996).

It is generally accepted that individual and/or household income is a powerful determinant of *individual* health (Subramanian & Kawachi, 2004). What is controversial is whether income inequality at the societal or community level is bad for both population and individual health. A number of studies and reviews have found no association between income inequality and life expectancy in other developed countries (Deaton, 2003; Lynch et al., 2001; McLeod et al., 2003; Ross et al., 2000). The United States is the country in which the relationship between income inequality and premature death at the population level has been most consistent. It has been suggested that this is because the United States does less to mitigate the effects of income inequality than many other countries (Adler et al., 1994). Sweden, in contrast, possesses a more comprehensive social welfare system than the United States, which weakens the negative effects of income inequality. Its citizens also on average live four years longer than Americans (Kawachi & Kennedy, 2002). Individual states with the most income inequality within the United States not only offer the fewest benefits but also invest the least in infrastructure that can improve health, such as education, transportation, child care, public health services, and the environment. This may be why a significant correlation exists between state inequality levels and rates of premature deaths in some studies (Kaplan et al., 1996).

Although studies continue to appear that support the role of income inequality in explaining various health outcomes (De Vogli et al., 2005; Wilkinson & Pickett, 2009), the tide of opinion is against it, at least for the moment. (Deaton, 2003; Eberstadt & Satel, 2004; Fiscella & Franks, 1997; Lynch et al., 2000; Mackenbach, 2002; McLeod et al., 2003). The data are too inconsistent and contradictory. Deaton's (2003) authoritative review of the topic summarizes the issue this way:

> It is low incomes that are important, not inequality, and there is no evidence that making the rich richer, however undesirable that may be on other grounds, is hazardous to the health of the poor, *provided that their own incomes are maintained* [emphasis added]. (p. 151)

Deaton cautions that these conclusions should not be misinterpreted, however:

While they do imply that income inequality is not important per se, *other than its effects through poverty* [emphasis added], they do not imply that the social environment is not important for individual health, let alone that individual health is determined by individual characteristics and the provision of personal medical care. (p. 151)

Income inequality's effects through poverty are very important, though. Fiscella and Franks (1997) comment:

[Our] findings suggest that community income inequality does not have large effects on mortality independent of the effects of family income. However, income inequality and family income are closely intertwined. Countries, states, or communities with large income inequalities are likely to have more poverty. Countries whose explicit goal has been eradication of poverty also have less income inequality. Thus, whether public policy focuses primarily on the elimination of poverty or on reduction of income disparity, neither goal is likely to be achieved in the absence of the other. (p. 17)

Place

Income largely determines where one can live. Neighbourhood matters for both mental and physical health. Ross and Mirowsky (2001) and others (Hill, Ross, & Angell, 2005; Latkin & Curry, 2003; Mirowsky & Ross, 2002) have found that people have high rates of depressive symptoms in disadvantaged neighbourhoods because of what Ross and Mirowsky term 'disorder.' Disorder shows itself in streets that are dirty and noisy, buildings that are rundown or abandoned, residents who are indifferent, hostile, or hanging out and/or using drugs. It creates an atmosphere of incivility, distrust, and powerlessness (Ross & Mirowsky, 2009). These factors create chronic stress which activates psychological responses, in the form of anxiety and depression, and lead to sustained physiologic reactions that undermine health and well-being.

An important epidemiological work published in the last century was Alexander and Dorothea Leighton's Stirling County study, carried out in the Canadian province of Nova Scotia (Leighton et al., 1963). The Leightons initiated their study with the idea that the degree of social integration in a particular community (small rural communities, not neighbourhoods in large cities) affects the mental health of individuals living in it.[1] The degree of integration or disintegration was evaluated by measuring the number of broken homes, strength of social ties, adequacy of recreational facilities, quality of community leadership, and so on. Comparing several integrated communities with communities that showed a high degree of disintegration, the Leightons and their colleagues found that the rate of mental disorders – primarily anxiety, depression, psychosomatic, and personality disorders – was twice as high in the disintegrated communities. In fact, individuals in lower socioeconomic positions within the integrated communities were less at risk for psychiatric disorder than the high-ranking members in disintegrated communities. For Alexander Leighton (1960), the connection between society, at the level of a community, and the individual was clear: 'A disintegrated sociocultural environment will produce disintegrated personalities,' he said (p. 75).

A British study reported similar findings for neighbourhoods (McCulloch, 2001). Based on an annual survey of a representative sample of British households, neighbourhoods were ranked by their level of social capital and their degree of social disintegration. Social capital referred to 'those features of a community that promote cohesion and a sense of belonging and that enable its members to cooperate' (p. 208). Individuals were also asked about their psychiatric and physical health problems. Men and women in the lowest category of social capital reported psychiatric problems much more often than individuals of either sex living in neighbourhoods with high social capital. Men and women living in the neighbourhoods with the least disintegration were also less likely to report physical symptoms.

In New York City, a prospective, randomized, controlled study was carried out in which families in high-rise public housing in high-poverty neighbourhoods were moved into private housing in similar neighbourhoods or private housing in low poverty neighbourhoods (Leventhal & Brooks-Gunn, 2003). A comparison group stayed in public housing. All families were re-interviewed after three years. Parents of families that moved to low-poverty neighbourhoods reported significantly less distress, in the form of anxiety and depression, than the parents who remained in high-poverty neighbourhoods. The mental health impact of the program was even greater on the children in the group that moved to low-poverty neighbourhoods. This was especially true for boys between the ages of eight and thirteen, who showed a 25% reduction in depression, anxiety, and dependency problems (an excessive need to be with their parents, frequent crying). The main reason for this promising outcome, in the authors' view, was the higher median income in the neighbourhoods to which the experimental groups had moved, which was reflected not only in less disorder but also in better health care services, schools, housing, parks, sports facilities, and youth programs.

The effect of neighbourhoods on physical health was published in 2001 in *The New England Journal of Medicine* by Diez Roux and colleagues. With an impressive number of subjects in four different communities around the country and a median follow-up time for each patient of nine years, Diez Roux et al. (2001) found that individuals living in disadvantaged neighbourhoods (based on composite ratings of educational, occupational, and income levels) had significantly more heart problems than individuals living in advantaged neighbourhoods even after personal income, occupation, and education were controlled for. Those living in the most disadvantaged neighbourhoods had rates of heart disease that were three times higher than those living in the most advantaged places, a ratio that was unchanged even when established risk factors for heart disease were controlled for. The investigators also found that level of personal income was an independent risk factor for heart disease, but this was not the most surprising finding, since many other studies have shown an inverse relationship between heart disease and socioeconomic status (Kaplan & Keil, 1993). The most surprising finding was that the kind of neighbourhood one lives in is itself a risk factor for heart disease.

Diez Roux et al. (2001) speculated that characteristics of a neighbourhood interact with established risk factors to cause heart disease. Urban neighbourhoods with stores that advertise cigarettes and offer unhealthy food products promote smoking and poor eating habits. Lack of safe public spaces and recreational facilities discourages physical activity. Stress caused by chronic exposure to noise or violence represents another disadvantage of poor neighbourhoods.

Stress

The degree of exposure to stress and the resources available to cope with it explain many individual and group differences in mental health (Turner & Avison, 2003). An individual's position in the social hierarchy 'influences the probability of encountering stressors, which in turn increases the probability of becoming emotionally distressed' (Aneshensel, 1992, p. 19). Various kinds of stress tied to socioeconomic position have been the factor most often cited to explain the link between lower social class position, disorder, and distress (Eaton, 2001). Indeed, a comprehensive model of the stress process, often associated with the work of Leonard Pearlin (Pearlin 1989, 1999; Pearlin et al., 1981; Pearlin & Schooler, 1978), has played a dominant role in medical sociology in the last quarter-century. In seeking to elucidate the connections between social structure and the individual, this model emphasizes the class-related sources of stress, the ways that psychological distress and disorder are expressed, and the factors that mediate the relationship (Pearlin et al., 1981).

Lower socioeconomic position is generally associated with higher rates of stressful events (Brown, Bhrolchain, & Harris, 1975; Eaton & Muntaner, 1999; Warner, 2004). It is chronic strain, however, that is most consistently related to lower class position (Thoits, 1995). Individuals lower in the social hierarchy, for example, are more apt to experience marital problems, suffer financial hardship, unemployment, and job insecurity. Overall, lower status in the class hierarchy is associated with higher levels of stress, which are associated with higher rates of mental disorder and distress. Also, lower socioeconomic position is a greater risk factor for mental disorder than higher position at any given level of stress, and comparable levels of stress are more likely to precipitate mental illness in less, as opposed to more, privileged individuals (Eaton, 2001).

Just how adequately stress exposure can account for distress and disorder has been a matter of some debate. Some investigators have concluded that the association is modest rather than robust (Aneshensel, 1992; Link & Phelan, 1995; Rabkin & Struening, 1976). If only acute events are considered, this is true. But there are other sources of stress beside recent life events, and when chronic stressors, ambient stressors (living in places where there is concern about safety and access to services and transportation), and other sources of stress such as discrimination, daily hassles, and normal life transitions are included as sources of stress, the relationship is stronger (Baum & Garofalo, 1999; Pearlin et al., 2005; Turner & Avison, 2003; Turner, Wheaton, & Lloyd, 1995). Still, stress, while consistently and reliably related to mental health problems, does not account for all of the relationship between social class and health. For one thing, adverse consequences for mental health from exposure to stressors are not inherent in the stressors themselves (Aneshensel, 1999). They have to go through an individual, who determines their meaning in a complex process of appraisal which determines whether an event is threatening, harmful, or benign. Kessler and Cleary (1980) believe that differences in reactiveness to stress are more important for explaining distress than just exposure to it. Both innate temperamental and other factors such as poor self-esteem or a low sense of control that can be associated with class position can contribute to greater stress reactivity.

Coping resources are yet another part of the stress process. Medical sociologists make a distinction between coping resources and coping strategies, which are behavioural and cognitive responses to stress (Pearlin & Schooler, 1978; Thoits, 2010). The main coping resources are a sense of control (or efficacy), social support, and – to a lesser extent because less studied than the other two – self-esteem. The number of individual coping strategies is very large, but they are usually divided into two types, problem-centred and emotion-centred. Problem-centred coping is aimed at reducing the stressful demands themselves, while emotion-centred coping aims at changing one's emotional reactions to the stressful demands. Most people use a combination of resources and strategies when dealing with stress, and which ones work best depend on the particular situation. For example, strains associated with marriage and parenting are best coped with by active problem-solving approaches rather than strategies of avoidance and withdrawal. In marriage, reflective probing of problems reduces strain more effectively than emotional venting, while in parenting a belief that one has influence over one's children is more effective than an attitude of helplessness (Pearlin & Schooler, 1978).

Pearlin and Schooler found that socioeconomic differences exist for coping resources and strategies: less privileged individuals possessed fewer resources and employed less effective coping strategies. This represents double jeopardy. It would be unsurprising to learn that socioeconomic position linked to more stressors and less effective coping might be associated with negative emotions such as depression, hopelessness, anxiety, sometimes hostility; and such is the case. As well as being symptoms of different conditions, these emotions have their own adverse effects on health and well-being (Gallo & Matthews, 1999). For Cohen (2002) and Williams (1998), emotions are bridges that connect social structure to emotional, physical, and even cognitive problems. That is, unfavourable positions in the stratification system generate feelings and emotions that activate physiological pathways such as the sympathetic nervous system and the hypothalamic-pituitary-adrenal axis. In the short run, in the face of acute stress, for example, such activation is a normal physiologic response, but over the longer run, the stress placed on these pathways uninterruptedly (referred to as the 'allostatic load') can be harmful to health and well-being (Kristenson et al., 2004). Activation of these two systems in response to acute and chronic stress has been the topic studied most extensively, but haematological, immune, and inflammatory responses that affect various organs and systems have been shown to be harmful. McEwen (2003), for example, has shown how depressive states may cause anatomical changes in brain areas such as the hippocampus, amygdala, and the dentate gyrus, areas which are associated with memory and the processing of emotions. Other investigators have described how chronic stress is responsible for cardiovascular disease by raising blood pressure, increasing fibrinogen levels in the blood, and elevating interleukin-6, an inflammatory cytokine, in the plasma (Cohen et al., 2007; McEwen, 1998; Roose, Glassman, & Seidman, 2001; Siegrist & Theorell, 2006).

In sum, good coping resources and effective coping strategies exert an important moderating influence on the stress process. The two resources that have received the most attention as stress mediators are a sense of control, or efficacy, and social support. In Kosteniuk and Dickinson's (2003) view, these are crucial secondary determinants of health and well-being, the primary ones being socioeconomic (income, education) and demographic (age, gender) in nature. The quality and quantity of both control and social support are strongly connected to socioeconomic position. In their study, household income was found to be the primary determinant that most strongly predicted levels of control and social support. Control, in turn, turned out to be the secondary determinant with the most significant effect on well-being and health. In other words, more income predicted more control which predicted better health and well-being.

Control

A sense of control is the 'learned expectation that outcomes are contingent on one's own choices and actions – that one can master, control, or effectively alter one's environment' (Ross & Wu, 1995, p. 722). It is the opposite of powerlessness, the belief that one's actions do not affect anything. The concept of personal control is known by many names in the sociological and psychological literature: mastery, locus of control, self-efficacy, autonomy, self-directedness, hardiness, competence, and agency (Bandura, 1997; Ross & Wu, 1995; Syme, 1989).

A sense of control is a large part of morale. Individuals with high morale are confident of their ability to direct their own lives and carry out their plans as well as to get along with others. They enjoy life, their friends, they feel good, have energy, and look forward to the future (Mirowsky & Ross, 2003b). The opposite of good morale is a state of mind Frank (1975) calls 'demoralization.' This is characterized by a feeling of powerlessness or a loss of control over events or the direction of one's life. It results from a sense that one is unable to cope effectively. Frank has argued that demoralization is a common factor in all forms of distress and mental illness, regardless of what specific forms they take. This state of mind is what brings people for help, and all types of effective therapy diminish it. Marmot (2004) believes that class-based differences in a sense of control, at work and in other aspects of life, contribute heavily to the social gradient in health and well-being.

Mirowsky and Ross (2003b) consider a sense of control to be the primary link between psychological distress and low socioeconomic position. They show that lack of control or powerlessness is implicated in most of the distress connected with lower social position. All of the components of higher socioeconomic position – more education, better occupation, decent income – can be regarded as beneficial to health and well-being because they increase an individual's sense of control. Eaton (2001) says it concisely: 'Socioeconomic stratification affects the degree to which individuals can control their environment' (p. 180).

Marmot's (2004) Whitehall studies, as well as Karasek and Theorell's (1990) investigation of the effects of working conditions on heart disease and the Northwestern National Life Insurance Company (1991) survey of employee burnout mentioned in chapter 5, firmly implicate low control at work as a major risk factor for illness and distress. This also represents a major structural problem in society since what distinguishes the working class in the United States is 'its lack of power over the terms and conditions of employment' (Aronowitz, 2003, p. 26).

Social Support

People feel socially supported when they feel 'cared for and loved, esteemed, and a member of a network of mutual obligations' that can be counted on (Cobb, 1976, p. 300). Most definitions of social support refer to the ability of individuals to get their basic social needs – affection, esteem, belonging, identity, security – met through interaction with other people (Aneshensel, 1992). Instrumental, informational, and emotional types of support, which are highly correlated with each other, are usually referred to as 'perceived support' (Thoits, 1995). Most of the studies that look at the relationship between support and health use this construct (Turner & Brown, 2010).

Perceived support is inversely related to psychological distress, physical disorder, and mortality (Aneshensel, 1992). Higher levels of support are associated with fewer depressive, anxiety, or other psychological problems, while lower levels show more (Kessler & McLeod, 1985; LaRocco, House, & French, 1980). When major depression occurs, high levels of support reduce the length of time to recovery and predict higher odds of recovery (George, 2006; George et al., 1989). Individuals with more support also have fewer heart attacks, live longer after a heart attack, recover more completely from strokes, and catch fewer colds than those with less support (Putnam, 2000).

In the Whitehall studies, social support was related to position in the occupational hierarchy. Men and women at upper levels had more relationships that provided emotional support than individuals at lower levels. Upper-class men (but not women) also had more instrumental support. Moreover, negative aspects of close relationships were more often reported among the lower grades for men (but not for women) (Stansfeld, 1999). In general, higher income and education is associated with more social support, larger social networks, and more contact among members (Fischer, 1982).

The social/psychological mechanisms by which social support affects health and well-being are several. First, it seems to enhance self-esteem and a sense of control through affirmation and validation (Pearlin et al., 1981). Second, it bolsters problem-solving abilities and helps individuals make better decisions, thus enhancing their sense of efficacy and helping them avoid the stress that comes with bad choices. People who are supportive contribute information, help with evaluation of situations and problems, suggest sensible plans, and consider likely consequences (McFarlane et al., 1983). Third, support has a buffering effect on stress, reflecting the maxim that a trouble shared is a trouble halved. Fourth, supportive relationships may discourage bad health habits such as heavy drinking, smoking, or drug use (Ross & Wu, 1995; Umberson, 1987).

Low levels of social support have demonstrably negative effects on health and well-being (House, Landis, & Umberson, 1988). Diminished social support predicts poorer mental health generally and depression in particular (Turner & Brown, 2010). Age-adjusted mortality for men with few social connections is over twice as high as it is for men with many connections; for women it is almost three times as high (Berkman & Breslow, 1983).

Beyond a low level of social support is a qualitatively different form of social interaction that clinicians should also be aware of. It was originally described in connection with the prognosis of schizophrenia. This form has been conceptualized under the awkward term 'expressed emotion' (EE). Relatives of schizophrenic patients are considered to express high levels of expressed emotion when they, in relation to the patients, (a) make frequent critical comments about them, (b) are overinvolved with them, and (c) show hostility toward them (Brown et al., 1962). In one of the early studies, hospitalized schizophrenics who returned home to relatives who showed high levels of expressed emotion had much higher relapse rates within nine months than patients who returned to households with low levels: 58% versus 16% (Brown et al., 1972). Vaughn and Leff (1976) replicated this study four years later. They also found, as did Brown and colleagues, that patients in high EE homes could protect themselves from relapse in two ways: by taking antipsychotic medication regularly and by avoiding relatives who showed high levels of expressed emotion. In fact, there was an additive effect for patients who employed both strategies such that their relapse rates were reduced even more than patients who employed only one or the other. McCreadie (1992), following schizophrenic patients for five years, found that those in high EE homes relapsed about once a year while those in low EE environments relapsed only once every three years. Since then, high levels of EE have been shown to affect outcome adversely not only for schizophrenia but also for other mental disorders such as depression, bipolar illness, eating disorders, alcohol abuse, and post-traumatic stress disorder. The course of medical disorders such as diabetes and epilepsy is also affected negatively by high levels of expressed emotion (Leff, 2001).

High EE environments constitute chronic stress, not support, for schizophrenics and other patients. Leff initially viewed caregivers who showed low levels of expressed emotion as detached and neutral. He found this assumption to be false. Low EE relatives had a supportive, calming effect on schizophrenic patients. High EE relatives did not. Leff's work has done a great deal to advance the awareness that the quality of social interaction influences the course of schizophrenia and several other psychiatric and medical disorders.

Early Social Class Influences

Socioeconomic position at all ages strongly defines the social contexts to which individuals are exposed (Turner & Avison, 2003), and the influence of socioeconomic position begins before birth. White women who are poor, for example, have a higher chance of giving birth to a low weight baby than those who are not (Power & Matthews, 1997; Wood, 2003). Low birth weight or a diminished growth rate during the first year of life, presumably the result of adverse intrauterine influences, increases the risk for hypertension, diabetes, and cardiovascular disease in later life (Barker, 1998).

One of the most persuasive pieces of evidence that socioeconomic position at birth is related to risk factors for health and well-being in later life is the British birth cohort study of 1958 (Power et al., 1997; Power & Matthews, 1997).

The study included all children – 17,414 – born in the United Kingdom during one week in March 1958. Follow-up surveys were conducted when they were seven, eleven, sixteen, twenty-three, and thirty-three years old, at which time there were still 11,404 (65%) of the participants in the study. They were categorized at birth on the basis of their father's occupation (a marker of social class) into six groups, of which the top and bottom two were combined. Thus the final four groups were classes I and II (professional and intermediate), III-nm (skilled, non-manual), III-m (skilled manual), and classes IV and V (semi-skilled and unskilled manual workers). When they reached the age of thirty-three, they were asked to rate themselves on fifteen measures of health. Among these ratings were items related to overall health and current level of psychological distress.

Psychological distress and risk factors for poor health at thirty-three were associated with social class at birth. The prevalence of both showed a clear gradient: distress and health risk factors increased incrementally as paternal socioeconomic position declined. Hay fever was the only condition that showed a higher prevalence in the more privileged group. Many other personal and environmental characteristics were associated with class position at birth also, as shown in table 6.1. Thus, in addition to health status and psychological distress at age thirty-three, economic circumstances, health-related behaviours, social and family functioning, marriage, educational achievement, and job status were all significantly correlated with social class of origin. Strongly linked to later distress were poorer economic circumstances during early life,

Table 6.1

Characteristics of British Birth Cohort study sample associated with social class of origin

Aspect	Remarks
Birth weight	Higher in UC*
Body mass index	Higher LC,[†] age 33
Height	Taller in UC at ages 7 and 33
Household overcrowding (> I person/room)	UP[‡]
Lacking household amenities (bathroom, indoor toilet, hot water supply)	UP
Free school meals	UP
Poor outdoor play facilities	UP
Economic circumstances as adults, including below average income at 23, no savings, mortgage or rent in arrears, renting vs owning house, receiving income support/unemployment benefits at 33	UP
Smoking, including maternal smoking during pregnancy, regular smoking ages 23 and 33	UP
Heavy alcohol consumption (units/week > 50 for men, > 35 for women)	No difference for men at age 23; higher for LC men at age 33; no differences for women at either age
Unhealthy diet (white bread, no fruit, vegetables, salad)	UP
Parental divorce before age 16	UP
Infrequent reading at home, measured at age 7	UP
Lack of parental encouragement	UP
No expressed parental aspirations, measured at age 11	UP
Poor social/emotional adjustment at ages 7, 11, and 16 (rated by teachers)	UP
Relationships (living with someone before age 20, early parenthood, divorced/separated, single parenthood by age 33, poor emotional and practical social support age 33	UP, except no class difference for men re single parenthood at age 33
No educational qualifications by age 23	UP
Unemployed	UP, trend stronger for men than women to age 23
Job insecurity	UP except no difference for women at age 23
Laid off at some point between ages 23 and 33	UP, trend stronger for men
Adverse work conditions (monotony, lack of learning opportunities, etc.)	UP

Source: C. Power & S. Matthews. (1997). Origins of health inequalities in a national population sample. *Lancet, 350*, 1584–9.

* Upper classes

† Lower classes

‡ Usual pattern, with LC disadvantaged relative to UC at *p* < .001 significance level

less social support, less education, less secure employment, and more job stress once the work force had been entered. Power and Matthews (1997) comment:

> By adulthood, participants born into lower social classes had experienced more biological and psychosocial risk factors than those born into higher ones. Specifically, those from lower social classes had poorer growth in childhood, combined with greater likelihood of obesity in adulthood; poorer economic conditions in both childhood and adulthood; a less favourable cultural and behavioural environment in the parental home with, for example, greater exposure to passive smoking and, subsequently, a higher likelihood of acquiring health-damaging behaviours in early adulthood; less social and emotional support and stimulation from their own families of origin and, in turn, in their own families; and, finally, few educational qualifications and less secure employment with greater psychosocial job strain. (p. 1588)

This quotation in effect lists the wide range of conditions that mediate the relationship between SES and poor health. Power and Matthews were careful to point out that since the individuals in their study were still only thirty-three years old they would not be yet be expected to show significant medical problems – coronary heart disease, cancer, strokes. But they did emphasize that even at age thirty-three important risk factors for physical and mental problems were firmly established.

Different models seek to explain how earlier life experiences connect to adult health status (Hertzman, 1994; Power & Hertzman, 1997). In the *latency* model, events or experiences that occur at sensitive periods of childhood are thought to have a lifetime effect on health and well-being regardless of subsequent experiences. There is evidence, for example, that development of language and social skills has sensitive periods in the first five years of life; anything that interferes with development during those times results in permanent impairment. In the *cumulative* model, experiences beneficial or harmful to health accumulate over time and depend on the duration and intensity of exposure to factors that have the potential to confer advantage or disadvantage. For example, low social class at three different times in life – at birth, on entering the labour market, and in later adulthood – carries a higher risk of early death than low social class at any one of those times alone (Davey Smith et al., 1997). In the *pathway* model, different experiences in childhood put children on different life trajectories. For example, lower social class at birth is correlated with lower levels of security and stability in early childhood. This leads to unreadiness for school at ages five or six. Lack of readiness for schooling contributes to behavioural problems and failure at school. Behavioural problems and school failure lead to low levels of well-being in early adulthood (Hertzman, 1994). In terms of physical health, poorer social circumstances in childhood have stronger effects on some disorders of later life than others. The relationship is particularly strong for stomach cancer and hemorrhagic stroke, for example (Galobardes et al., 2004). The work of Power and Matthews (1997), cited earlier, is an example of both the cumulative and pathway processes (though it can be hard to differentiate the two), whereas David Barker's (1998) work illustrates the latency model.

By whatever model, however, the evidence to show that parents' class status significantly affects their children's lives is strong. Social conditioning, initiated in the family, begins at birth and has long-lasting effects. David Mechanic (1986) observes:

> Advantage at birth in terms of income and parental education in modern societies continues to elevate the opportunities for survival and health, educational attainment, a more favorable occupation, and a privileged social position. While innate abilities and motivation may compensate for social disadvantage, those launched from a position of greater privilege do better at any level of measurable ability. (p. 3)

The life course perspective on health makes the case that adult health and well-being are influenced by a continuous interaction of biological and social elements at every stage of life, that biological development takes place within a social context, that social conditions at all stages of life are important for health (Blane, 2006), and that risks and advantage accumulate over time. Early and later life trajectories can also be modified in ways that either increase or decrease advantage (Power & Hertzman, 1997).

A particularly striking example of this last point was illustrated in a paper published by Nancy Krieger and colleagues in 2005. They looked at 308 twin pairs, all women. The majority were monozygotic, as opposed to dizygotic, twins. All of the twins were raised together, in the same family, at least until age fourteen, and thus shared the same social class background. In addition to social class position in childhood and adulthood, information was collected from them about a number of cardiovascular risk factors (blood pressure, body mass index, and so forth) and, as adults, how they rated their health. By the time they were older, slightly over forty years of age on average, a third of the pairs were in different occupational class categories from each other. That is, one twin was working class (for example, she held a non-supervisory job), the other was not (for example, she managed or supervised others). The investigators found that there were significant differences in the cardiovascular risk factors and self-reported health in the group of twins who were in different social classes. The working-class twins showed higher scores on risk factors and reported poorer health than their more highly-placed sisters. In this study, then, the socioeconomic status the women achieved as adults, not childhood status or shared genetic makeup, accounted for the differences in health outcomes. This suggests that cumulative experiences over the life course, after adolescence and sometimes after the completion of education, that result in disparate socioeconomic positions (even among identical twins) significantly affect adult health.

Socioeconomic position also exerts its influence through child-rearing practices. In a series of publications, Annette Lareau (1989, 2003; Lareau & Weininger, 2008) has shown that there are significant class-related differences in the way that middle-class and working-class parents raise their children that pertain to three areas: school involvement, time use, and language.

In her first book, Lareau (1989) showed that parents' involvement in their children's schooling was strongly correlated with social class. There is evidence that the best predictor of children's performance in school is the level of parental interest in their education (Wadsworth, 1991).

A major difference between middle- and working-class parents was the degree of their involvement in their children's schooling.[2] Middle-class parents actively 'supervised, supplemented, and intervened' (Lareau, 1989, p. 169) in their children's education. There was an interconnection between school and family life: Parents were interested in all aspects of school life and welcomed, if not demanded, interaction with teachers. They felt free to monitor teachers' and school administrators' activities, and did not hesitate to intervene on their children's behalf.

In contrast, working-class parents rarely intervened in their children's schooling. They trusted the educators to train their children. They viewed school and the family as separate domains, and invitations from teachers to parents to participate in their children's schooling were often turned down. Conley (2008) believes that working-class parents tend to instil a sharp division between the world of children and the world of adults, which puts working-class children at a disadvantage later on.

This involvement in school on the part of middle- and upper-middle-class parents reflects class-related differences in resources and dispositions. When parents have more education themselves, for example, they have the ability to understand the language used by teachers as well as the social confidence to help their children in school. Middle-class parents approach teachers as social equals and are not intimidated by them; this is often not the case with working-class or poor parents. Higher status parents believe they have a right and a responsibility to involve themselves in their child's education, and it is easier for them to do so because they have more resources, among them time and, if they are working, more flexible work schedules.

In a later study that followed the same group of children and their parents through the fifth grade, Lareau (2003) documented further the class-related patterns of raising children that distinguished middle-class parents from working-class parents. The biggest difference between the two was a class-based difference in the organization of daily life in which middle-class children followed a hectic schedule of adult-organized activities. In contrast, the less privileged children were given a more open-ended agenda that was not as tightly controlled by adults. Middle-class parents practise what Lareau calls 'concerted cultivation.' They view their children as projects. They continuously support and encourage their personal growth. These children participate in myriad extracurricular activities, many of them involving organized sports, which results in a very busy schedule for both children and parents. As Camille Paglia (2010) has said, 'Contemporary moms have become virtuoso super-managers of a complex operation focused on the care and transport of children' (p. 12). Parents take the lead in the organization of activities and monitor their children closely. In turn, the children get used to the presence of adult involvement and supervision. Also, since their lives are taken seriously by their parents, they learn to expect that other adults will take their thoughts and opinions seriously and are more apt to challenge adults, including teachers. In middle-class families, also, parents volunteer for school activities and interact easily with teachers outside the classroom. And outside school, at home, conversation is encouraged, verbal jousting is frequent, direct orders are rarely given, and parents often answer questions with questions, leading their children to develop their own reasoning and verbal abilities. Middle-class parents are more likely to have reading materials around the house and their children are encouraged to read.

Lareau believes that this style of parenting is instrumental in helping prepare children for middle- (and upper-middle-) class adult life. They learn to cooperate with peers and adults. They come to feel that they have the right to participate in various activities. They learn to manage time, to plan, and to perform in public, which prepares them for performance-based assessments in school and in later life.

In contrast, working-class (and poor) parents follow what Lareau calls a 'natural growth' paradigm with their children. Their philosophy more often seems to assume that if they provide for the basic needs of their children, the children will grow up satisfactorily by themselves. The parents are often strapped themselves and have neither the resources nor time to devote to their children's development in the same way that middle- and upper-middle-class parents do. In the absence of multiple activities orchestrated by adults, their children have more choice about how to spend their time. As Lareau observes, this often makes for a more relaxed childhood, but it deprives them of opportunities to develop skills that will be useful later. Working-class parents take less of an interest in their children's daily lives and monitor them less. More of the verbal exchanges between parent and child are in the form of orders rather than questions. Working-class adults rarely challenge authority overtly and are more deferential to it. Their children, in turn, develop a more passive and withdrawn stance toward authority than do middle-class children.

Concerted cultivation is a recent phenomenon in American society. Lareau remarks that today's parents are not transmitting child-rearing practices that they learned in their families of origin. Most of them were born in the 1950s and 1960s and were raised according to the natural growth model. Why are middle-class parents more anxious and more intensely involved with their children's lives and education today? The social context has changed, Lareau argues. The position of the United States in the world economy is different now than it was thirty or forty years ago. The loss of higher-paying manufacturing jobs and the increase of lower-paying service jobs mean that good jobs are scarcer than they once were which results in more competition for them. Aware of this, middle- and upper-class parents make whatever efforts necessary to insure that their children have access to the kind of education that will give them a competitive edge.

Lareau did not relate her findings to health outcomes. She was careful to point out that the parenting style that typifies the middle-class does not succeed with all children, but it is not hard to see how this style, which can promote confidence, control, and social participation, could be related to a sense of well-being in later life.

In Summary

No one factor explains the inverse relationship between socioeconomic position or social class and physical health, mental health, and well-being. There are many factors, which are interactive and cumulative over time. Education is a pivotal link between class and health since it increases the chances of good work, more income, a good neighbourhood, and a higher standard of living. Social position is linked to the amount and type of stress one is subject to, the way one responds to stress, and the external resources available to cope with stress when it occurs. Education, steady employment, rewarding work, and adequate financial resources correlate highly with the amount of control and autonomy one can exercise; a sense of control appears to be a key factor that links overall social class and well-being. Class position is also associated with the quality and quantity of social ties and where one lives, both of which are linked to health and well-being. The effect of class is important early in life because parental socioeconomic position is connected with resources and patterns of childrearing that set a trajectory for experiences that impair or enhance well-being and health in later life. The social class one achieves in adult life also affects health. It is, finally, cumulative exposure to good or bad conditions over a lifetime that result in health and well-being or their opposites.

7 Class Differences in Psychotherapy

In the previous chapters I have endeavoured to present a social perspective whose main aim is to show how the structure of society affects well-being and health. Well-being and health reflect differences in the distribution of important resources. The class system in America embodies inequalities of resources that have been pushed to extremes in recent years. This is the picture at the macro and meso levels. In this and the following chapters I want to give more attention to the micro level – to the clinician, the patient, and the interaction between the two – and show the effect of social perspective there, too. In addition, in chapter 8, I return to the issue, raised in the introduction, of why a social perspective has remained largely outside of psychiatry and clinical psychology.

Role of the Therapist

At the level of the individual patient, the role of the therapist or clinician is straightforward. His or her task is to relieve distress (Engel, 1980). This is carried out by sympathetic talk, various kinds of psychotherapy and, often, medication. Most patients, whatever their specific problems, come to psychiatrists and psychologists when they are in crisis. What they most want is relief.

Discussion – and criticism – of psychiatry's larger role in society has existed since its beginnings as a profession (P. Miller & Rose, 1986). Of several authors (Kleinman, 1988; Light, 1980; Luhrmann, 2000) who have written notable books in the past thirty years about psychiatrists and their training, it is Kleinman and Light who have been most explicit about psychiatry's role in, as Kleinman says, 'affirming the status quo and converting social predicaments into psychological conflicts and thereby blinding us to the political roots of our all too human dilemmas' (p. 129).

Unfortunately there are no studies I am aware of that document how larger economic and social issues that contribute to distress and disorder are played out in the consulting rooms of psychiatrists and clinical psychologists. Howard Waitzkin, however, himself both a sociologist and practising internist, studied transcripts of conversations between physicians and patients over a period of years (Waitzkin, 1991). Though Waitzkin studied internists and family practitioners, not mental health professionals, his work is worth some attention in the present context because it is one of the few studies documenting how clinicians deal with social issues in the privacy of their offices and clinics.

Waitzkin (1991) was impressed with how infrequently social context even came up in most interviews and how often clinicians made comments to their patients that either reinforced the prevailing (privileged class) ideology of American society or that attempted to influence patients' behaviour in ways that were consistent with mainstream expectations of how people should behave.

It was the Italian social theorist Antonio Gramsci, Waitzkin (1991) points out, who argued that groups in power control and maintain existing power relationships in society by two means. The first is direct coercion through a monopoly of the legal means of violence, represented by the police and the military. The second, more important and more subtle, is by ideological hegemony. Institutions such as schools, churches, the professional classes, the mass media, and family inculcate and reinforce a system of values and beliefs that by and large supports the established order and the class interests that dominate it.

In his book, Waitzkin (1991) cites numerous examples of how practitioners serve to transmit the prevailing American ideology through the expression of specific attitudes about the importance of work for health (even in the face of evidence that some jobs are detrimental to health), the negative effects of idleness or too much leisure, the need to take personal responsibility for actions, the proper roles (according to physicians) of men and women, and, of course, the ways to lead a healthier life.

Waitzkin also found that practitioners systematically excluded social issues, when they did arise, from their dialogue with patients. This was achieved through interruption, change of subject, the use of close-ended questions, and reinterpretation of social difficulties into the language of symptoms such as anxiety and depression, thus making them amenable to a technical approach, such as prescription of medications. Waitzkin, borrowing a term from Marx, labelled this as 'reification,' a process in which social relations and social processes become transformed into other things – symptoms and diagnoses in this case. A related term for it is 'medicalization,' the process by which non-medical problems become defined and treated as medical disorders (Conrad, 2007). Reification is apt to occur when clinicians pay attention only to signs and symptoms and fail to inquire about the social problems or situations that often lie behind them.

Psychiatrists, clinical psychologists, and other mental health professionals are usually more cognizant of social context than physicians. However, anyone doing clinical work with individual patients cannot entirely escape the influence of the medical model and the dominance of the psychiatric diagnostic system, both of which locate the primary problem squarely within the individual. Physicians, psychiatrists, and clinical psychologists all see patients whose difficult life circumstances are responsible for their symptoms. But patients' social circumstances tend to be secondary to the main interest of physicians, which is to identify organic pathology. In their world, the underlying pathology that causes the symptoms, not the symptoms themselves, is the diagnosis, Unfortunately for psychiatry, no organic causes have been found for any of the serious or common mental disorders. Still, like physicians, psychiatrists often assume the presence of an organic defect – a neurochemical imbalance – behind psychological symptoms. In both cases clinicians' minds tend to be occupied with individual pathology (this is the medical model). Nevertheless, this creates a mindset in which important non-biological factors, such as troublesome life experiences of which depression, anxiety, and somatic complaints are the expressions, slip out of the picture. Waitzkin (1991) comments

> Symptoms, signs, and treatments take on an aura of scientific fact, rather than of subjective manifestations of a troubled social reality. The medical processing of social problems ... constricts the level of attention to the disturbed individual, rather than the social structures impinging on the individual. (p. 16)

If a person is experiencing depression, anxiety, or problems with sleep because of conditions at work – too much overtime, shift work, or little control on the job, for example – the symptoms all too often become the exclusive focus of evaluation and treatment, and the occupational or social sources of distress are left undisturbed.

It could be, as Waitzkin suggests, that clinicians are playing out, in a limited way, the politics of class society by ignoring, overlooking, or reifying social conditions. In doing so, they obscure the existence of social inequities that adversely affect health and well-being. Indeed, Waitzkin's conclusion is that one of medicine's major roles in society, perhaps inadvertently, is to defuse, or blunt, socially caused distress. Kleinman (1986) maintains that psychiatry does the same.

As a concrete example, Waitzkin cites the case of a fifty-five-year-old married man who worked as a radial drill operator and was visiting his doctor several months after he had suffered a heart attack. The patient was a high school graduate who was married and had an eighteen-year-old daughter. He had known his doctor, a thirty-eight-year-old internist, for over five years. The doctor, who had diagnosed his patient as having coronary artery disease and 'severe recurrent depression,' had previously told his patient that the patient's disability insurance following the heart attack would end by a certain period. The patient told the doctor that his union might go on strike soon, which would mean that his disability payments would end and, because of the strike, he would have no income. The doctor asked the patient if going back to work was 'bugging' him. The patient replied, 'Actually I think I want to go back' to which the doctor replied, 'Yeah, I think you should go back.' But then the patient expressed ambivalence about going back to work. He told the doctor that he was bothered by the thought of going back to work and then immediately having to go on strike. The doctor asserted that if he [the patient] went back to work by a certain time it wouldn't bother him(!). The patient rather reluctantly agreed. A bit later the doctor turned to the man's wife and told her that if her husband didn't go back to work his depression would get worse: 'I tell you if this guy stays home, he's going to curl in a ball, you know, he's going to be unreachable.'

In this small excerpt from a much longer transcript, the implication is clearly that, for this patient, working is good. Waitzkin (1991) comments that this doctor may believe that working is good for everyone. While employment is indeed generally good for health, distinctions must be made. The doctor either ignores or is oblivious to the financial problems his patient will face if in fact the union strikes after the patient returns to work. The doctor transmits the message that work is beneficial to the patient's health despite apparently knowing little about conditions at the patient's workplace or the added stress created by the threat of a strike, both topics that could lead to a fruitful discussion and a more considered response from the doctor. Could a high-level of demand coupled with a low-level of control, or an imbalance between effort and rewards (see chapter 5), have played a role in causing the patient's heart disease or his depression in the first place? Waitzkin says that discussions between physicians and patients, such as the one illustrated here, are common. Nor is this problem confined to physicians and psychiatrists.

Isaac Prilleltensky, a Canadian psychologist, has come to much the same conclusion about clinical psychologists (Prilleltensky, 1989, 1994, 1997). Psychologists' preoccupation with only the psychological dimension of life enables the social order to go about its business unchallenged, he asserts. Most psychological models that therapists use, whether analytic, cognitive, or behavioural, are quite innocent of social, economic, or political context. For example, in what Prilleltensky calls the traditional approach to psychotherapy, the one most psychiatrists and psychologists subscribe to, the goal of therapy is one of personal adjustment. Changes in the individual are required so that he or she can fit into a social order whose value, meaning, and possible contribution to the problem at hand are unquestioned. There is a tendency, with this model, to see individual problems as intrapsychic, implying a defect in the individual, or, at most, interpersonal. When social factors are neglected, Prilleltensky argues, the traditional approach creates at least two problems. The first is that the source of difficulties will always be found within the individual since, when the role of society is overlooked, there is nowhere else to look. The second is that energy and resources that might more profitably be put into social change are diverted into personal, private issues (Prilleltensky, 1997).

Prilleltensky (1997) believes that the influence of psychologists' class backgrounds on their practices has been seriously underestimated, a judgment that probably applies to psychiatrists as well. A long socialization process that has established them in the privileged class has taught psychologists to accept society as it is and not to question social arrangements. The more prolonged, systematic, and effective the socialization, the less self-conscious people are about the factors and forces that have shaped them for their roles. Prilleltensky (1994) quotes Yale psychologist Seymour Sarason: 'To be socialized means that one has absorbed and accommodated to predetermined conceptions of the way things are and ought to be' (p. 27). Prilleltensky (1989) maintains that clinical psychology is instrumental in maintaining the status quo by (a) endorsing and not questioning dominant social values and beliefs, (b) advocating these values and beliefs under the guise of professional expertise, and (c) subscribing to a model of human functioning that is asocial in that it represents the individual as independent of social and historical circumstances.

George Albee (1998, 2000; Perry & Albee, 1994), who was a professor of psychology at the University of Vermont, was also critical of the role that clinical psychologists played in maintaining the status quo. He pointed out that uncritical acceptance of the medical model by clinical psychologists many years ago committed them to the same organic/deficit model of mental disorder that psychiatrists use. As a result, they failed to consider a social model that emphasized the role of chronic stress in mental disorder. The major sources of this stress were related to imbalances of power associated with lower social class status (including poverty, unemployment, and poor living conditions) in addition to exploitation, discrimination, and minority status (Albee, 1986, 1990). Social and political action was needed to counter these inequities but had largely been ignored by psychologists because of the prevailing deficit model. In Albee's (2000) view, clinical psychology not only supported the status quo, but 'by aligning itself with the conservative view of causation, [it] has joined the forces that perpetuate social injustice' (p. 248).

Class Differences and Consequences

Mean pretax income for psychiatrists in the United States in 2009 was $163,660. For psychologists (including clinical, counselling, and school psychologists) it was $72,310, while for all occupations in the United States it was $43,460 (U.S. Department of Labor, 2009). These income differences are only a part of other differences between socioeconomic strata that have consequences for psychotherapy.

In her 1989 book on the professional middle class – the credentialed segment of the privileged class in Perrucci and Wysong's classification – Barbara Ehrenreich pointed out that outside of the workplace (where they labour under the supervision of credentialed class managers) most working-class people encounter credentialed class individuals not as friends or neighbours but as 'helping professionals' such as teachers, social workers, therapists, physicians. These roles confer authority and the power to make judgments. The dialogue is one-directional, in the form of diagnoses, evaluations, and instructions. The credentialed class, Ehrenreich charges, views itself as the sole repository of useful information.

Significant differences in working conditions and lifestyle exist between classes. Like most members of the credentialed class, clinicians must earn their livings. But unlike working-class people, they have considerably more autonomy and are usually not directly supervised. Both the professional and managerial segments of the credentialed class have a guild-like quality in that they are open only to people who have completed a lengthy education and have achieved certain credentials. Their wealth enables them to live in neighbourhoods with members of their own class, pay for college educations for their children, take regular vacations, and partake in various cultural activities (Ehrenreich, 1989).

How work is regarded is largely a class phenomenon. Only in the credentialed class is work seen as intrinsically rewarding, creative, and important (Ehrenreich, 1989). For much of the working class their work is increasingly stressful and insecure (Ciulla, 2000; De Santis, 1999; Head, 2003; Fraser, 2001; Shulman, 2003). It is members of the privileged class who possess the active or challenging jobs, those characterized by high demand but also high control. It is the working class who do the high strain jobs, where demand is high and control is low, or the jobs that make few demands or challenges and still offer little control or autonomy. Personal responsibility and effort are important, but it is access to resources, not only individual effort, that leads to success. Dependency has a negative connotation in a society that strongly values self-reliance, and social dependence is often attributed to personal failing. But the majority of people who find themselves in a position of social dependency and apply for welfare find themselves there more often because of economic and political conditions beyond their control than because of personal misjudgment, personality disorder, or mental illness. The single most common cause of a fall into poverty is a reduction of work hours that lowers family income (Mishel et al., 2005).

What part clinicians' credentialed class status plays in therapy is also reflected in the kinds of patients that psychiatrists and psychologists prefer to treat. This preference reflects class differences, though it is rarely put like that. Psychiatrists, at least in the past, have unsurprisingly been shown to prefer patients who can afford their fees and who are most often like themselves, with similar values and outlooks (Rogow, 1970). The YAVIS syndrome – patients who are considered most suitable for therapy are Young, Attractive, Verbal, Intelligent, and Successful – has long been part of psychological and psychiatric lore (Schofield, 1964). These are the characteristics, with perhaps the exception of age and appearance, of psychiatrists and psychologists themselves.

Hollingshead and Redlich's (1958) study, though now old, revealed differences between therapists and lower-class patients that were dismaying but do not sound entirely out of date. They found that therapists rated patients in classes I through III as 'liked,' patients in classes IV and V as 'disliked.' As a group, the therapists were irritated by the inability of lower-class patients to think in their (the therapists') terms and were critical of lower-class values. Unsurprisingly, this caused higher drop-out rates among lower-class neurotic patients. The most frequent source of difficulty between therapists and lower-class patients was a misunderstanding about what to expect from psychotherapy. These patients expected therapists to be directive, like medical doctors, while therapists wanted patients to achieve insight. This is unlikely to be a problem now, when so many more psychiatric drugs are prescribed and the goal of insight, with the demise of analysis, is a thing of the past. Hollingshead and Redlich acknowledged that psychoanalysis was limited to patients from classes I and II because they were 'the only ones where individuals are not preoccupied with overwhelming external pressures and conflicts' (p. 347) and because they were the only patients who could afford to pay for such treatment. They also cautioned that the values of the therapist and the patient did not need to be identical, only that they should not be too far apart.

These findings, or variants of them, have been duplicated in the psychiatric and psychological literature. In a comprehensive review, E. Jones (1974)[1] documented the negative attitudes and stereotypes that therapists exhibited toward lower-class patients, who were less often accepted for therapy, who were regarded as being less psychologically minded and possessed of unrealistic expectations, who were thought to require more concrete forms of therapy, and who were prone to drop out sooner than more affluent patients. Little thought seemed to have been given to the possibility that therapists' negative attitudes toward the poor may have had something to do with drop-out rates. Jones also confirmed that most therapists preferred patients who were from the same social stratum as themselves. Similar findings have been reported by Storck (2002).

There are several problems that privileged-class therapists face when they see working-class patients. It can be hard for a credentialed-class professional raised in an affluent family to appreciate the social and economic constraints that less affluent individuals face, such as the stress on a single mother with children who lives in a bad neighbourhood with poor schools or the impact of an abusive relationship on a woman who cannot leave her abuser because she needs his financial support. Sums of money so small they have literally no meaning to a professional may be the difference between making it through the month or not for poorer families.

Differences in life styles, attitudes, ideologies, and the use of language can create gaps in understanding between members of different classes that are hard to bridge in psychotherapy. Speech patterns are tailored to the upper rather than the lower end of the class spectrum. Even differences in dress may cause problems, as in the case of a thirty-five-year-old skilled blue-collar employee who consulted a psychologist for marital problems. He had recently seen a psychiatrist for the same problem but had decided not to go back after two sessions. When asked why, he said, 'It was his clothes. They were so nice, not like anything I'd ever wear. I didn't feel comfortable.'

Clinicians prefer not only to treat patients like themselves; they also give them more optimistic prognoses than less privileged patients, which may be realistic given the differences in resources (Magnus & Mick, 2000). Still, clinicians give worse prognoses to patients they *perceive* as being lower rather than middle class in experimental studies when they do not have accurate information about the actual social class background of the patients (Haase as cited in E. Jones, 1974). Problems may be compounded when patients, in addition to being poor, are either black or Hispanic, who 'must [then] overcome the biases, cultural blind spots, reactive guilt, and unconscious prejudice of the person to whom he [sic] comes for help' (Peck, 1974, p. 526).

Bias against the poor is called 'classism' (Lott, 2002; L. Smith, 2005). The term refers to assumptions or misconceptions that therapists make or have about lower-class patients that hinder their access to psychological services. Smith lists four misconceptions that, for her, exemplify classism in practice. The first is that the poor[2] are so overwhelmed with everyday problems that they cannot make use of psychological counselling. The second is that therapeutic help is of lesser value to lower-class patients in light of the overwhelming, reality-based problems of living that they face. The third is that therapists are dragged down by the realities of lower-class existence, and the fourth is that psychological services do not benefit the poor because lower-class patients are neither familiar with nor accept them.

Smith (2005) addresses these misconceptions. With respect to the third of these, for example, she points out that, indeed, working with less privileged patients does expose comfortable upper-middle-class therapists to realities that they would rather not see. Smith lists some of the hardships that such people face: persistent involuntary unemployment, jobs that do not pay enough, deteriorating public housing, overcrowded schools, racism, violence, and inconsistent police presence, which undermines safety. She continues,

> I do not imply that this avoidance [of acknowledging the realities of life lower on the social ladder] is conscious. I believe that we avert our gaze from the poor as an unconscious way of preserving our ability to enjoy our relative good fortune amid an unequal distribution of resources. When we from the middle-class go into poor neighborhoods to work, we must admit into consciousness a vivid comprehension of the disparity between their lives and ours. (p. 693)

In 2000 the American Psychological Association (APA) published a resolution on poverty and socioeconomic status that acknowledged the increasing income gap between the rich and the poor, the high rate of child poverty, the particular vulnerability of women and certain minority groups, the many developmental, psychological and physical problems associated with poverty, and the increased rate of mental illness among the poor. The APA noted the lack of a wider perspective in thinking about the poor: 'Perceptions of the poor and of welfare – by those not in those circumstances – tend to reflect attitudes and stereotypes that attribute poverty to personal failings rather than socioeconomic structures and systems.' (APA, 2000, p. 2). A program of advocacy for research, training, education, and public policy directed toward the poor was formulated. Two of the seventeen recommendations had to do with increased access to mental health services, but the majority were concerned with other improvements in the form of better social provision, including education, income, food and nutrition, housing, insurance, good jobs, and child care.

The report was more concerned with the poor than it was with, for example, the adverse consequences of social class disparities in general. The advantage of this focus is that the lowest group on the social hierarchy, clearly the one in greatest need, is the one that receives attention. A drawback was that it reinforced the impression that health and social problems are limited to a disadvantaged minority – the poor – rather than distributed in gradient fashion across society. As we have seen, the middle class is being squeezed also. In its categorical approach to the rich and the poor, the resolution reflected a viewpoint, more common before 1985, that assumed the existence of a threshold (the poverty line) below which increasing resources, particularly income, would improve health and well-being but above which significant improvements would not occur. We now know, thanks primarily to the Whitehall studies, that socioeconomic factors affect health and well-being all the way from the bottom to the top of the social ladder.

In 2007, another report issued by the APA recommended that a committee on socioeconomic status be established within the organization with the goal of raising awareness of socioeconomic and class issues pertaining to health and well-being (American Psychological Association, 2007). It also urged that classism be regarded and taught as a major form of discrimination.

A year later, in 2008, a task force of the APA published a report on resources available for the inclusion of social class into psychology curricula (American Psychological Association, 2008). It acknowledged that issues of social class and socioeconomic status had been absent from textbooks of psychology and from university and college curricula as well as 'invisible' in discussions, in teaching, and in research within the field. The report contained suggestions about how to raise class consciousness, presented examples of undergraduate and graduate syllabi pertaining to socioeconomic issues, gave references to works of fiction and non-fiction, popular media outlets, websites, scholarly articles, and included a guide to researching public policy related to SES.

In Summary

Clinicians – whether physicians, psychiatrists, or clinical psychologists – often fail to question problematic social arrangements because of their own social background and because the biomedical model and the psychiatric diagnostic system emphasize individual problems and pathologies. This would not matter if social arrangements were not responsible for disparities in the distribution of resources that have an impact on health and well-being. Class-based differences between clinicians and patients can interfere with treatment. An awareness of these differences, however, can mitigate the problem.

8 The *DSM*, Disorder, and Distress

At the beginning of the book I mentioned that there were two reasons that a social perspective has been neglected in clinical work. The first was that it had not been clearly defined. I hope this is no longer the case. With an awareness of how the class system works, a grasp of why roles are important, and how economic policies and political decisions affect groups differently, a wider understanding of the individual should now be possible. I would now like to turn to the other reason that social perspective has been stunted: the psychiatric *Diagnostic and Statistical Manual of Mental Disorders*, the well-known *DSM*. I want to spend some time on this since the topic has important implications for both clinicians and patients. In this discussion I rely primarily and heavily on the work of Horwitz (2002), but the publications of Wakefield (1992) as well as Horwitz and Wakefield (2005, 2007) have also been helpful.

The Horwitz and Wakefield Argument

The first order of business in clinical work in psychiatry and much of clinical psychology is to make an axis I diagnosis, if there is one. Axis I is the category reserved for clinical disorders. This involves eliciting symptoms, counting them up, taking account of the length of time they have been present, judging the disability they cause, and ruling out other symptoms or conditions that might better account for the diagnosis. Other axes that provide different kinds of information that may help the clinician plan treatment and predict outcome are reserved for personality disorder, medical disorder, psychosocial and environmental problems, and assessment of current functioning. The axis

I diagnosis is paramount in the diagnostic process, however, It is the symptoms that count, literally.

Increased reliability of diagnosis is one advantage of this approach. Clinicians and researchers can more easily agree on what they are talking about. A weakness is that such an emphasis on symptom-based diagnoses neglects the role of social circumstances for many disorders and symptoms and lumps normal emotional responses together with serious mental illnesses.

Horwitz (2002)[1] and Wakefield (1992) point out that the present classification system is based on a model of disorder that uses serious mental illness as the prototype. In this model, symptoms are indicative of a brain-based defect, presumably genetic or neurochemical in nature, that has distinct symptoms, a predictable course, and a specific treatment. This model is appropriate for such conditions as schizophrenia and bipolar illness. These disorders manifest basic behavioural and psychological dysfunctions – of thought, of mood – associated with distress and disability. They are neither expectable nor culturally understandable responses to a particular event, nor do they represent conflicts between the individual and society.

The problem with the diagnostic system is overreach. This occurs not only because of the assumption that the basic cause of the disorder is in the brain but also because the diagnostic system leaves out meaningful considerations of context. The result is that real mental disorders; states of distress that are expected, understandable, and normal; and even deviancy are thrown together and called mental disorders. The capture and conversion of distress, in particular, by the psychiatric profession have a number of beneficial consequences for the psychiatric profession, patients, drug manufacturers, and advocates for the mentally ill. But it also has several disadvantages, among which are inflated rates of mental disorder in the community, stigmatization of patients, and neglect of social factors in the causation and shaping of distress and disorder.

Brief History

How and why we got to this state of affairs is well told by Horwitz (2002) and Horwitz and Wakefield (2007). Horwitz (2002) reminds us that throughout most of its history psychiatry in the United States was asylum-based. Psychiatrists cared for patients who suffered from a variety of serious disorders, including schizophrenia, mania, depression, syphilis, epilepsy, mental retardation, and dementia. The treatment of syphilis and epilepsy was taken over by other specialists as the organic aetiologies of these diseases became understood, but psychiatrists retained responsibility for the care of seriously mentally ill patients. Mental illness was equated with madness. When the first formal list of psychiatric disorders was published in the United States in 1918, it contained twenty-two categories of mental illness, twenty-one of which referred to different forms of psychosis. The remaining category was reserved for those who were not psychotic (Horwitz, 2002, p. 39; White, 1924). Mental disorders were regarded as brain diseases, and symptoms were assumed to be manifestations of some type of organic condition.

For various reasons, including the influx of Freudian-trained analysts into the United States in the years before World War II and a culture receptive to analysis, Freud's theory caught on in America during the thirties and forties. For a profession that had been languishing, literally, in mental hospitals along with its clients and watching its patients being channelled into other specialties, for a profession that offered little except custodial care to its charges and low status to its practitioners, the arrival of psychoanalysis – Horwitz (2002) refers to it as dynamic psychiatry – was a godsend. It offered a new and promising treatment along with a vastly expanded client base. It completely altered the landscape of psychiatry.

Dynamic[2] psychiatry expanded its client base by linking neurotic behaviour with normal behaviour and by classifying both as variants of a common developmental process. This served to blur the distinction between the neurotic and the normal but maintained the distinction between psychoses and other disorders. Neuroses, according to Freud, were rooted in universal childhood experiences, such as the Oedipus conflict or conflict over toilet training, and the differences between normal and abnormal behaviour were differences of degree, not kind. For example, obsessive-compulsiveness shaded gradually into the well-organized normal (though perhaps a bit compulsive) individual. Freud's aim was to provide a general psychology that explained all, not just neurotic, behaviour.

Symptoms now came to be considered indicators of symbolic conflicts that arose as a result of a complex interaction between unconscious dynamics and a process of repression that could only be understood in the context of the individual's biography. As a result, the causal process that produced symptoms rather than the nature of the symptoms became the focus of analytic therapy. Unconscious conflicts about aggression and sexuality were the usual targets of treatment. Symptoms themselves were regarded as 'chameleon-like' (Horwitz, 2002, p. 45) expressions of unconscious conflicts. The same symptoms could indicate different underlying conflicts and the same conflict could be expressed through different symptoms. Because of this, and because overt symptoms represented only the most socially accepted way of expressing a conflict, precise classification schemes based on symptoms were unimportant. Diagnosis had only a minor role in therapy and was hardly ever the starting point of treatment.[3] A search for the unconscious underlying conflicts that produced the symptoms was. The first *DSM* in 1952 viewed symptoms as indicative of either broad underlying dynamic conditions or as reactions to difficult life circumstances.

Just as today, when the prevailing cultural milieu interprets certain symptoms as clinical depression that can be relieved by fluoxetine (Prozac), so in that era one's problems were interpreted as manifestations of conflicts that could be resolved through psychoanalysis.

But this era ended, too, again for a variety of reasons. One was a shift in scientific standards. The clinical anecdote and the case study were no longer sufficient. Acceptable data had to be empirically based, using clearly defined diagnostic categories, random controlled trials, and sophisticated statistical techniques. Analysts were at first disdainful of these demands. As a result, psychoanalytic psychiatrists, who had protected themselves from competition from other psychoprofessionals (psychologists, social workers) through their status as physicians, found themselves increasingly looked down on by their medical colleagues, who regarded the psychiatric approach to diagnosis and treatment as unscientific. Another factor in the diagnostic revolution was that therapists of whatever qualification (and some with very few) were entering the field of psychotherapy in increasingly large numbers. The analytic movement had created a need for therapy that was greater than psychiatrists alone could meet. Criticized by medical practitioners and besieged by other mental health professionals who could learn and practise dynamic psychiatry as well as psychiatrists, psychiatry returned to the biomedical model that the dynamic model had originally displaced. This served to re-establish professional legitimacy with the rest of medicine and to differentiate psychiatry from its competitors.

Advent of Diagnostic Psychiatry

What Horwitz refers to as the diagnostic revolution began in 1972 with the publication of the Feighner criteria for mental disorders (Feighner et al., 1972). This modest list contained only fourteen distinct categories of mental illness. It emphasized direct observation of signs and symptoms, categorical separation of symptoms so that disease categories did not overlap, and inter-rater reliability. No particular set of causes was given priority – they could be social, psychological, or biological – but there was a strong presumption that the causes were biological and/or genetic and that these were more powerful influences for the development of mental illness than social or psychological factors. The vague unconscious mechanisms of the analytic system were replaced by a symptom-based classification of mental disorder. This was undertaken in order to eliminate psychodynamic assumptions (such as unconscious conflicts being the cause of symptoms) that had always reduced the reliability of diagnosis. Disorders were now defined by lists of overt symptoms, regardless of cause. Like medical illnesses – and now based on the same biomedical model – psychiatric disorders were viewed as natural entities that existed in the body and produced the symptoms from which the individual suffered, usually independent of influences beyond the individual's immediate social environment. Disturbed brains rather than deep-seated conflicts were viewed as the primary cause of disorder. As for therapy, the search for the best medication replaced the lengthy and expensive psychodynamic exploration of a patient's life.

The *DSM–III* (*Diagnostic and Statistical Manual*, third edition) task force was given the task of revising the diagnostic manual. Chaired by Robert Spitzer beginning in 1974, the committee built on the Feighner criteria. The goals were different, however. Spitzer's mandate was to create a diagnostic system that would serve not only researchers but also therapists in the sense that it would allow them to retain the large patient population that had already been captured by dynamic psychiatry. Both goals were achieved by focusing on reliability, the ability to produce a consistent replicable result. Researchers needed reliable diagnoses so that they could agree on which patients were ill and what they were suffering from. Indeed, 'the success of all the other justifications for diagnoses – aetiology, prognosis, and treatment – depends on whether a category identifies a distinct condition' (Horwitz, 2002,

p. 109). Standardized definitions of mental disorders were needed. Since schizophrenia and bipolar disorder were more clearly defined and distinct than the other disorders in two earlier versions of the manual, these became the model for the other diagnostic categories. Ironically, psychotic disorders, marginalized by dynamic psychiatry, returned in diagnostic psychiatry as the prototypes for the usefulness of categorical thinking in diagnosis. But in order to include the patient population that had been generated over the years by dynamic psychiatry, fourteen diagnostic entities were too few. The new *DSM–III* was meant to be inclusive, not exclusive, so that practitioners did not lose patients on the grounds that patients' problems were no longer psychiatric.

The diverse and often normal human difficulties that analytically oriented therapists treated that distinguished them so decisively from asylum-based psychiatrists – problems of living, of social relationships, of marriage, of children, and symptoms of unhappiness, anxiety, value conflicts, depression, somatic problems, even deviance – were reconfigured into discrete forms of individual pathology, defined by lists of symptoms and incorporated into the *DSM–III*. This provided complete coverage of the population of patients who consulted psychiatrists. No wonder that Spitzer (1991) said 'Limiting the DSM-III to only those categories that had been fully validated by empirical studies would be at the least a serious obstacle to the widespread use of the manual by mental health professionals' (p. 294). With the addition of acute stress reaction, adjustment disorders, and other categories that included atypical clinical presentations (depression, not otherwise specified, for example), almost all imaginable psychological distress could now be defined as some kind of psychiatric disorder.

There is no question that diagnostic psychiatry possesses a number of advantages over dynamic psychiatry. Reliability of psychiatric diagnosis has improved, which is particularly important for psychiatric research. With the elimination of vague diagnostic categories, like the neuroses, and the need to look for the supposed conflicts lying behind symptoms, diagnostic psychiatry has made the process of diagnosis more straightforward for clinicians and thereby enhances their confidence in it. For some patients, knowing they have a disorder that is clearly defined and explains their distress is often a relief. For others, the attribution of their symptoms to an underlying neurochemical disorder can explain underachievement or failure, provide an alternative to punishment, and even lead to special provision, as in the case of learning disability.

Horwitz (2002) reminds us that diagnoses have important social functions. They represent modes by which individuals can interpret and make sense of their symptoms. They are legitimate societal scripts for illness and distress that structure how psychiatrists and patients alike learn which symptoms to pay attention to or ignore, to respond to or dismiss. Psychiatric diagnoses – interpretations of symptoms – are the means by which psychiatrists, doctors, clinical psychologist, patients, and the general public make sense of troubling experiences.

Problems with Diagnostic Psychiatry

There are, however, problems with the symptom-based classification system that the *DSM* embodies. When symptoms are classified without regard to their causes, there is no limit to the kinds of conditions, including normal but troubling experiences, that can be included in the *DSM*.

The transformation of some cases of normal but intense sadness into the diagnosis of major depression is an especially clear example of how the diagnostic system can capture normal and expectable responses to stress. Horwitz and Wakefield (2005, 2007) point out that for two-and-a-half millennia normal human nature was regarded as having a propensity toward intense sadness after certain kinds of losses. Such feelings were regarded as disordered only when they persisted longer than normal or were disproportionately intense. Using the current *DSM* criteria, all a patient has to do to receive the diagnosis of a major depressive disorder is to report five of nine criteria that have been present for a two-week period. The only times that a cause can be taken into consideration is when the symptoms are judged to be the result of a medical condition, a pharmacologic agent, or bereavement. Yet normal sadness with symptoms identical to those that define major depressive disorder is not confined to bereavement, Horwitz and Wakefield (2005) emphasize. 'Betrayal by romantic partners, being passed over for an anticipated promotion, failure to achieve long-anticipated goals, or discovering a life-threatening illness in oneself or a loved one' (p. 49) are examples of other events that can cause symptoms identical to major depression. Yet all such symptoms, regardless, of context, are classified as major depressive disorder. Perhaps other social circumstances besides bereavement that lead to symptoms of major depression should also be excluded from the category of major depression and thus of mental disorder, Horwitz and Wakefield suggest.

In 2007 Wakefield and his colleagues published a study that addressed this issue. They compared individuals with normal bereavement responses after the death of a loved one with individuals who suffered major losses from other causes, including rejection by a loved one, financial misfortune, failure to attain valued goals, and severe physical illness. In the current edition of the *DSM*, normal grief – whose signs and symptoms may mimic major depression exactly – is not considered a mental disorder. Only if bereavement lasts an unexpectedly long time and/or shows unusual symptoms will it be diagnosed as a mental disorder – major depression or something more serious such as a psychotic disorder. What Wakefield and colleagues found was that losses other than death caused virtually the same symptoms that loss from death did. If uncomplicated bereavement is not a mental disorder and other losses cause identical symptoms, why should those other kinds of losses also not be excluded from the category of mental illness, they asked. They are not excluded at the moment, which means that a certain number of patients with intense normal sadness experiences are being categorized as major depression under current diagnostic criteria. Based on their study, the authors estimated that the rate of diagnosed major depression would have been about 25% lower had other losses been excluded. Their proposal to exclude other conditions has drawn various reactions from psychiatrists (Kendler et al., 2008; Maj, 2008; Pies, 2008).

Horwitz (2002) argues that there are in fact very few true mental illnesses that fit the categorical, disease-based model of the *DSM*. Many of the disorders in the current *DSM* represent not true mental illness but, instead, normal reactions to stressful circumstances, deviant behaviour, or general human unhappiness and dissatisfaction. They are all regarded as individual mental disorders in the *Diagnostic and Statistical Manual*.

To some extent experienced psychiatrists and psychologists can compensate clinically for this problem,[4] but epidemiological surveys, using a *DSM*-inspired approach to diagnosis, cannot. Unrealistically inflated rates of psychiatric disorder in the community are the result. This invites not only public scepticism but also increases the probability that medical treatment will replace sound social policy (Horwitz & Wakefield, 2005).

It may be, too, that the current diagnostic system promotes the treatment of life problems at the expense of serious mental illness with internal dysfunctions (Horwitz, 2002) so that psychiatric and psychological services are diverted away from patients with serious mental illness toward those with problems of living.

The current system may also hinder research. By lumping together all sorts of conditions on the assumption that they have a biological basis when in fact only a few probably do, the search for biological factors – in genes or a combination of genes – will be fruitless. It may be, instead, that genes produce only broad vulnerabilities to depressive, compulsive, or addictive traits which are then given a particular form by social and cultural forces, not that specific genes are responsible for such conditions as anorexia, non-psychotic depression, or several types of anxiety disorders.[5]

The most troublesome problem with the *DSM*, in light of my argument in this book, is its logic that steers clinicians in the direction of regarding common symptoms, such as anxiety and depression, only as indicators of psychiatric disorder. Simultaneously, it steers them away from considering that symptoms may be indicators of difficult social circumstances and the social arrangements that structure them. This causes the social context to be scanted and obscures the contribution of social arrangements to suffering. And by converting what is probably a significant amount of distress into categories of individual psychiatric disorder, the *DSM* sacrifices validity, the true state of affairs, for reliability, the ability of two independent observers to check the same symptoms off a checklist and come to the same conclusion.

Mental Disorder and Distress

The easiest way to address these problems is to stick consistently to the definition of mental illness that the *DSM* advocates. For, in fact, the *DSM*'s definition of mental illness is very similar to Horwitz and Wakefield's in stressing that mental disorders are internal dysfunctions and not expectable responses to particular events (Horwitz, 2002, p. 21). The problem, as mentioned earlier, is that the *DSM* has expanded, for political and professional reasons, to include many conditions that do not meet the definition. Horwitz (2002) and Wakefield (1992) argue that mental disorder has two components, one universal, the other cultural or social. The universal component is an internal dysfunction. An internal dysfunction exists when one or more psychological systems – of cognition, perception, motivation, memory, language, attachment, affect – are unable to function as they were designed to do evolutionarily, by the process of natural selection. Clinicians should suspect the presence of an internal dysfunction when '[symptoms] either arise in the absence of any stressor that would expectably produce them or persist with greater than normal severity and for a longer time after the initial stressor has disappeared' (Horwitz, 2002, p. 31). The presence of symptoms alone is never enough to define mental disorder. A social context is also required. Social context and cultural standards determine what behaviours are normal or abnormal. These standards are not the same across societies or cultures. They are culturally specific. Adjectives in the *DSM* such as 'inappropriate,' 'maladaptive,' or 'bizarre' identify the culturally based value judgments that comprise the second, social, component of the definition of mental disorder. Hallucinations, prolonged grief, fear of snakes, or paranoia are not considered abnormal in all cultures. It is the combination of the universal and social components that adds up to what Horwitz and Wakefield (2007) call true mental disorder, which is a 'harmful dysfunction' (p. 17). Table 8.1 summarizes the various terms and groups of conditions used by Horwitz (2002) that are relevant to the following discussion.

Schizophrenia, bipolar disorder, other psychotic illnesses (for example, delusional disorder), and recurrent endogenous depression fulfil the two criteria for mental disorder best, in Horwitz's (2002) view. These conditions are probably mental diseases in the same way that diabetes and hyperthyroidism are medical diseases: their symptoms serve to identify a specific and distinct underlying disorder. The internal dysfunction involves dysmodulation of affect in manic and depressive disorders, and of cognition and working memory (Silver et al., 2003) in schizophrenia. The symptoms of both disorders are considered unusual, excessive, and inappropriate in light of any social situation that might explain them. Horwitz argues that these disorders are composed of distinct groups of symptoms that do not have a great deal of overlap between them.[6] Their form and occurrence are similar across cultures[7] and their course and treatment are relatively specific. Antipsychotics are the long-term pharmacologic treatment of choice for schizophrenia, for example, while mood stabilizers such as lithium or divalproex are still the first choice for prevention of the manic phase of bipolar disorder.

A second category of problems also meets the criteria for mental disorder – Horwitz (2002) calls it non-psychotic disorder – that has characteristics that distinguish it from the mental diseases of the first category. The boundaries of the disorders in this category, in contrast to the psychotic category, are often indistinct. For example, symptoms

Table 8.1
Different terms used by Horwitz in description of mental conditions

Term	Features	Examples
I. Mental disease	Symptoms reflect underlying organic disorder; distinct cause (?), prognosis, and treatment; occurs world-wide regardless of social context	Schizophrenia, bipolar affective disorder, recurrent endogenous depression, delusional disorders
II. Non-psychotic disorders: culturally structured vulnerabilities	Symptoms structured according to societal norms, identity categories, and psychiatric nosology; underlying vulnerability caused by risk factors; common – not distinct – causes, prognosis, treatment; symptoms vary widely over place and time	Non-psychotic depression, anxiety, eating disorders, phobias, OCD, panic, PTSD
Mental disorder	Includes both categories above since both represent psychological dysfunctions that are socially inappropriate or harmful	
III. Distress	Symptoms secondary to social causes; not valid form of mental illness because appearance of symptoms appear and disappear with stress	Acute stress reaction, depression, anxiety, psycho-physiologic disorders
IV. Deviance	Any violation of social norms, regulated by law or not	Substance misuse, antisocial behaviour, promiscuity, crime
Mental illness	Whatever a particular social group defines as such	*DSM IV*

Source: A.V. Horwitz. (2002). *Creating mental illness*. Chicago, IL: University of Chicago Press.

of anxiety and depression usually occur together. Significant crossover of diagnoses occurs over time. Patients with anxiety disorder become depressed, patients with phobias become obsessive, and those with depression may become somatisizers. The medications used in their treatment are not specific to any one disorder in this group of disorders but are instead effective for all of them. The selective serotonin reuptake inhibitors (SSRIs), for example, are prescribed successfully for depression, panic, generalized anxiety, eating disorders, obsessive-compulsive illness, post-traumatic stress disorder (PTSD), and substance abuse. While genetic, family, and neurochemical studies of psychotic disorders lend support to the idea that their cause contains, or will turn out to contain, a large biological component, the case is quite different with the non-psychotic disorders, for which there are virtually no specific aetiologies.

Horwitz's (2002) and others'[8] interpretation of this finding is that individuals with non-psychotic disorders have a general vulnerability to psychological dysfunction that is associated with common, not specific, risk factors. These include a family history of any psychiatric disorder, early trauma, difficult life circumstances at the time the disorder appears, weak social support systems, and female gender. They are common to all sorts of disorders and may create a vulnerability to psychiatric symptoms in general, not to any one specific disorder. 'With the exception of the psychotic disorders, biological, psychological, and social stresses make people vulnerable to psychological disorders in general, not to particular kinds of disorders' (Horwitz 2002, p. 113).

Social and cultural influences shape these vulnerabilities into specific forms. A powerful force is the diagnostic system itself, the *DSM*, which provides categories through which people can interpret their distress in ways that make sense to them and that are acceptable to others. Specific examples of vulnerabilities that are shaped in culturally bound ways include hysteria, which is now rare but which was once common among young women in a particular time and place; eating disorders, arising from a society with access to more food than it needs and cultural norms of thinness, beauty, and fitness; and depression, 'the most ubiquitous form of human suffering' (Horwitz 2002, p. 126), which reflects a vulnerability that takes widely different forms in different cultures. The role of culture or society in shaping symptoms of mental disorder does not mean, however, that the underlying disorder, the vulnerability, is artificial or unassociated with real suffering. But neither do these kinds of mental disorder fit the model in which specific symptoms indicate a specific underlying disease process, as the few major (psychotic) mental disorders come close to doing.

It is usually taken for granted that internal dysfunctions are innate and biological in nature. This may well turn out to be true for the most serious mental disorders, although stress and social circumstances may affect the time of their appearance and their course. But in the case of non-psychotic disorders, internal dysfunctions may be the result of social causes. Virtually any of the various acute and chronic stressors that cause emotional distress, falling with enough force at a vulnerable period of life on a vulnerable personality, can cause an internal dysfunction. These stressors include acute events such as divorce, unemployment, physical illness, and the death of friends and family. Events that are negative and uncontrollable are especially harmful. So are severe chronic strains, such as those caused by very troubled marriages and unusually difficult work situations.

A social cause of internal dysfunction should be suspected when a traumatic event has occurred but the symptoms behave just as they would in any case of internal dysfunction: they last too long, even after the event has receded, and are disproportionate in severity. Individuals with PTSD or victims of violence who suffer from persistent fears and anxieties years after the event are among the clearest examples. Severe phobias, panic disorder, obsessive-compulsive disorder, somatization disorders, alcoholism, eating disorders, and drug dependence are examples of non-psychotic disorders that meet the internal dysfunction criterion.

The first two categories in table 8.1, mental diseases (or psychotic disorders) and non-psychotic disorders, comprise true mental disorder, Horwitz (2002) argues. These are the categories that fit the definition of harmful dysfunctions. However, the most serious of these, the psychotic disorders, are also relatively uncommon. Using ECA data, Kessler and colleagues (1997) defined rates of serious and persistent mental disorder using four criteria: (1) non-affective psychosis (primarily schizophrenia) or mania, (2) major depression or panic disorder with either hospitalization or use of psychiatric medication, (3) planned or attempted suicide within the past twelve months, (4) a *DSM–IV* disorder associated with substantial vocational or interpersonal impairment. They found that, by these criteria, only 2.6% of the population had a serious and persistent mental disorder. Another 5.4% suffered from a serious (but not necessarily persistent) mental disorder. These percentages are far smaller than the 29%–48% (though many of the cases in the higher estimates are mild in severity) lifetime prevalence rates reported for all mental disorders in epidemiological studies (Kessler et al., 1994; Robins et al., 1984).

Two other categories of problems included as mental disorders in the *DSM* do not meet the definition for mental illness because, according to Horwitz (2002), they do not meet the criteria for a harmful dysfunction. These categories are psychological responses, usually a combination of depression and anxiety, to stressful circumstances (such as marital strife, separation, and occupational problems) and social deviance. Various forms of distress are not mental disorders when they dissipate after the events or conditions that caused them disappear. To reiterate:

only conditions that emerge without cause, that are disproportionate to the event, or that remain after the stress has passed, so indicating an internal dysfunction, should be considered mental disorders.

It is difficult to know how often cases of distress involving symptoms of depression and anxiety are transformed into psychiatric disorder. In the case of normal intense sadness and depressive disorder, we now at least have a figure, cited earlier, that tells us what per cent of the time major depression is overdiagnosed if normal losses (that may result in intense sadness) besides bereavement are excluded from the category of major depression: 25% (Wakefield et al., 2007). Regier et al. (1993) found that nearly half of people who receive treatment from mental health professionals do not have a diagnosable mental disorder (though the majority of this group had received a psychiatric diagnosis in the past). The National Comorbidity Survey showed that the use of mental health services was high in the half of the population with *no* lifetime history of mental disorder (Katz et al., 1997). Another survey (Olfsun & Pincus, 1994a, 1994b) discovered that most heavy users of psychotherapy (more than twenty visits in the previous year) were in good health, did not report serious psychiatric symptoms, and did not have major functional impairments. Horwitz (2002) concludes:

> Although data about the conditions of the users of mental health services are very poor, they suggest that many of the clients of mental health professionals are distressed but not mentally disordered. If the argument of this book is correct, many of the 50 million Americans who meet the criteria for a mental disorder in community studies do not have valid disorders but suffer from distress that is rooted in stressful social arrangements and that will disappear when these situations improve. (p. 222)

Deviance in the form of personality disorders and drug problems is the fourth and final category that is currently incorporated into the diagnostic system. It refers to behaviours that violate social norms of right and wrong. Horwitz (2002) acknowledges that how to regard heavy drinking, juvenile delinquency, or disruptive behaviour raises difficult questions. Should they be considered to be psychiatric disorders and given names such as substance abuse, conduct disorder, or attention deficit disorder? Or should they be seen merely as deviant acts? Social value judgments, he points out, will play an important part in whether such conditions are treated as volitional, and thus subject to punishment, or whether they will be considered a mental disorder, thus suitable for treatment. His larger point, however, is that the symptom-based logic of the *DSM* does not allow for a distinction between the two.

Horwitz's (2002) and Wakefield's (1992) efforts to define mental ill-nesses in such a way that makes them, as well as other entities currently included in the *DSM*, more valid categories (and in a way that is consistent with the *DSM*'s definition of what mental illness is) represent an important body of work. David Mechanic (2003) has pointed out, however, that there are two problems with the harmful dysfunction criterion: (1) uncertainty about when internal processes are inconsistent with evolutionary development and (2) the absence of more empirical ways – no chemical test, no imaging procedure – to identify internal dysfunction (Mechanic, 2002). The absence of a concrete marker means that there can always be uncertainty about whether an internal dysfunction is present or not, particularly in the case of non-psychotic conditions. Does the persistent inability of some people to cope with their lives long after a loss, from death or divorce, represent an internal dysfunction or chronic demoralization? Does the incessant craving of the addict for his drug of choice represent damage to some internal system, a bad habit, or just deviant behaviour? It can be hard to decide. Mechanic (2003) points out that 'in extreme cases the dysfunction may be obvious, but the practical challenge is in defining ambiguous cases and not the extreme' (p. 14). Other psychiatrists have also weighed in on this debate (Fulford, 1999; Klein, 1999; Lilienfeld & Marino, 1995; Maj, 2008; Richters & Hinshaw, 1999; Sadler, 1999).

The identification of a biological basis for dysfunction has been the goal of psychiatric research for a long time yet still remains a hope for the future. But for the present, Horwitz's and Wakefield's proposal to use certain characteristics of symptoms (those that come on without cause, those that last too long, and so forth) as indicators of a true dysfunction is a useful guide. Better delineation of what is and what is not a mental disorder would resolve some of the problems associated with the current diagnostic system. The number of disorders would be reduced and admission of new disorders into the *DSM* would be more rigorous. Rates of mental illness in the population would be lower and more realistic. Psychiatric researchers would be able to concentrate their efforts on the nature and causes of the internal dysfunctions that lie behind true psychiatric illness. And if patients with mental illness, by Horwitz/Wakefield's definition, were consistently distinguished from patients with distress, the extent of the population of patients experiencing distress because of social circumstances would become apparent. It might also make clinicians and policy makers more sensitive to the role of social factors in both distress and mental disorder.

In Summary

The current psychiatric diagnostic system is based on a disease model, in which specific symptoms are indicative of a natural underlying organic disorder. This model, however, may be appropriate for only a relatively few of the more serious psychiatric disorders. The presence of particular symptoms is never enough for a diagnosis of mental disorder without consideration of cause and context because individuals who show appropriate but intense responses to stressful situations, particularly with symptoms of anxiety and depression, cannot be differentiated reliably from individuals who meet the criteria – as proposed by Horwitz and Wakefield and, indeed, by the *DSM* itself – for true mental illness. That is, their symptoms appear in the absence of external stressors, the symptoms are disproportionate to the situation, or they last too long, indicating an internal dysfunction.

One result of current diagnostic practice, Horwitz and Wakefield argue, is that a substantial number of cases of normal but intense distress as well as other types of personal and interpersonal difficulties are all included in the same large category of individual mental disorder. This emphasis on individual disorder does not represent a true state of affairs in many cases and draws attention away from the social realities that should also be implicated in the genesis of symptoms. But it also helps explain why the social dimension has remained relatively neglected in clinical practice.

9 Social Perspective in Practice

In this chapter I show how a social perspective can be incorporated, first by description and then by example, into clinicians' thinking in order to round out the conceptual framework that currently emphasizes biological and psychological approaches.

Incorporating a Social Perspective

Social Roles

The first meeting between a clinician and a patient usually begins with the clinician asking the patient about the problem that brought him or her to seek professional help. This is followed by a survey of symptoms that are bothering the patient. Possible precipitating events are asked about as well as past psychiatric history, family history of psychiatric disorder, use of drugs and alcohol, personality characteristics, and such background information as upbringing, education, job, and marital history. These are topics all clinicians are familiar with.

Acute life events are certainly a reason that patients come to clinicians and therapists, but they often occur in conjunction with chronic role strains, and it is this combination that motivates a patient to get help. Unlike acute events, chronic strains associated with roles have been relatively neglected in the clinical setting. Thus a review of these strains is a good place to start.

Individuals play multiple roles, usually sequentially and sometimes simultaneously. In the course of a day or a week, for example, a person may be a parent, a child, a spouse, a teacher, a supervisor, an employee, a department member, a friend, a therapist, a club member, a runner, or a patient. These roles may be sources of satisfaction or strain, and sometimes both. Most chronic strains come from family or work-related roles, the ones that occupy most of our time. Following are the major sources of role strain (Gallagher, 1995; Pearlin, 1989):

- role overload – too much work, either at home, at work, or both
- conflicts within complementary roles – friction between husband and wife, child and parent, employer and employee
- competing demands between different roles – conflict within one individual about the time to devote to spouse, parental, or work roles
- role captivity – inability to leave a difficult relationship because of financial constraints or moral considerations
- restructured role – an adult child who assumes the parental role with an impaired parent
- role incompatibility – discrepancy between achievement in one role and not another, for example, a high educational level and a low-status job.
- loss of a major role – as a spouse, parent, employee

To illustrate: a sixty-five-year-old soon-to-retire white female retail clerk living with her eighty-seven-year-old mother sought help because she felt depressed, had difficulty concentrating on routine tasks at work, and felt unable to make important decisions. She was also having trouble sleeping, with many awakenings during the night. She experienced tension during the day and noticed that she did not enjoy many of the activities she had previously looked forward to. These symptoms had been present for a year. She had no history of depression or of chronic medical problems.

The immediate cause of her problems was conflict with her mother. She lived with her mother in order to take care of her, but her mother criticized her constantly and, the patient felt, took her for granted. The mother refused to accept a substitute caregiver and the daughter felt unable to take any substantial break, such as a vacation. If she did and something happened to her mother, she thought, she would not be able to live with the guilt that would result from the feeling that she was unavailable when her mother needed her. In addition, work had become steadily more stressful in the last three years because the large retail department store that the patient worked for had reorganized. She was now the only retail clerk in a section of the store that five years before had employed three clerks. She was eager to retire, but also anxious about it, worrying that her modest pension would not be enough to live on adequately and that spending more time in retirement in the house with her mother might well increase their friction.

In this example, it was not an acute event but the chronic strain of living with her mother, combined with symptoms of distress (in the form of depressive symptoms) and a feeling that she was not coping very well that led this patient to seek help. Role overload at work and at home, conflict about the patient's restructured role with her mother (who refused to acknowledge that her daughter was now her caregiver), and role captivity (the patient felt she couldn't leave her mother) were the major strains for this woman, worsened by the prospect of retirement with limited financial means. It was this constellation of conditions that led to her distress.

This woman did not have trouble identifying the context of her distress, but this is not always the case with patients. If patients have significant symptoms of anxiety and/or depression and deny any problems in the proximal parts of their lives – family, work, friends – this itself should cause the clinician to wonder since few, if any, individuals enjoy problem-free lives. When a social context for symptoms cannot be identified, the focus of treatment often becomes the patient's state of mind and how it can be improved with the help of medications, usually antidepressants. A biological vulnerability that accounts for the symptoms is usually assumed. Problems without known or obvious causes exist, particularly in the case of serious mental illness, but therapists should be cautious about accepting this conclusion in non-psychotic disorders and distress, especially early in treatment.

Time sometimes has to go by before the true significance of role strains can be appreciated in a person's life. It can also be helpful to consult with relatives and friends, if permission can be obtained, who may provide important insights into a patient's problem.

Class Position and Political-Economic Factors

When acute events and/or chronic strains are paired with specific elements of the stratification system, such as lower socioeconomic position, female gender, or minority status, strains are likely to be magnified. But distress can be associated with stratification factors and political-economic circumstances independently. Lack of financial resources associated with lower socioeconomic position is a stress in itself. Political and economic circumstances, such as threats to reduce or cut Medicaid, can be a great source of distress to the poor. Questions that help bring out the social dimension of a person's life are included in table 9.1. These serve not only to uncover sources of distress but also allow the clinician to form an idea of a patient's resources.

Several of these areas of inquiry are already part of the traditional clinical interview in psychiatry and clinical psychology. However, they are often treated more as demographic data than as substantive information. I hope that the material I have presented in this book demonstrates unequivocally why a notation of a patient's education ('Completed the 11th grade') without understanding its significance in setting off a potential train of events – for jobs, housing, or standard of

Table 9.1
The social dimension in the clinical interview

Area or factor	Initial questions	Rationale
Childhood social class	What did your father/ mother do for a living? What were the circumstances in which you grew up?	Sense of self, security, opportunities, choices, view of the world
Education	How far did you go in school?	Marker of attainment
Occupation	What kind of work do you do? Satisfactions and discontents? Working conditions?	Marker of resources; source of satisfaction or distress
Income	What is the average amount of income a year you or your family makes?	Marker of resources; source of satisfaction or distress
Place of residence	Where do you live? What's the neighbourhood like?	Buffer or source of chronic and sometimes acute stress
Stress (acute and chronic)	Have any unexpected events occurred recently? Chronic strain, roles or otherwise?	Causes of psychological distress
Control	How much control do you have (in a particular situation)?	Important mediator of stress
Social support	Who do you rely on for emotional and practical help? Do you belong to any clubs or groups?	Buffers stress; isolation can be source of distress

living – is inadequate. Questions about employment status and current working conditions, problems, degree of control and demand, and whether rewards are commensurate with effort are also important in light of findings that link premature death, depression, and distress to employment status and job conditions.

Questions about income, sense of control at home, and place of residence also help define potential problems and their context. If I have a good idea of a patient's socioeconomic position or the neighbourhood s/he lives in because of my knowledge of the local community, I will not ask about income or the neighbourhood. But if I am unsure, or if money is identified as a problem, I ask about both. With regard to the neighbourhood, I ask what it looks like, whether it's safe, whether it's kept up or not, who the neighbours are, what the noise level is, and whether any of the neighbours are friends.

With respect to income, I am interested in what the person makes in a year and what the household income is. If a direct question feels awkward, I might introduce the issue by asking 'Do you feel comfortable telling me what you earn in a year?' Questions, when appropriate, about savings, size of home mortgage, credit card debt, and other major expenses help fill in the financial picture. Financial problems can hardly be overestimated as a source of individual and family distress.

A patient's sense of control is assessed by asking about autonomy at work and at home: 'How much control do you have at work?' and 'Do you have much say in family decisions?' The quality and extent of individuals' social support network can be gauged by asking how many close friends they have, who they are, whom they rely on in an emergency, whom they feel comfortable asking favours of ('If you had to leave your car in the shop and get home, who would you ask to pick you up?'), whom they talk to when they have problems, and whom they would ask if they were in need of money.

In addition to these person-level questions, maintaining a social perspective also involves keeping in mind the economic and political developments in society that affect people's lives. The number and kinds of jobs the economy is generating, the prevailing level of wages and benefits, the rate of inflation, the cost of goods and services, governmental policies pertaining to taxation and the enforcement of regulations, and which part of the class spectrum these different policies and decisions favour are some of the considerations that give substance to the category of more distal social factors that are always hovering around more proximal circumstances. How these factors in turn intersect with social roles and the stratification system, after all, comprise the social perspective.

Direct links between distal social forces and personal distress are often seen most clearly in the workplace. Pressures to work harder and longer, reductions in benefits, outsourcing, company restructuring, and closures are common causes of insecurity and anxiety that are often generated at a distance – in the national economy or the global marketplace – and experienced personally, as discussed in chapter 5.

Case Presentation

The following case presentation illustrates an application of social perspective to clinical work.

Mrs. J., a forty-one-year-old married women, the mother of two children ages twenty-two and eighteen, was referred to me by a neurologist for the evaluation and possible treatment of depression. The patient dated her mood decline to three years before, when she and her husband, a forty-eight-year-old college graduate with a middle-management job in state government, moved from a small to a medium-sized town. She looked forward to the move but had not felt well since. Her symptoms were a chronically low mood, worse in the last four to six months, lack of energy, inability to finish projects around the house, little enjoyment in knitting and calligraphy, which she previously enjoyed, trouble sleeping because of pain in her left shoulder, lack of motivation, and some minor problems with her memory. She had no thoughts of suicide, her appetite and weight were unchanged, and she had no trouble concentrating or making decisions. Asked how she felt at the moment, she said, 'I feel cut off from joy, passion, and anger.' She did not recall earlier episodes of depression.

As she defined them, her problems fell into three categories:

1 Physical health: for the past three years she had suffered from pain in her left shoulder. Repeated investigations revealed no obvious pathology. The pain was discouraging but did not limit her physically. A recent course of physical therapy provided some relief. However, medical expenses connected with investigation of her shoulder problem had worried her husband. For the past five years she had also had fainting spells about twice a year for which medical and neurological examinations had been unrevealing.

2 Marriage: she was married when she was eighteen, shortly after completing high school. For most of the marriage she has been dependent on her husband, relying on him for decisions about money, when to make appointments, what clothes to wear, and what to watch on television. When she went out with a friend in the evening, which was rare, her husband demanded a careful accounting of how the time was spent and became suspicious whenever she was late.

In the last year or two, she had begun to realize that she needed more independence and control. She had always wanted to be a dental hygienist, which would require going back to work before she could return to school since her husband would not finance her training. She had one close friend but felt the need for more. She felt isolated. Talking about her goals, particularly going back to work, caused friction with her husband. She has been unhappy with her marriage for the past two years. Her daughter had married two years before and her son planned to attend community college but remain living at home; she had good relationships with both.

3 Parents: they were still living in their own home but her mother had dementia. Mrs. J. visited her parents almost every day and often consulted on the phone with caregivers who would come in daily to help her parents. She helped her father pay the bills and occasionally went to church with them on Sundays.

Mrs. J. was a tall, light-brown-haired woman who was animated and talked easily. She did not initially look sad, but she cried throughout most of the first meeting as she talked about her problems. When asked what expectations she had of psychotherapy, she said that she wanted some insight into why she was behaving as she was. She said that her husband, in turn, wanted to know what was behind her 'destructive' behaviour, meaning her desire for more independence. She scored twenty on a Beck Depression Inventory (BDI), which put her in the mildly to moderately depressed category. I made an axis I diagnosis of dysthymia (chronic depression) at the end of the first interview, with a differential diagnosis that included mild major depressive disorder and adjustment disorder with depression. Mood disorder due to a medical condition such as hypothyroidism was considered but ruled out after a review of her medical records showed no unusual physical or laboratory findings.

In thinking about Mrs. J. with a social perspective in mind, it was obvious that role strains were prominent. Foremost were those associated with her marriage. Her type of marriage, a traditional one, is known to be one that is strongly associated with distress for women (Mirowsky & Ross, 2003b). These are the marriages in which the woman does not work outside the home and has responsibility for all of the housework. Lack of employment for women is associated with more stress than being employed, even when this causes conflict between work and family roles. Within the marriage, moreover, Mrs. J. was at a socioeconomic disadvantage in comparison with her husband in terms of earning power and control. She was relatively powerless. Unfulfilled expectations about her marriage, lack of reciprocity on the part of her husband in terms of sharing decisions, and his lack of acceptance of her wish for more independence constituted other chronic strains within the marriage. Mrs. J.'s social network was small and her sources of social support few, both because she had little opportunity to meet people and because of her husband's controlling behaviour. Strain was also evident in Mrs. J.'s role as a caretaker for her mother since it involved a redefinition of the relationship between her and her parents as well as an additional responsibility for Mrs. J. Still, the strain so generated was minor compared to that caused by her marriage.

In terms of class position, Mrs. J. and her husband were between the lower part of the privileged class and the upper part of the new working class – the comfort class. Her husband had a secure, stable job with benefits, but they had not been able to save a great deal, which was another reason, beside her wish for more independence, that she wanted to go back to school. Having only a high school education is a risk factor for distress, not as much as not having completed high school, but significantly more than having finished college. The fact that Mrs. J. was married as a teenager, which often disrupts the sequence of development leading from education to a desirable job, is another potential source of disadvantage for both men and women. Even though her son was planning to go to community college, he planned to remain living at home, and couples with children at home are, on average, more distressed than childless couples, largely for financial reasons.

The role strains that distressed Mrs. J. were numerous, but other social factors affected her life positively. Her husband's secure job, with a decent salary and good benefits, provided the couple with a reasonable standard of living. It also insulated them against economic downturns and governmental policy decisions that could negatively affect less financially secure couples. Their socioeconomic position provided a base that gave Mrs. J. the opportunity to pursue her own vocational goals rather than being forced to take any job available just to keep the family financially afloat – the plight of many women re-entering the workforce. She had the means to seek psychiatric help, which could potentially provide help in the way of support, encouragement, and relief of depressive symptoms. The state in which Mrs. J. lived was a joint property state, which meant that she would receive half the couple's assets if a divorce were to take place. This was also a form of security in that Mrs. J. knew she would not be destitute even if she were divorced. Mrs. J. had a good relationship with her children, which gave her confidence about her parental role, and one good friend, who provided social support as well serving as an outlet for Mrs. J.'s dissatisfaction.

Finally, distal social factors were also involved. A combination of social, economic, and political changes over the course of the last century prepared the ground for Mrs. J.'s decision to join the labour force. In the earlier part of the century it is likely that neither society nor Mrs. J.'s husband would have accepted such a decision. Indeed, such was the social climate that not even Mrs. J. herself would have thought of returning to work as a solution to her problems. The efforts of the women's rights movement have made it acceptable for women to aspire to identities of their own, not just identities tied to their husbands'. Economic factors, such as stagnant wages for working-class men in the latter third of the last century, made it acceptable, even mandatory in many cases, for women to work if family living standards were to be maintained. These developments were on Mrs. J.'s side.

On the third visit Mrs. J. asked me how long therapy would take. Her husband wanted to know because he was worried about the expense, though the couple had good insurance. By this point I was convinced that Mrs. J.'s marital problems were the main cause of her distress. When asked how she wanted her husband to change, she said that she wanted him to be less critical of her, to show some interest in her plans, and to drop his demand that she account for her time when she went out with friends. I proposed that Mrs. J. and her husband meet with me for two or three sessions to see if we could work on these issues. She was doubtful that he would agree. She returned the next week and told me that her husband had not only refused the invitation, he had also told her that the current visit with me was to be the last.

In the meantime, she was thinking about getting a part-time job in order to earn some money for school instead of tackling her marital problems more directly. 'I think it's better to avoid landmines,' she said. I thought this sounded reasonable. If it worked, fine. And if it did not, the information gained might be helpful in either approaching the problem in another way or providing an impetus to move on to another problem.

In our last scheduled meeting, the fourth, I was still impressed with how sad Mrs. J. was. She cried throughout the session. I was reminded of her score on the depression inventory. Reviewing Mrs. J.'s symptoms, I was able to make the case, by stretching the criteria a bit, that Mrs. J. was suffering from a mild major depressive disorder. She met five of the nine criteria for the diagnosis if her sleep problem was attributed to depression rather than pain and if her inability to complete household tasks was interpreted as lack of concentration. Because one of the main treatments for major depression is medication, I wondered aloud if it might not help her. At first, Mrs. J. baulked, saying she didn't like to take pills, but she then asked about the rationale and the side effects. She also said, 'I don't see how that's going to change my situation.' I said, 'If you feel better and have more energy, you may be in a better position to do something about it. At least that's my hope.'

Mrs. J. called back the next day and said she would like to try the medication, fluoxetine (Prozac). She agreed to be in touch by telephone for the next several weeks and thought that her husband might agree to one more visit in the future. Almost three weeks later she wrote a note, saying that she had managed to stop her constant crying and get her dishes done. She said she had little energy and had trouble sleeping, but that her interest in the holidays had picked up, at least intermittently. She closed by saying, 'I feel that the medication pulls me above those very dark emotions but when I am here I am not dealing with them. Which place is reality?'

I might have offered Mrs. J. medication even had I stuck with the original diagnosis of dysthymia, particularly once the possibility of couples therapy had been eliminated. I was impressed with the intensity of her distress. But the diagnosis of major depression, in conjunction with her BDI score and her persistent weeping, made a stronger case for medication in my mind than did dysthymia. However, both these conditions are considered mental disorders in the *DSM*. In retrospect, and by now having read Horwitz (2002), I can ask: Was it accurate, or even fair, to include Mrs. J. among the mentally disordered? Or was she a normal person who was unhappy, primarily because of an oppressive marriage which made her feel powerless? Applying the criteria for mental disorder that Horwitz suggested and as outlined in chapter 8 – symptoms that come on for no apparent reason or are disproportionate to the precipitating event, symptoms that persist even though the stress disappears – it certainly appears that Mrs. J. did not fit into a mental disorder category. Rather, since her symptoms were associated with a difficult marriage and were in proportion to her circumstances, Mrs J. fell more appropriately into the category of normal intense sadness rather than major depressive disorder or dysthymia. Her symptoms were the result of chronic role strains (as a wife and daughter) and stratification factors (female, high school education) rather than an acute unexpected negative life event. The diagnosis of normal sadness would carry none of the stigmatizing connotations of a mental disorder, either. The only problem in giving her this diagnosis – besides violating hospital and clinic policy that mandates the use of the formal diagnostic system – would be that reimbursement would not be forthcoming, since insurance companies will not pay for conditions not considered disorders in the *DSM*.

As discussed in the last chapter, diagnostic psychiatry regards symptoms as evidence of an underlying entity (major depression in this case) which then becomes defined as the problem and so the focus of treatment. In contrast, a social perspective approach urges clinicians to consider symptoms not always as evidence of a presumptive underlying biological disorder but, instead, as an intense response to difficult situations and circumstances. A social perspective gives as much weight to the social context from which symptoms arise as it does to the symptoms themselves.

Does the name of a condition matter to patients? It depends, partly on the nature of the problem, partly on the patient. Some patients, when they attribute their distress primarily to adverse circumstances, feel that a diagnosis of mental disorder is the last thing they need. Mental disorder, for many of them, connotes a biological problem and chronicity. It focuses on the wrong thing – individual defect, which makes them feel, in turn, defective. There is also the problem of stigmatization. Diagnoses follow people around, and I doubt that having to fill in a space on an application that asks if you have been treated for a psychiatric condition ever facilitates a job search. Patients have told me that they prefer terms such as 'distress' or 'demoralization' not only because those terms describe their conditions more accurately than mental disorder, but also because they avoid the potential (and actual) stigmatization that mental disorder diagnoses can cause. (But there is always the problem of what diagnosis to put down on the billing form if insurance is involved.) Sometimes patients are relieved by a *DSM* diagnosis, at least if it is not too serious, since it connotes that their condition is known about and can be treated. The idea that mental problems can be the result of chemical imbalance in the brain may have reduced the resistance to mental disorder diagnoses in recent years, but whether this is a good thing is debatable if it extends to all mental disorders and not just the most serious ones. A putative chemical imbalance as the cause of, for example, depressive symptoms implies that the person has no control over them. I have seen this come as a relief to some.

I do not think that the presence of social or interpersonal problems should preclude the use of medications – or anything else that might help, for that matter. In the case of Mrs. J., prescribing a medication did not imply that no marital problems existed, that Mrs. J. was not overloaded, or that the problem was primarily hers – and those details were discussed explicitly. Medications are meant to provide symptom relief. Since we usually tend to regard symptoms as constituting a formal mental disorder, it is easy to infer that medications act specifically on disorder. But it is probable that medication also helps some people with unhappiness or normal but intense sadness. Horwitz (2002) points out that, given the non-specific effects of the serotonin-enhancing drugs like fluoxetine, which are used to treat a wide range of conditions as well as to enhance the personalities of normal people (Kramer, 1993), they could as well be called 'anti-neurotics' or 'psychic energizers' as antidepressants (Horwitz, 2002, p. 191). Why not 'wellness pills'? Whatever. The process of improving one's life starts when symptoms of distress or depression diminish.

Mrs. J. came for one further visit four months later. She said that her mood and her overall state of mind were 80% better. She was able to do the housework again because her energy had returned, she felt able to concentrate, and her sleep had improved. She attributed this improvement to the antidepressant medication. It had dulled her libido, but she regarded this as a small price to pay for feeling better. Also, she said she had been more assertive with her husband about her plans and felt that he was trying to be more accepting of them. She added that, once most of her depressive symptoms disappeared, she had realized that she had had several episodes of depression earlier in her life, though none were as severe or long-lasting as the present episode; all, however, seemed to be related to feelings of being socially isolated.

Eight months after this visit, I received a note in the mail from Mrs. J. She wrote, 'Do you remember me? Things have changed since I sat crying on your couch. I am now attending community college working for the certificate I told you about. I am also working part-time at Target to pay for it. My marriage has improved a lot since I have been able to face some of the issues and stop giving away my power. Thank you for listening to me and helping me get back on the track.'

The next time I talked on the telephone to Mrs J. was ten years later. She had received her certificate as a dental hygienist four years after our last meeting and had been working full-time in a private dental office ever since. She attributed her initial improvement to fluoxetine and had taken it for a year afterwards before discontinuing it on her own. She and her husband still had their differences, but she acknowledged that he had changed in some ways. He complained less about her expenses because of the salary she was now earning. He no longer demanded that she give him an account of how she spent her time, at work or with friends. Compartmentalizing parts of their lives together had also helped. For example, they ate meals with each other but watched television in separate rooms. She also said that some of her reactions to him had softened: 'I take his criticism less seriously.' Mrs. J had had no further episodes of depression in the intervening ten years nor had she had further fainting episodes. Other strains besides the marital ones had subsided. Her mother had died. Her father still required some attention, but providing it to him was less difficult than it had been with her mother. Her shoulder pain had diminished though it had never completely disappeared.

Looking back, she thought that obtaining full-time employment was the best long-term course of action she could have taken. It eliminated her sense of social isolation, allowed her to make new friends, gave her a sense of independence, and made it easier for her to stand up for herself. As she said at the end of our conversation, 'I'm much more in control now.'

Her outcome was obviously a good one. She was unusual in the sense that many people who take medication for distress feel better, at least for a while, but few of them undertake and carry out the long-range changes in their lives that Mrs. J. did.

A social perspective on Mrs. J. highlights the various role strains that caused her distress as well as her achievement of a new and valued role that gave her self-confidence, reduced her dependence on her husband, and gave her some income of her own. It brings out the elements of stratification that both ameliorated stress (the family's social class position) and made her more vulnerable to it (female gender) and the larger political-economic circumstances (the women's rights movement, stagnant wages for working-class males over the past thirty years) that have made it more acceptable and, indeed, often necessary for many wives to work

10 In Closing

1 Social disparities produce health disparities.
2 The clinical professions have largely ignored the impact of social
  disparities on health and well-being.

These are the two sentences I would use if I were asked to condense this book. Throughout it I have emphasized that individuals are embedded in society through their roles shaped within the institutions of society, through the stratification system, and through their places as citizens subject to economic-political circumstances. Daily life is experienced through various roles, which bring satisfactions and strains. Stratification refers to a system of ranking individuals on hierarchies from high to low. The main stratification hierarchies in American society are class, race, and gender. Along the lines of these hierarchies resources are distributed by various forms of exclusion. Economic policies and political decisions affect everyone – but differently, depending on their places in the stratification system,

Health and well-being are patterned. Specifically, health, including mental health and well-being, is inversely related to lower socioeconomic status in a gradient-like fashion. Acute and chronic stress, impaired coping and lack of a sense of control, lack of social support, and lack of opportunities are risk factors for disorders and distress. All are correlated with lower social class position. Many chronic stressors are associated with lack of resources, such as money, education and skills, social ties, and social connections. Lack of material and psychosocial resources is what links mental disorder and emotional distress to social class and socioeconomic position, just as possession of them leads to health and well-being.

Social class is defined by the kinds and amounts of resources that individuals and families possess and are able to make use of over time. Two main classes (with various sub-classes) currently define American society. During the last thirty years the privileged class, particularly the top part of it, has increased its income and wealth resources enormously compared to the working class, which has suffered from stagnant incomes, loss of benefits, and insecurity. This trend is reflected in health statistics that show, for example, that individuals higher on the social scale have gained more years of life than those lower on it and that several markers of social well-being have deteriorated. A number of explanations have also been advanced for this growth of inequality, but the most important ones are connected to the privileged class's power to control the economy and commandeer the government to their advantage. The unequal distribution of resources lies behind the unequal distribution of physical and mental health; the social gradient is reflected in the health gradient.

It has not been the immediate social contexts – precipitating events, interpersonal difficulties, living circumstances – that have been neglected in psychiatry and clinical psychology so much as it has been the larger social arrangements and circumstances that structure these immediate contexts: the macro-sphere (political-economic contexts, the stratification system) that structures the meso-sphere (family and community) and the micro-sphere (the individual).

The aim of this book is to bring together in one place information that is dispersed over many fields so that clinicians can become more aware of the relationships between society and the individual and how those relationships affect health and well-being. This awareness represents a social perspective. Perspective, according to the *New Oxford Dictionary of English* (1998), refers to a 'true understanding of the relative importance of things; a sense of proportion' (p. 1386). Biology (genetics, neurochemistry) and psychology have received ample attention in the literature of psychiatry and clinical psychology, to the extent that our thinking about individual problems has largely remained confined to those areas. The contents of this book add the third element to the biopsychosocial model that Engel (1977) presented over thirty years ago.

From the point of view of individual clinicians, there are always questions of what to do in the clinical setting with the kinds of awareness that social perspective brings. Most immediately, with individual patients, I think that clinicians should remember to do what they've always done: to provide relief and help in whatever ways they can. As far back as 1904 Freud (as cited in Roazen, 1974) said, 'There are many ways and means of practising psychotherapy. All that lead to recovery are good' (p. 112). This was before the advent of modern psychiatric drugs, but such broadmindedness would probably have included the judicious use of medication in treatment also. Patients are usually discouraged when they come for help, and whatever means that help restore their morale will lessen symptoms and improve quality of life.

It is difficult to be prescriptive about the extent a clinician should share his or her social perspective with patients. I am sparing with it, not because I want to hoard important information but because patients come for help, not a social perspective. Probably the best advice is to use it when the occasion arises and when it seems appropriate. I consider mentioning one or another aspect of social perspective if the information helps patients view their situations in new and potentially helpful ways, if it promotes a sense of universality, the realization that many people are in the same boat, or if it helps relieve a sense of personal failure for a situation over which the patient has little control. I am thinking specifically of a fifty-five-year-old mid-level manager at an international corporation who consulted me for anxiety and depression. His company had recently merged with a larger corporation. His authority at work had been reduced at the same time that his work demands had increased. He was depressed, he said, and attributed his state not to his changed working conditions but to his inability to cope as successfully with these changes as many of his co-workers had seemed to. This feeling of failure seemed to diminish when I told him that it was well-known that distress in the form of uncertainty, insecurity, anxiety, and depression was common among employees when companies merged and job descriptions changed.

While social perspective certainly informed my thinking about Mrs. J., the person I discussed at length in the last chapter, there was little time or reason to explicitly talk with her about the larger social implications of her situation. It is true that an understanding of social structures and social dynamics makes one aware of how they can constrain the possibilities of action, but it is helpful to remember also that social structures, while influential, are not determinative. Mrs. J. showed that.

Personal and interpersonal problems can be ameliorated with professional help, but the larger social context in which personal problems are embedded cannot be altered by individual psychotherapy. Only social action can accomplish that. The topic is beyond the scope of this book, but I feel that clinicians should acquaint themselves with some of the proposals that have been made to mitigate the central social problem that lies behind the disparities in health and well-being: inequality.[1] There are many, and most of them would not only reduce inequality but would also reduce poverty and help improve the economy. These range, for example, from establishing a more realistic minimum wage, creating a reverse income tax, and raising the cap on the payroll tax to increasing marginal tax rates on the highest earners, enforcing laws that prohibit anti-union activities, and establishing publicly funded elections (Krugman, 2007; Madrick, 2009; Reich, 2010). An acquaintance with these proposals can serve to allay the feeling of helplessness that clinicians often express when issues beyond the individual come up. 'What can you do about *those?*' they ask.

Some clinicians devote a substantial amount of their time to social activism, but I think it is unrealistic to think that most could or would. I would hope that reading a book like this one would encourage clinicians to deepen their understanding of the ways that society distributes advantages and disadvantages and the effects this has on health. With this knowledge, clinicians can support or join politicians, programs, organizations, and full-time advocates whose goal is to advance a progressive social agenda. As Nancy Krieger and her colleagues (1997) have pointed out, 'The better health and longer lives of the better off imply possibilities of what health for all could truly mean' (p. 343). Michael Marmot (2006) comments:

> Our profession seeks not only to understand but to improve things. Some doctors feel queasy about the prospect of social action to improve health, which smacks of social engineering. Yet, a physician faced with a suffering patient has an obligation to make things better. If she sees 100 patients the obligation extends to all of them. And if a society is making people sick? We have a duty to do what we can to improve the public health and to reduce health inequalities in social groups where these are avoidable and hence inequitable or unfair. This duty is a moral obligation, a matter of social justice. (p. 2082)

Clinicians can put social perspective into practice by analysing the social origins of distress with their patients, by remembering that not all symptoms indicate mental disorder, and that not all problems are entirely personal, even though they are experienced personally. Many are social, for others a social contribution is great, and all have social consequences. And for professions that focus so intensely on individual treatment, it should be kept in mind that social remedies can also reduce personal distress. To paraphrase Howard Waitzkin (1991, p. 277) only slightly: When stress at work or job insecurity produces symptoms, labour organizing may be the preferred therapy. For the tension headaches and psychosomatic complaints (such as fainting spells and shoulder pain in the case of Mrs. J.) that result from dissatisfaction with the housewife's role, sexual politics may be a solution. For alcoholism and other addictions that represent a search for oblivion from the strains of social life, organizing at the level of local communities can convert isolation to fraternity.

As clinicians, we do not usually think this way. We are trained to treat the individual and that is what we do, that is our role. For the genuine well-being of patients, and for all of us for that matter, more than individual approaches will be necessary.

Appendix: Reading for a Social Perspective

Important and accessible professional books about social class are Leonard Beegley's (2007) *The Structure of Social Stratification in the United States*, **5th edition**; Perrucci and Wysong's (2002) *The New Class Society*, **2nd edition**; and Richard Scase's (1984) *Class*. Sociology and mental illness are addressed in William Eaton's (2003) *The Sociology of Mental Illness* and Tausig, Michello, and Subedi's (2004) *A Sociology of Mental Illness*, **2nd edition.** The best general volumes on the relationship of society and mental health are Horwitz and Scheid's (1999) *A Handbook for the Study of Mental Health;* Avison, McLeod, and Pescosolido's (2006) *Mental Health, Social Mirror;* and Scheid and Brown's (2010) *A Handbook for the Study of Mental Health*, **2nd edition.** The most extended treatment of the social gradient for health is found in Michael Marmot's (2004) *The Status Syndrome.* Donald Barr's (2008) *Health Disparities in the United States* contains a clear discussion of health, class, and race. Two books published by the Russell Sage Foundation, Richard Freeman's (2007) *America Works* and Douglas Massey's (2007) *Categorically Unequal,* an exceptional book about the American stratification system, are strongly recommended. All of the books above are referenced in the bibliography.

The *New York Times* reports much news of social interest. The *Atlantic, Harper's,* and the *New York Review of Books* occasionally contain articles that relate strongly to a social perspective. In general, however, one has to go to the liberal and the alternative press for that, to magazines like the *Nation, Dollars and Sense,* the *Progressive, Z* magazine, *In These Times,* and particularly the *American Prospect.* Among professional journals, the *British Medical Journal, Social Science & Medicine,* the *American Journal of Public Health,* the *American Psychologist,*

Health Affairs, the *Journal of Social Issues*, the *American Sociological Review*, *Epidemiologic Reviews*, and the *Journal of Health and Social Behavior* often contain important articles that advance the social perspective.

For more general reading about class, social issues, and the state of American society, many books can be recommended. They can be looked up on the website of Amazon.com and in most libraries. Herbert Gans's *The War Against the Poor*, Michael Lind's *The Next American Nation*, Barbara Ehrenreich's *Fear of Falling* (as well as her more recent account of trying to make a living in several low-paying jobs around the country, *Nickel and Dimed*), and Robert Putnam's *Bowling Alone* are important. Alex Kotlowitz's *There Are No Children Here* and William Julius Wilson's *The Underclass* are noteworthy. Larry Bartels's *Unequal Democracy*, Robert Reich's *Supercapitalism*, Peter Gosselin's *High Wire*, Steven Greenhouse's *The Big Squeeze*, Paul Krugman's *The Conscience of a Liberal*, Louis Uchitelle's *The Disposable American*, Robert and Carolyn Perrucci's *America at Risk*, Jacob Hacker and Paul Pierson's *Winner-Take-All Politics*, and Chris Hedges's *Death of the Liberal Class* are also books to be recommended. For a humorous but telling account of class in America, Paul Fussell's *Class* is in a category by itself. Novels I have enjoyed that contain strong social themes are Tom Wolfe's *A Man in Full* and *The Bonfire of the Vanities*, as well as Russell Banks's *Continental Drift*, J.C. Boyle's *Tortilla Curtain*, and Richard Russo's *Empire Falls*.

Websites useful for understanding the political and economic factors relevant to a social perspective include those of the **Economic Policy Institute** (www.epi.org), **United for a Fair Economy** (www.faireconomy.org), **AlterNet** (www.alternet.org), the **Mark Thoma's Economist's View** (www.economistsview.typepad.com), **TAX.com** (www.tax.com), the **Center for Economic and Policy Research** (www.cepr.net), and **Paul Krugman's blog** (http://krugman.blogs.nytimes.com).

Notes

Introduction

1 When used as a single word 'health' without an adjective is the generic term for physical health, mental health, and psychological well-being. When used in conjunction with well-being, as in 'health and well-being,' it refers to physical health and psychological well-being. Occasionally 'health and well-being,' refers to 'health and well-being, disorder and distress.' This is too long a phrase to repeat very often, so I will just say 'health and well-being' and hope the context suggests the full phrase when appropriate. 'Well-being' refers to psychological or emotional well-being, the absence of psychiatric disorder and/or emotional distress. The word 'disorder' without an adjective refers to either physical and mental disorder. Again, the context should help. I distinguish between distress and disorder throughout the book.

2 I owe the idea of embeddedness to Leonard Pearlin (1989).

1 Social Perspective

1 For a thorough discussion of the different kinds of stressors, see Wheaton (1999).

2 Wheaton (1997) has a somewhat different typology for the causes of chronic stress. They include, with examples, (a) threats – abuse, violence; (b) demands – facing levels of expectation that cannot be met with existing resources which lead to role overload; (c) structural constraints – lack of opportunities or means to achieve desired ends; (d) under-reward – as in a relationship or at work in terms of recognition or pay; (e) complexity – number of sources of demand, conflict of responsibilities

among roles, instability in life arrangements; (f) uncertainty – unwanted waiting for an outcome; (g) conflict – when it occurs regularly in relationships without resolution.

3 When talking about stratification, I will be explicit about the type: class, gender, or ethnic stratification.

4 It is admittedly uncomfortable to speak of 'lower' or 'higher' classes since it often connotes a negative value judgment on one, a positive judgment on the other. It is not always easy to get around these terms, but when I cannot I will use them descriptively and not judgmentally.

5 To distinguish between these two models of class, the practical question relevant to the social class model is 'What does he do?' This question focuses on a person's place in the occupational order and reflects his/her place in the social relationship of the production process. Relevant to the attributes model is the question 'What does he have?' (Therborn, 1982). This question captures the attributes (economic, educational, social) that define a person as belonging to one socioeconomic stratum or another. It is not unusual to see these two different concepts of social class used synonymously, which is understandable since social class proper can be considered a form of stratification: one class dominant, one class subordinate (Eaton et al., 2010). In this book, when it matters, I will be clear when I am using either social class in the social class proper sense or the attributes model (SES) sense. At other times, when it matters less and class in either the SES or social class proper sense will do equally well, I will use the words 'class' or 'class position.'

6 Social class theorizing is extensive and controversial. See Beeghley (2005), Coser (1973), Gilbert (2010), Kerbo (2003), Levine (2006), Scase (1992), and Wright (1997, 2008, 2009).

7 For discussions of this issue, see Aneshensel et al. (1991); Aneshensel (2002); Horwitz (2002), Kessler (2002), and Mirowsky and Ross (2002).

8 Recently, however, Caspi's first publication has been refuted. Risch et al. (2009) found no evidence that a genetic factor alone or in combination with stressful life events was associated with depression. Only the number of stressful life events was.

2 Socioeconomic Status, Psychiatric Disorder, and Psychological Distress

1 An exception occurred in the National Comorbidity Survey (NCS) (Kessler et al., 1994), which showed that the lifetime prevalence of substance abuse was significantly higher in the middle classes (as measured by educational level) than in either the lower or upper classes.

2 All figures quoted in dollars refer to U.S. currency unless otherwise stated.

3 Household incomes are less than family incomes. Family income only takes households with two or more people related by blood or marriage into account whereas household income includes all households, which contain many single earners. See http://census.gov/population/www.cps.cpsdef.html.

4 To show how complicated this issue for other disorders can be: Miech et al. (1999) found that different disorders had a unique relationship with SES in young adults because of selection effects, the extent to which adolescents ended up in lower socioeconomic positions because their education was shortened. There were no selection effects for anxiety, which showed exclusive social causation, and depression, which showed neither selection nor causation because individuals had not yet been exposed to the stresses that cause depression in adults. Strong selection effects were shown for attention deficit disorder, exclusively, while antisocial personality disorder showed the effects of both causation and selection.

3 Social Class

1 'Generative' because it 'can produce more of the same resource when invested, or in other cases [it] can contribute to the production of another resource,' as when social capital leads to income (Wysong & Perrucci, 2007, p. 219).

2 Terry Eagleton (2001), a former professor of English at Oxford who grew up in a working-class family, observes, 'Though money is not everything, it is an indispensable condition of almost everything. There are indeed a great many more things in life than money, and it is money that gives us access to most of them' (p. 48).

3 Through direct ownership or through possession of enough corporate shares to give them a voice in running the company.

4 For more detailed descriptions of how the distributive order works, see Domhoff (1983) and Wysong and Perrucci (2007).

5 The media and popular culture, in addition to the educational system, constitute the cultural sphere.

6 For another description of the privileged class, see Michael Lind's (1995) *The Next American Nation*. His terms for the privileged class and the superclass are the 'white overclass' and the 'institutional elite.' The top officials in federal and state governments, university executives, military officers, judges, diplomats, financial and industrial executives, publishers, and intellectuals constitute the institutional elite (p. 144). The top 20% of the population

constitutes the white overclass, from which most of the institutional elite is drawn.

The white overclass tends to be concentrated in east- and west-coast metropolitan areas. They can be culturally distinguished from the American majority by a fairly uniform accent, diet (careful attention to), sports (squash and tennis), Anglophilia, delayed marriage, and distinctive forms of emotional problems including co-dependency, anorexia, bulimia, and diet pill addiction. As a class, they tend to be liberal, perhaps even libertarian, on social issues and conservative economically.

The white overclass's near-monopoly of the private sector and political branches of the institutional elite is the basis of its power in society. In the private sector, the major group of the white overclass is composed of lawyers, bankers, and corporate executives who set the style and tone of elite life. Entry into this group is largely determined by admission to prestigious universities, facilitated by legacy preferences, and maintained by state systems of professional accreditation, which protects the interests of the managerial-professional elite. In the public sector, the white overclass dominates political life in the United States through its dominant role in campaign financing and its occupation of the higher executive and judicial offices in the federal government. Lind argues that the key figures in the white overclass are institutional officers and professionals of one kind or another, not investors and individual owners of property. The essential class distinction, he believes, is not between the bourgeoisie and the proletariat but between the professional-managerial class and the wage-earning salaried class, the non-unionized employees who can be fired at any time, who lack a college degree, are paid by the hour, have few managerial responsibilities, and who constitute the great majority of working Americans (Lind, 1995, 151–2).

7 As does the cost of college education. It was predicted, before the Great Recession, that the cost of an Ivy League education in 2016 would be $364,800 (in 1997 dollars). A public university would cost $114,786. The monthly amount a family would have to save, from the day of the child's birth, to afford a public university education in 2016 would have been $319 (Collins & Yeskel, 2000, p. 35). Expensive, yes, but when these predictions were made, the lifetime earnings of those without a high school degree were $1 million. For those with a high school diploma, a college diploma, and a professional degree, the amounts were $1.2 million, 2.1 million, and 4.4 million (Kahlenberg, 2004). More recently, Mark Taylor (2010) has pointed out that if recent trends in the cost of higher education continue, the cost of four years at a top-tier school will be $330,000 in 2020, $525,000 in 2028, and $785,000 in 2035.

8 'Outsourcing' and 'offshoring' are often used synonymously, but they refer
  to different processes. Outsourcing occurs when a company hires another
  company to carry out a business function it no longer wants to carry out
  itself. The second company may be next door or across the sea. Offshoring
  occurs when a company shifts a portion of its business operation abroad. It
  may then carry out this operation itself or outsource it to another company
  (Miller, 2007).

4 Growing Inequality: Causes and Consequences

1 Linsky, Bachman, and Straus (1995) showed that economic stress, measured by rate of unemployment, business failures, personal bankruptcies,
  and mortgage foreclosures increased by almost 50% in the United States
  between 1976 and 1982. Schor (1991) found that between 1969 and 1987 the
  annual working hours for U.S. employees rose from 1,786 hours to 1,949,
  an increase of nine hours every year. The figure by 1998 had risen further,
  to 1967 hours a year (Streeck & Heinze, 1999). By 2002, however, the figure
  had fallen back to 1815 hours because of the 2001 recession and subsequent
  jobless recovery. Even though the Japanese have a special word for death
  from overwork – 'karoshi' – workers in the U.S. put in more hours per year
  in 2002 than workers in any other industrialized country except Australia
  and New Zealand. In 2000, when Americans put in more time than they
  do now – 1,877 hours per year – German workers, by contrast, put in 1,480
  hours, which amounted to a total of 50 fewer days a year than Americans.
  The Japanese worked 1,840 hours annually in 2000 (Mishel et al., 2005; Phillips, 2002; Sanger, 1990). The 2008–9 recession reduced annual work hours
  in America to 1650, however (Lowenstein, 2009).
2 Wherever the line is drawn among the privileged, Thomas Frank (2008)
  believes that this increasing accumulation of wealth at the top end has far
  reaching political effects in producing the 'leading political fact of our time:
  the replacement of our middle-class republic by a plutocracy' (p. A17), the
  rule or control of society by the wealthy.
3 The cost of tuition at the University of Oregon has increased 341% since
  1979 (Pardington, 2009). However, tuition and fees at all colleges that published the figures increased 439% between 1982 and 2007. This figure was
  adjusted for inflation and far outpaced the modest growth of family income
  during the same period (Lewin, 2008).
4 There is little consensus among economists about how much weight to
  accord the different factors that have been implicated in rising levels of inequality. In Mishel and colleagues' (2005) opinion, a third of the increasing

wage inequality is due to decreased unionization and failure to maintain the minimum wage; a third to globalization including trade, immigration, capital mobility, and the employment shift toward service industries; and a third to other factors, such as the unemployment rate.

5 A remarkable feature of the economy in recent years has been the dramatic gap between the growth of productivity and the growth of wages, which as mentioned has been relatively stagnant. Productivity refers to the economy's output of goods and services per hour of work. The average income in the United States is governed mainly by the level of productivity. Productivity by historical standards was low between 1973 and 1995 (Madrick, 1995). It picked up significantly afterwards but incomes lagged far behind for most wage earners. The explanations for this development vary (Levy & Temin, 2007; Mishel et al, 2007). In any event, it is clear that a smaller share of economic output is going to labour, a larger share to capital (Bradsher, 1995b; Mishel et al., 2005, 2009; Phelps, 1997).

6 Links between Social Class, Well-Being, and Distress

1 The study was inspired in part by Durkheim's (1897/1951) study of suicide, in which he formulated one of the few laws of sociology: the suicide rate varies inversely with the individual's degree of integration with his or her society.

2 Families were considered middle class if at least one parent worked in a position that involved substantial managerial authority or performed work that was based on complex, educationally certified skills. Families were categorized as working class if neither parent met the criteria for a middle-class position and at least one worked at a job that neither granted managerial authority nor required educational credentials.

7 Class Differences in Psychotherapy

1 The great majority of the articles on social class and psychotherapy listed in a Google Scholar search in December 2010 were published prior to 1970.

2 Smith (2005) points out that the poor comprise a category without sharp boundaries that includes the unemployed, the partially employed, and the lower-income members of the working class.

8 The *DSM*, Disorder, and Distress

1 I have followed and paraphrased Horwitz (2002) closely in this chapter. Within its compass I cannot hope to do justice to the richness of his account.

He has something interesting to say on every page. His book should be read by everyone interested in the ways that mental illness is constructed.

2 The terms 'dynamic' and 'analytic' are synonymous.

3 A well-known psychotherapist, Irvin Yalom (2002, pp. xxi, 5–6), who himself trained during the era of dynamic psychiatry, advises therapists to avoid diagnoses except when dealing with insurance companies. He believes that a diagnosis diminishes the therapist's ability to relate to the patient because it encourages selective attention to the symptoms and behaviours that confirm the diagnosis at the expense of other kinds of information. Also, over-attention to symptoms of such conditions as recovered memory disorder and multiple personality disorder may perpetrate the very symptoms or traits that one is treating. He acknowledges, however, the importance of diagnosis in the treatment of severe mental disorder and organic conditions.

4 But not all. For a telling example of how a psychiatrist with a biological orientation to diagnosis and treatment fails to appreciate the context of a patient's life see Kleinman (1988, pp. 77–94). The problem in this example is not social class difference – both psychiatrist and patient are physicians – but lack of social perspective.

5 In psychiatric practice, the frequency with which psychiatrists shoehorn patients into formal psychiatric diagnostic categories – usually adjustment reactions or mood disorders of various types – for the purposes of record-keeping and reimbursement also supports Horwitz's (2002) point that many normal problems of living have been inappropriately captured by the diagnostic manual.

6 Torrey (1999) presents evidence to show that there is more overlap than previously thought, that the two disorders may represent the ends of a spectrum.

7 An assertion that is controversial. See McGrath et al. (2008).

8 For example, see Kendler, Myers, and Zisook (1987).

10 In Closing

1 See the Appendix as well as Edwards, Crain, & Kalleberg (2007); Madrick (2009); Marmot (2004); Marmot et al. (2008); Page & Simmons (2000).

References

Adler, N.E., Boyce, T., Chesney, M.A., et al. (1994). Socioeconomic status and health: The challenge of the gradient. *American Psychologist, 49*, 15–24.

Adler, N.E., & Ostrove, J.M. (1999). Socioeconomic status and health: What we know and what we don't. *Annals of the New York Academy of Sciences, 896*, 3–15.

Albee, G.W. (1986). Toward a just society: Lessons from observations on the primary prevention of psychopathology. *American Psychologist, 41*, 891–8.

– (1990). The futility of psychotherapy. *Journal of Mind and Behavior, 11*, 369–84.

– (1998). Fifty years of clinical psychology: Selling our soul to the devil. *Applied and Preventive Psychology, 7*, 189–94.

– (2000). The Boulder model's fatal flaw. *American Psychologist, 55*, 247–8.

Altman, D. (2004). *Neoconomy: George Bush's revolutionary gamble with America's future*. New York, NY: Public Affairs Press.

American Psychiatric Association. (2000). *Diagnostic and statistical manual of mental disorders: DSM-IV-TR* (4th ed., text revision). Washington, DC: Author.

American Psychological Association (2000). *Resolution on poverty and socioeconomic status*. Retrieved from http://www.apa.org/about/governance/council/policy/poverty-resolution.aspx

– (2007). *Report of the APA task force on socioeconomic status*. Washington, DC: American Psychological Association.

– (2008). Report of the task force on resources for the inclusion of social class in psychology curricula. Washington, DC; American Psychological Association.

Andrews, E.L. (2003a, January 7). White House aides launch a defense of Bush tax plan. *New York Times*, pp. A1, A16.

– (2003b, January 8). Plan gives most benefits to wealthy and families. *New York Times,* p. A17

– (2003c, January 14). Fight looms over who bears the biggest tax burden. *New York Times,* pp. C1, C8.

– (2003d, December 7). Imports don't deserve all that blame. *New York Times,* Section 3, p. 4.

Aneshensel, C.S. (1992). Social stress: Theory and research. *Annual Review of Sociology, 18,* 15–38.

– (1999). Outcomes of the stress process. In A.V. Horwitz & T.C. Scheid (Eds.), *A handbook for the study of mental health* (pp. 211–27). New York, NY: Cambridge University Press.

– (2002). Commentary: Answers and questions in the sociology of mental health. *Journal of Health and Social Behavior, 43,* 236–46.

Aneshensel, C.S., Rutter, C.M., & Lachenbruch, P.A. (1991). Social structure, stress, and mental health: Competing conceptual and analytic models. *American Sociological Review, 56,* 166–88.

Antonovsky, A. (1967). Social class, life expectancy and overall mortality. *Milbank Memorial Fund Quarterly, 65,* 31–73.

Arenson, K.W. (2004, February 29). Harvard says poor parents won't have to pay. *New York Times,* p. 12.

Aronowitz, S. (2003). *How class works: Power and social movement.* New Haven, CT: Yale University Press.

Avison, W.R., & Turner, R.J. (1988). Stressful life events and depressive symptoms: Disaggregating the effects of acute stressors and chronic strains. *Journal of Health and Social Behavior, 29,* 253–64.

Bachrach, L.L. (1993). American experience in social psychiatry. In D. Bhugra & J. Leff (Eds.), *Principles of social psychiatry* (pp. 534–8). Oxford: Blackwell Scientific Publications.

Bandura, A. (1997). *Self-efficacy: The exercise of control.* New York, NY: Worth.

Barbour, A.G. (1995). *Caring for patients: A critique of the medical model.* Stanford, CA: Stanford University Press.

Barker, D.J.P. (1998). *Mothers, babies, and health in later life.* Edinburgh: Churchill Livingstone.

Barondess, J.A. (2007, Winter). Danse macabre: Poverty, social status, and health. *The Pharos,* pp. 4–9.

Barr, D.A. (2008). *Health disparities in the United States: Social class, race, ethnicity, and health.* Baltimore, MD: Johns Hopkins University Press.

Bartels, L.M. (2008). *Unequal democracy: The political economy of the new gilded age.* Princeton, NJ: Princeton University Press.

Bartley, M., Ferrie, J., & Montgomery, S.M. (1999). Living in a high-unemployment economy: Understanding the health differences. In M.G. Marmot & R.G. Wilkinson (Eds.), *Social determinants of health* (pp. 81–104). New York, NY: Oxford University Press.

– (2006). Health and market disadvantage, non-employment, and job insecurity. In M. Marmot & R.G. Wilkinson (Eds.), *Social determinants of health* (2nd ed., pp. 78–96). New York, NY: Oxford University Press.

Baum, A., Garofalo, J.P., & Yali, A.M. (1999). Socioeconomic status and chronic stress: Does stress account for SES effects on health? *Annals of the New York Academy of Sciences, 896,* 131–44.

Beeghley, L. (2005). *The structure of social stratification in the United States* (5th ed.). Boston, MA: Allyn & Bacon.

Berger, P. (1986). *The capitalist revolution.* New York, NY: Basic Books.

Berkman, L.F., & Breslow, L. (1983). *Health and way of living: The Alameda County study.* New York, NY: Oxford University Press.

Blane, D. (1995). Editorial: Social determinants of health—socioeconomic status, social class, and ethnicity. *American Journal of Public Health, 85,* 903–5.

– (2006). The life course, the social gradient, and health. In M.G. Marmot & R.G. Wilkinson (Eds.), *Social determinants of health* (2nd ed., pp. 54–77). New York, NY: Oxford University Press.

Blank, R.M. (1997). *It takes a nation: A new agenda for fighting poverty.* Princeton, NJ: Princeton University Press.

Blazer, D., Hughes, D., & George, L.K. (1988). Stressful life events and the onset of a generalized anxiety syndrome. *American Journal of Psychiatry, 144,* 1178–83.

Blumenthal, R. (2003, October 19). As Levi's work is exported, stress stays at home. *New York Times,* p. 14.

Boshara, R. (2002, September 29). Poverty is more than a matter of income. *New York Times,* Section 4, p. 13.

Bosma, H., Marmot, M.G., Hemingway, H., et al. (1997). Low job control and risk of coronary heart disease in the Whitehall II (prospective study) cohort. *British Medical Journal, 314,* 558–65.

Bradsher, K. (1995a, April 17). Gap in wealth in U.S. called widest in west. *New York Times,* pp. Al, C4.

– (1995b, June 25). Productivity is all, but it doesn't pay well. *New York Times,* p. E4.

Brody, J. (1991, July 10). As employee benefits and staffs shrink, on-the-job stress grows. *New York Times,* p. B6.

Brown, G.W. (2000). Medical sociology and issues of aetiology. In M.G. Gelder, J.J. Lopez-Ibor, & N.C. Andreason (Eds.), *New Oxford textbook of psychiatry* (pp. 293–300). Oxford: Oxford University Press.

Brown, G.W., Bhrolchain, M.N., & Harris, T. (1975). Social class and psychiatric disturbance in women in an urban population. *Sociology, 9,* 225–54.

Brown, G.W., Birley, J.L.T., & Wing, J.K. (1972). Influence of family life on the course of schizophrenic disorders: A replication. *British Journal of Psychiatry, 121,* 241–58.

Brown, G.W., & Harris, T. (1978). *The social origins of depression.* London: Tavistock.

Brown, G.W., Monck, E.M., Carstairs, G.M., et al. (1962). Influence of family life on the cause of schizophrenic illness. *Journal of Preventive and Social Medicine, 16,* 55–68.

Brown, L. (1994). *Subversive dialogues: Theory in feminist therapy.* New York, NY: Basic Books.

Bruce, M.L., Takeuchi, D.T., & Leaf, P.J. (1991). Poverty and psychiatric status. *Archives of General Psychiatry, 48,* 470–4.

Bureau of Labor Statistics. (2004). *Union affiliation of employed wage and salary workers by selected characteristics.* Retrieved from http://www.bls.gov/news.release/union2.t01.htm

Carpiano, R.M., Link, B.G., & Phelan, J.C. (2008). Social inequality and health: Future directions for the fundamental cause explanation. In A. Lareau & D. Conley (Eds.), *Social class: How does it work?* (pp. 232–63). New York, NY: Russell Sage.

Caspi, A., McClay, J., Moffitt, T.E., et al. (2002). Role of genotype in the cycle of violence in maltreated children. *Science, 297,* 851–4.

Caspi, A., Sugden, K., Moffitt, T.E., et al. (2003). Influence of life stress on depression: Moderation by a polymorphism in the 5-HTT gene. *Science, 301,* 386–9.

Caspi, A., Williams, B., Kim-Cohen, J., et al. (2007). Moderation of breastfeeding effects on the IQ by genetic variation in fatty acid metabolism. *Proceedings of the National Academy of Sciences, 104,* 18860–5.

Cawley, A.H. (1992). The logic of macrosociology. *Annual Review of Sociology, 18,* 1–14.

Chesler, P. (1973). *Women and madness.* New York, NY: Avon Books.

Ciulla, J.B. (2000). *The working life.* New York, NY: Three Rivers Press.

Cobb, S. (1976). Social support as a moderator of life stress. *Psychosomatic Medicine, 38,* 300–14.

Cohen, C.I. (2002). Social inequality and health: Will psychiatry assume center stage? *Psychiatric Services, 53,* 937–9.

Cohen, S., Janicki-Deverts, D., & Miller, G.E. (2007). Psychological stress and disease. *Journal of the American Medical Association, 298,* 1685–7.

Cohen-Cole, S.A., Brown, F.W., & McDaniel, J.S. (1993). Assessment of depression and grief reactions in the medically ill. In A. Stoudemire & B.S. Fogel (Eds.), *Psychiatric care of the medical patient* (pp. 52–69). New York, NY: Oxford University Press.

Collins, C., & Yeskel, F. (2000). *Economic apartheid in America.* New York, NY: New Press.

Conley, D. (2008). Reading between the lines (of this volume): A reflection of why we should stick to folk concepts of social class. In A. Lareau & D. Conley, D. (Eds.), *Social class: How does it work?* (pp. 366–73). New York, NY: Russell Sage.

Connery, I., Shapiro, P.A., McLaughlin, J.S., Bagiella, E., et al. (2001). Relationship between depression after coronary bypass surgery and 12-month outcome: A prospective study. *Lancet, 358,* 1766–71.

Conrad, P. (2007). *The medicalization of society.* Baltimore, MD: Johns Hopkins University Press.

Cooper, B. (1992). Sociology in the context of social psychiatry. *British Journal of Psychiatry, 161,* 594–8.

Coser, L.A. (1973). Class. In P.P. Wiener (Ed.), *Dictionary of the history of ideas: Studies of selected pivotal ideas* (Vol. 1, pp. 441–9). New York, NY: Charles Scribner's Sons.

Craig, T.J., & Van Natta, P.A. (1979). Influence of demographic characteristics on two measures of depressive symptoms. *Archives of General Psychiatry, 36,* 149–54.

Davey Smith, G., Hart, C., Blane, D., et al. (1997). Lifetime socioeconomic position and mortality: Prospective observational study. *British Medical Journal, 314,* 547–52.

Davey Smith, G., Neaton, J.D., Wentworth, D., et al. (1996). Socioeconomic differentials in mortality risk among men screened for the Multiple Risk Intervention Trial: I. White Men. *American Journal of Public Health, 86,* 486–96.

Deaton, A. (2002). Policy implications of the gradient of health and wealth. *Health Affairs, 21,* 13–30.

– (2003). Health, inequality, and economic development. *Journal of Economic Literature 41,* 113–58.

DeNavas-Walt, C., Proctor, B.D., & Smith, J.C. (2009). *Income, poverty, and health insurance coverage in the United States: 2008* [U.S. Census Bureau, Current Population Reports, P60–236]. Washington, DC: U.S. Government Printing Office.

De Santis, S. (1999). *Life on the line.* New York, NY: Anchor Books.

De Vogli, R., Mistry, R, Gaesotta, R. et al. (2005). Has the relation between income inequality and life expectancy disappeared? Evidence from Italy and top industrialized countries. *Journal of Epidemiology and Community Health, 59,* 158–62.

Diez Roux, A.V., Stein Merkin, S., Arnett, D., et al. (2001). Neighborhood of residence and incidence of coronary artery disease. *New England Journal of Medicine, 345,* 99–106.

Di Leo, L., & Sparshott, J. (2010, November 24). Corporate profits rise to record annual rate. *Wall Street Journal,* p. A5.

Does trade help or hurt workers? (2004, January 17). *New York Times,* p. A 30.

Dohrenwend, B.P., & Dohrenwend, B.S. (1969). *Social status and psychological disorder.* New York, NY: Wiley.

Dohrenwend, B.P., Dohrenwend, B.S., Gould, M.S., et al. (1980). *Mental illness in the United States: Epidemiological estimates.* New York, NY: Praeger.

Dohrenwend, B.P., Levav, P.W., Shrout, S., et al. (1992). Socioeconomic status and psychiatric disorders: The causative-selection issue. *Science, 255,* 946–52.

Domhoff, G.W. (1983). *Who rules America now?* Englewood Cliffs, NJ: Prentice-Hall, 1983.

– (2010). *Who rules America? Power in America: Wealth, income, power.* Retrieved from http://sociology.ucsc.edu/whorulesamerica/power/wealth.html.

Dragano, N., Verde, P.E., & Siegrist, J. (2005). Organisational downsizing and work stress: Testing synergistic health effects in employed men and women. *Journal of Epidemiology and Community Health, 59,* 694–9.

Durkheim, E. (1951). *Suicide: A study in sociology* (G. Simpson, Ed. & Trans.). New York, NY: Free Press. (Original work published in 1897)

Eagleton, T. (2001). *The gatekeeper.* New York, NY: St. Martin's Press.

Eaton, W.W. (2001). *The sociology of mental disorders* (3rd ed.). Westport, CT: Praeger.

Eaton, W.W., Martins, S.S., Nestadt, G., et al. (2008). The burden of mental disorders. *Epidiologic Reviews, 30,* 1–14.

Eaton, W.W., & Muntaner, C. (1999). Socioeconomic stratification and mental disorder. In A.V. Horwitz & T.C. Scheid (Eds.), *A handbook for the study of mental health* (pp. 259–83). New York, NY: Cambridge University Press.

Eaton, W.W., Muntaner, C., & Sapag, J.C. (2010). Socioeconomic stratification and mental disorder. In T.L. Scheid & T.N. Brown (Eds.), *A handbook for the study of mental health: Social contexts, theories, and systems* (2nd ed., pp. 226–5). New York, NY: Cambridge University Press.

Eberstadt, N., & Satel, S. (2004). *Health and the income inequality hypothesis.* Washington, DC: AEI Press.

Eckenrode, J. (1984). Impact of chronic and acute stressors on daily reports of mood. *Journal of Personality and Social Psychology, 46,* 907–18.

Editorial: The escalating price of politics. (2010, March 8). *New York Times,* p. A18.

Edwards, J., Crain, M., & Kalleberg, A.L. (Eds.). (2007). *Ending poverty: How to restore the American Dream.* New York, NY: New Press.

Ehrenreich, B. (1989). *Fear of falling: The inner life of the middle class.* New York, NY: Pantheon.

Elliot, L., & Atkinson, D. (1999). *The age of insecurity.* London: Verso.

Emmott, B. (2003). *20:21 Vision.* New York, NY: Farrar, Straus and Giroux.

The end of the company pension. (1999, May 15). *Economist,* pp. 85–7.

Engel, G.L. (1977). The need for a new medical model: A challenge for biomedicine. *Science, 196,* 129–36.

– (1980). The clinical application of the biopsychosocial model. *American Journal of Psychiatry, 137,* 535–44.

Everson, S.A., Roberts, R.E., & Goldberg, D. E. (1998). Depressive symptoms and increased risk of stroke mortality. *Archives of Internal Medicine, 158,* 1133–8.

Feighner, J.P., Robins, E., Guze, S.B., et al. (1972). Diagnostic criteria for use in psychiatric research. *Archives of General Psychiatry, 26,* 57–63.

Feldman, J.J., Makuc, D.M., Kleinman J.C., et al. (1989). National trends in educational differentials in mortality. *American Journal of Epidemiology, 129,* 919–33.

Fenwick, R., & Tausig, M. (2008). Work and the political economy of stress: Recontextualizing the study of mental health/illness in sociology. In W.R Avison, J.D. McLeod, & B.A. Pescosolido (Eds.), *Mental health, social mirror* (pp. 143–67). New York, NY: Springer.

Fernandez, R., & Rogerson, R. (2001). Sorting and long-run inequality. *Quarterly Journal of Economics, 116,* 1305–41.

Ferrie, J.E., Shipley, M.J., Marmot, M.G., et al. (1995). Health effects of anticipation of job change and non-employment: Longitudinal data from the Whitehall II study. *British Medical Journal, 311,* 1264–9.

Finn, J., & Jacobson, M. (2003). *Just practice: A social justice approach to social work.* Peosta, IA: Eddie Bowers.

Fiscella, K., & Franks, P. (1997). Poverty or income inequality as predictor of mortality: Longitudinal cohort study. *British Medical Journal, 314,* 1724–7.

Fischer, C.S. (1982). *To dwell among friends.* Chicago, IL: University of Chicago Press.

Fokken, U. (2007, July). Little help for the working poor. *German Times,* p. 13.

Folbre, N. (1995). *The new field guide to the U.S. economy.* New York, NY: New Press.

Forelle, C. (2004, May 14). On the road again, but now the boss is sitting beside you. *Wall Street Journal,* pp. A1, A6.

Forero, J. (2003, September 3). Mexico manufacturers lose business to China. *International Herald Tribune,* p. 11.

Fox, D., & Prilleltensky, I. (1997). Critical psychology: An introduction. London: Sage.

Frank, J. (1975). General psychotherapy: The restoration of morale. In S. Arieti (Series Ed), D.X. Friedman & J.E. Dyrud (Vol. Eds.), *American handbook of psychiatry: Vol. 5: Treatment* (2nd ed., pp. 117–132). New York, NY: Basic Books.

Frank, R.H. (2007). *Falling behind: How rising inequality hurts the middle class.* Berkeley, CA: University of California Press.

Frank, R.H., & Cook, P.J. (1995). *The winner-take-all society.* New York, NY: Penguin.

Frank, T. (2008, April 21). Obama's touch of class. *Wall Street Journal,* p. A17.

Fraser, J.A. (2001). *White-collar sweatshop: The deterioration of work and its rewards in corporate America.* New York, NY: Norton

Freeman, R.B. (2007). *America works: Critical thoughts on the exceptional U.S. labor market.* New York, NY: Russell Sage.

Friedman, B.M. (1998, October 8). The new demon. *New York Review of Books,* pp. 32–6.

Fryers, T., Melzer, D., & Jenkins, R. (2003). Social inequalities and the common mental disorders: A systematic review of the evidence. *Social Psychiatry & Psychiatric Epidemiology 38,* 229–37.

Fulcher, J. (2004). *Capitalism: A very short introduction.* New York, NY: Oxford University Press.

Fulford, K.W.M. (1999). Nine variations and a coda on the theme of an evolutionary definition of dysfunction. *Journal of Abnormal Psychology, 108,* 412–20.

Galbraith, J.K. (1998). *Created unequal: The crisis in American pay.* New York, NY: The Free Press.

Gallagher, B.J. (1995). *The sociology of mental illness* (3rd ed.). Englewood Cliffs, NJ: Prentice-Hall.

Gallo, L.C., & Matthews, K.A. (1999). Do negative emotions mediate the association between socioeconomic status and health? *Annals of the New York Academy of Sciences, 896,* 226–45.

Galobardes, B., Lynch, J.W.W., & Davey Smith, G. (2004). Childhood socioeconomic circumstances and cause-specific mortality in adulthood; Systematic review and interpretation. *Epidemiologic Reviews, 26,* 7–21.

George, L.K. (2006). Life course perspectives on social factors. In W.R. Avison, J.D. McLeod, & B.A. Pescosolido (Eds.), *Mental health, social mirror* (pp. 191–218). New York, NY: Springer.

George, L.K., Blazer, D.G., Hughes, D.C., et al. (1989). Social support and the outcome of major depression. *British Journal of Psychiatry, 154,* 478–85.

Gerth, H., & Mills, C.W. (1953). *Character and social structure: The psychology of social institutions.* New York, NY: Harcourt, Brace & World.

Gift, T.E., Strauss, J.S., Ritzler, B.A., et al. (1986). Social class and psychiatric outcome. *American Journal of Psychiatry, 143,* 222–5.

Gilbert, D. (2010). *The American class structure in an age of growing inequality* (8th ed.). Thousand Oaks, CA: Pine Forge Press.

Glaberson, W. (1987). Misery on the meatpacking line. *New York Times,* pp. F1, F3.

Golden, D. (2003a, January 15). Admissions preferences given to alumni children draws fire. *Wall Street Journal,* pp A1, A2.

– (2003b, May 14). For Supreme Court, affirmative action isn't just academics. *Wall Street Journal,* pp. A1, A11.

Goldin, C., & Katz, L.F. (2008). *The race between education and technology.* Cambridge, MA: Belknap Press of Harvard University Press.

Goodwin, F.K., & Jamison, K.R. (2007). *Manic-depressive illness: Bipolar disorders and recurrent depression* (2nd ed.). New York, NY: Oxford University Press.

Gordon, D. (1996). *Fat and mean: The corporate squeeze of working Americans and the myth of managerial 'downsizing.'* New York, NY: The Free Press.

Greenhouse, S. (2008). *The big squeeze: Tough times for American workers.* New York, NY: Knopf.

– (2009, May 20). Study says antiunion tactics are becoming more common. *New York Times,* p. B5.

– (2010, June 20). In Indiana, centerpiece for a city closes shop. *New York Times,* p. 14.

Greenspan, M. (1983). *A new approach to women and therapy.* New York, NY: McGraw-Hill.

Gross, D. (2005, March 20). Social security as Dramamine. *New York Times,* Section 3, p. 6.

Group for the Advancement of Psychiatry. (1983). *Community psychiatry: A reappraisal.* New York, NY: Mental Health Materials Center.

Hacker, J.S. (2006). *The great risk shift: The assault on American jobs, families, health care, and retirement and how you can fight back.* New York, NY: Oxford University Press.

Hacker, J.S., & Pierson, P. (2010). *Winner-take-all politics: How Washington made the rich richer—and turned its back on the middle class.* New York, NY: Simon & Schuster.

Handel, M.J. (2005). Trends in perceived job quality, 1989 to 1998. *Work & Occupations, 32,* 66–94.

Hasin, D.S., Goodwin, R.D., Stinson, F.S., et al. (2005). Epidemiology of major depressive disorder. *Archives of General Psychiatry, 62,* 1097–106.

Hawley, A.H. (1992). The logic of macrosociology. *Annual Review of Sociology, 58,* 1–14.

Head, S. (2003). *The new ruthless economy: Work and power in the digital age.* New York, NY: Oxford University Press.

Heilbroner, R. (1985). *The nature and logic of capitalism.* New York, NY: Norton.

Henwood, D. (2004, March 22). Toward a progressive view of outsourcing. *Nation,* pp. 25–6.

Hertzman, C. (1994). The lifelong impact of childhood health experiences: A population health perspective. *Daedalus, 123,* 167–80.

Hill, T.D., Ross, C.E., & Angell, R.J. (2005). Neighborhood disorder, psychophysiological distress, and health. *Journal of Health and Social Behavior, 46,* 170–86.

Hilsenrath, J.E., & Freeman, S. (2004, July 20). So far, economic recovery tilts to highest-income Americans. *Wall Street Journal.* Retrieved from http://online.wsj.com/article/0,SB109027263697767730,00.html

Hodgson, G. (2004). *More equal than others.* Princeton, NJ: Princeton University Press.

Hollingshead, A.B., & Redlich, F.C. (1958). *Social class and mental illness: A community study.* New York, NY: Wiley.

Holmes, T.H., & Rahe, R.H. (1967). The social readjustment rating scale. *Journal of Psychosomatic Research, 11,* 213–18.

Holusha, J. (1989, January 29). No utopia, but to workers it's a job: Fear, not just Japanese-style management, drives Nummi workers to perform so well. *New York Times,* pp. F1, F3.

Holzer, C.E., Shea, B., Swanson, J.W., et al. (1986). The increased risk for specific psychiatric disorders among persons of low socioeconomic status. *American Journal of Social Psychiatry, 6,* 259–71.

Horwitz, A.V. (2002). *Creating mental illness.* Chicago, IL: University of Chicago Press.

Horwitz, A.V., & Scheid, T.L. (1999). *A handbook for the study of mental health: Social contexts, theories, and systems.* New York, NY: Cambridge University Press

Horwitz, A.V., & Wakefield, J.C. (2005, Winter). The age of depression. *The Public Interest,* pp. 39–58.

– (2007). *The loss of sadness.* New York, NY: Oxford University Press.

House, J.S. (2001). Understanding social factors and inequalities in health: 20th Century progress and 21st Century prospects. *Journal of Health & Social Behavior, 43,* 125–42.

House, J.S., Landis, K.R., & Umberson, D. (1988). Social relationships and health. *Science, 241*, 540–5.

Hutton, W. (2004). *A declaration of interdependence: Why American should join the world*. New York, NY: Norton.

Ilsley, R., & Baker, D. (1991). Contextual variations in the meaning of health inequality. *Social Science and Medicine, 32*, 211–19.

Ip, G. (2004, July 8) U.S. health tied more to work than productivity, report says. *Wall Street Journal*, p. A2

Isaacs, S.L., & Schroeder, S.A. (2004). Class—The ignored determinant of the nation's health. *New England Journal of Medicine 351*, 1137–42.

Jones, E. (1974). Social class and psychotherapy: A critical review of research. *Psychiatry, 37*, 307–20.

Joyce, P.R. (2000). Epidemiology of mood disorders. In M.G. Gelder, J.J. Lopez-Ibor, & N.C. Andreason (Eds.), *New Oxford textbook of psychiatry* (pp. 695–701). Oxford: Oxford University Press.

Kahlenberg, R.D. (2003). *All together now: Creating middle-class schools through public choice*. Washington, DC: Brookings/Century Foundation.

– (2004, May). Schools of hard knocks. *American Prospect*, pp. 44–5.

Kaplan, G.A. (2004). What's wrong with social epidemiology, and how can we make it better? *Epidemiologic Reviews, 26*, 124–35.

Kaplan G.A., & Keil, J.E. (1993). Socioeconomic factors and cardiovascular disease: A review of the literature. *Circulation, 88*, 1973–98.

Kaplan, G.A., Pamuk, E., Lynch, J.W., et al. (1996). Income inequality and mortality in the United States: Analysis of mortality and potential pathways. *British Medical Journal, 312*, 999–1003.

Karasek, R., & Theorell, T. (1990). *Healthy work: Stress, productivity, and the reconstruction of the working life*. New York, NY: Basic Books.

Katz, S.J., Kessler, R.G., Frank, P., et al. (1997). Utilization of mental health services in the United States and Canada: The impact of mental health morbidity and perceived need for care. *American Journal of Public Health, 87*, 1136–43.

Kawachi, I., & Kennedy, B. (2002). *The health of nations: Why inequality is harmful to your health*. New York, NY: New Press.

Kendler, K.S., Heath, A.C., Martin, N.C., et al. (1987). Symptoms of anxiety and symptoms of depression: Same genes, different environment? *Archives of General Psychiatry, 122*, 451–7.

Kendler, K.S., Hettema, J.M., Butera, F., et al. (2003). Life event dimensions of loss, humiliation, entrapment, and danger in the prediction of onsets of major depression and generalized anxiety. *Archives of General Psychiatry, 60*, 789–96.

Kendler, K.S., Myers, J., & Zisook, S. (2008). Does bereavement-related depression differ from major depression associated with other stressful life events? *American Journal of Psychiatry, 165*, 1449–55.

Kerbo, H.R. (2003). *Social stratification and inequality; Class conflict in historical, comparative, and global perspective* (5th ed.). Boston: McGraw-Hill.

Kerkhof, A.J.F.M., & Arensman, E. (2000). Attempted suicide and deliberate self-harm: Epidemiology and risk factors. In M.G., Gelder, J.J. Lopez-Ibor, & N.C. Andreason (Eds.), *New Oxford textbook of psychiatry* (pp. 1039–45). Oxford: Oxford University Press.

Kessler, R.C. (2002). The categorical versus dimensional assessment controversy in the sociology of mental illness. *Journal of Health and Social Behavior, 43,* 171–88.

Kessler, R.C., Berglund, P., Demler, O., et al. (2003). The epidemiology of major depressive disorder: Results from the National Comorbidity Survey Replication (NCS-R). *Journal of the American Medical Association, 289,* 3095–105.

Kessler, R.C., & Cleary, P.D. (1980). Social class and psychological distress. *American Sociological Review, 45,* 463–78.

Kessler, R.C., McGonagle, K.A., Zhao, S., et al. (1994). Lifetime and 12-month prevalence of DSM-III-R psychiatric disorders in the United States. Results from the National Comorbidity Survey. *Archives of General Psychiatry, 51,* 8–19.

Kessler, R.C., & McLeod, J.D. (1985). Social support and mental health in a community sample. In S. Cohen & S.L. Syme (Eds.), *Social Support and Health* (pp. 219–40). New York, NY: Academic Press.

Kessler, R.C., Zhao, S., Blazer, D.G., et al. (1997). Prevalence, correlates, and course of minor depression and major depression in the National Comorbidity Survey. *Journal of Affective Disorders, 45,* 19–30.

Kilborn, P.T. (1990a, June 3). Tales from the digital treadmill. *New York Times,* pp. E1, E3.

– (1990b, December 23). Workers using computers find a supervisor inside. *New York Times,* pp. 1, 11.

– (1995, July 3). Even in good times, it's hard times for workers. *New York Times,* pp. A1, A7.

Klein, D.F. (1999). Harmful dysfunction, disorder, disease, illness, and evolution. *Journal of Abnormal Psychology, 108,* 421–9.

Kleinman, A. (1986). Commentary. In D. Mechanic, Role of social factors in health and well being: Psychosocial model from a social perspective. *Integrative Psychiatry, 4,* 2–11.

– (1988). *Rethinking psychiatry: From cultural category to personal experience.* New York, NY: The Free Press.

Kohn, R., Dohrenwend, B.P., & Mirotznik, J. (1998). Epidemiologic findings on selected psychiatric disorders in the general population. In B.P.

Dohrenwend (Ed.), *Adversity, stress, and psychopathology* (pp. 233–83). New York, NY: Oxford University Press.

Korten, D.C. (1995). *When corporations rule the world*. West Hartford, CT: Kumarion Press.

Kosteniuk, J.G., & Dickinson, H.D. (2003). Tracing the social gradient in the health of Canadians: Primary and secondary determinants. *Social Science & Medicine, 57*, 263–76.

Kramer, P. (1993). *Listening to Prozac: A psychiatrist explores antidepressant drugs and the remaking of the self*. New York, NY: Viking.

Krieger, N., Chen, J.T., Coull, B.A., et al. (2005). Lifetime socioeconomic position and twins' health: An analysis of 308 pairs of United States women twins. *PLOS Medicine, 2*, 645–53.

Krieger, N., Williams, D.R., & Moss, N.E. (1997). Measuring social class in US public health research: Concepts, methodologies, and guidelines. *Annual Review of Public Health, 18*, 341–78.

Kristenson, M., Eriksen, H.R., Sluiter, J.K., et al. (2004). Psychobiological mechanisms of socioeconomic differences in health. *Social Science and Medicine, 58*, 1511–22.

Krueger, A. (2002, November 14). The apple falls close to the tree, even in the land of opportunity. *New York Times*, p. C2.

Krugman, P. (2002, October 20). For richer: How the permissive capitalism of the boom destroyed American equality. *New York Times Magazine*, pp. 62–142.

– (2007). *The conscience of a liberal*. New York, NY: Norton.

Kuttner, R. (1997). *Everything for sale: The virtues and limits of markets*. New York, NY: Knopf.

– (2007). *The squandering of America: How the failure of our politics undermines our prosperity*. New York, NY: Knopf.

Lareau, A. (1989). *Home advantage: Social class and parental intervention in elementary education*. New York, NY: Falmer Press.

– (2003). *Unequal Childhoods: Class, race, and family life*. Berkeley, CA: University of California Press.

Lareau, A., & Weininger, E.B. (2008). Class and the transition to adulthood. In A. Lareau & E.B. Weininger (Eds.), *Social class: How does it work?* (pp. 118–51). New York, NY: Russell Sage.

LaRocco, J.M., House, J.S., & French, J.R.P. (1980). Social support, occupational stress, and health. *Journal of Health and Social Behavior, 3*, 202–18.

Latkin, C.A., & Curry, A.D. (2003). Stressful neighborhoods and depression: A prospective study of the impact of neighborhood disorder. *Journal of Health and Social Behavior, 44*, 34–44.

Leff, J. (2001). *The unbalanced mind.* New York, NY: Columbia University Press.

Leighton, A.H. (1960). *An introduction to social psychiatry.* Springfield, IL: Charles C. Thomas.

Leighton, D.C., Harding, J.S., Macklin, D.B., et al. (1963). *The character of danger: Psychiatric symptoms in selected communities.* New York, NY: Basic Books.

Leonhardt, D. (2004, April 22). As wealthy fill top colleges, concerns grow over fairness. *New York Times,* pp. A1, A22.

Leventhal, T., & Brooks-Gunn, J. (2003). Moving to opportunity: An experimental study of neighborhood effects on mental health. *American Journal of Public Health, 93,* 1576–82.

Levine, R.F. (2006). *Social class and stratification: Classic statements and theoretical debates* (2nd ed.). Lanham, MD: Rowman & Littlefield.

Levy, F.S., & Temin, P. (2007). *Inequality and institutions in 20th century America* [MIT Department of Economics Working Paper No. 07–17]. Retrieved from http://ssrn.com/abstract=984330

Lewin, T. (2008, December 3). College may become unaffordable for most in U.S. *New York Times,* p. A19.

Light, D. (1980). *Becoming psychiatrists.* New York, NY: Norton.

Lilienfeld, S.O., & Marino, L. (1995). Mental disorder as a Roschian concept: A critique of Wakefield's 'harmful dysfunction' analysis. *Journal of Abnormal Psychology, 104,* 411–20.

Lind, M. (1995). *The next American nation: The new nationalism and the fourth American revolution.* New York, NY: Free Press.

Lindeman, S., Laara, E., Hakko, H., et al. (1996). A systematic review of gender-specific suicide mortality in medical doctors. *British Journal of Psychiatry 168,* 274–9.

Link, B.G., & Phelan, J. (1995). Social conditions as fundamental causes of disease. *Journal of Health and Social Behavior, Extra Issue,* 80–94.

Linsky, A.S., Bachman, R., & Straus, M.A. (1995). *Stress, culture, and aggression.* New Haven, CT: Yale University Press.

Litt, E. (1963). Civic education, community norms, and political indoctrination. *American Sociological Review, 28,* 69–75.

Lonnqvist, J.K. (2000). Epidemiology and causes of suicide. In M.G., Gelder, J.J., Lopez-Ibor, & N.C. Andreason (Eds.), *New Oxford textbook of psychiatry* (pp. 1033–9). Oxford: Oxford University Press.

Lorant, V., Deliege, D., Eaton, W., et al. (2003). Socioeconomic inequalities in depression: A meta-analysis. *American Journal of Epidemiology, 157,* 98–112.

Lott, B. (2002). Cognitive and behavioral distancing from the poor. *American Psychologist, 57,* 100–10.

Lowenstein, R. (2009, July 26). The new joblessness. *New York Times Magazine*, pp. 11–12.

Lubrano, A. (2004). *Limbo: Blue collar roots, white collar dreams.* Hoboken, NJ: Wiley.

Luhrmann, T.M. (2000). *Of two minds: The growing disorder in American psychiatry.* New York, NY: Knopf.

Lynch, J., Smith, G.D., Hillemeier, M., et al. (2001). Income inequality, the psychosocial environment, and health: Comparisons of wealthy nations. *Lancet, 358,* 194–200.

Lynch, J.W., Davey Smith, G., Kaplan, G.A., et al. (2000). Income inequality and mortality: Importance to health of individual income, psychosocial environment, or material conditions. *British Medical Journal, 320,* 1200–4.

Lynch, J.W., Kaplan, G.A., & Shema, S.J. (1997). Cumulative impact of sustained economic hardship on physical, cognitive, and social functioning. *New England Journal of Medicine, 337,* 1889–903.

Mackenbach, J.P. (2002). Income inequality and population health. *British Medical Journal, 324,* 1–2.

Madrick, J. (1995). *The end of affluence.* New York, NY: Random House.

– (2003, February 21). A bull market and a boom in 401(k)s must mean fat pensions? Think again. *New York Times,* p. C2.

– (2009). The case for big government. Princeton, NJ: Princeton University Press.

Magnus, S.A., & Mick, S.S. (2000). Medical schools, affirmative action, and the neglected role of social class. *American Journal of Public Health, 90,* 1197–201.

Maj, M. (2008). Depression, bereavement, and 'understandable' intense sadness: Should the DSM-IV approach be revisited? *American Journal of Psychiatry, 165,* 1373–5.

Marchand, A., Demers, A., & Durand, P. (2005). Does work really cause distress? The contribution of occupational structure and work organization to the experience of psychological distress. *Social Science & Medicine, 61,* 1–14.

Maris, R.W. (2002). Suicide. *Lancet, 360,* 319–26.

Marmot, M. (2004). *The status syndrome: How social standing affects our life and longevity.* New York, NY: Times Books.

– (2006). Health in an unequal world. *Lancet, 368,* 2081–94.

Marmot, M., Friel, S., Bell, R., et al. (2008). Closing the gap in a generation: Health equity through action on the social determinants of health. *Lancet, 372,* 1661–9.

Marmot, M.G., Bosma., H., Hemingway, H., Brunner, E., et al. (1997). Contribution of job control and other risk factors to social variations in coronary heart disease incidence. *Lancet, 350,* 235–9.

Marmot, M.G., Rose, G.R., Shipley, M., et al. (1978) Employment grade and coronary heart disease in British civil servants. *Journal of Epidemiology and Community Health, 32,* 244–9.

Marmot, M.G., & Shipley, M.J. (1996). Do socioeconomic differences in mortality persist after retirement? 25 year follow-up of civil servants from the first Whitehall Study. *British Medical Journal, 313,* 1177–80.

Martin-Baro, I. (1996). *Writings for a liberation psychology* (A. Aron & S. Corne, Eds.). Cambridge, MA: Harvard University Press.

Massey, D.S. (2006). Race, class, and markets: Social policy in the 21st century. In D.B. Grusky & R. Kanbur (Eds.), *Poverty and inequality* (pp. 117–32). Stanford, CA: Stanford University Press.

– (2007). *Categorically unequal: The American stratification system.* New York, NY: Russell Sage.

Mayer, J. (2001, March 20). Study tracks who pays how much Oregon taxes. *Oregonian,* pp. A1, A11.

McCreadie, R.G. (1992). The Nithsdale schizophrenia surveys: An overview. *Social Psychiatry and Psychiatric Epidemiology, 36,* 311–15.

McCulloch, A. (2001). Social environments and health: Cross sectional national survey. *British Medical Journal, 323,* 208–9.

McDonough, P., Duncan, G.J., Williams, D., et al. (1997). Income dynamics and adult mortality in the United States, 1972 through 1989. *American Journal of Public Health, 87,* 1476–83.

McEwan, B.S. (1998). Protective and damaging effects of stress mediators. *New England Journal of Medicine, 338,* 171–9.

– (2003). Mood disorders and allostatic load. *Biological Psychiatry, 54,* 200–7.

McFarlane, A.H., Norman, G.R., Streiner, D.L., et al. (1983). The process of social stress: Stable, reciprocal, and mediating relationships. *Journal of Health and Social Behavior, 24,* 160–173.

McGrath, J., Saha, S., Chant, D., et al. (2008). Schizophrenia; A concise overview of incidence, prevalence, and mortality. *Epidemiologic Reviews, 30,* 67–76.

McLeod, C.B., Lavis, J.N., Mustard, C.A., et al. (2003). Income inequality, household income, and health status in Canada: A prospective cohort study. *American Journal of Public Health, 93,* 1287–93.

Meara, E.R., Richards, S., & Cutler, D.M. (2008, March/April). The gap gets bigger: Changes in mortality and life expectancy, by education, 1989–2000. *Health Affairs, 27,* 350–60.

Mechanic, D. (1986). Role of social factors in health and well-being: A psychosocial model from a social perspective. *Integrative Psychiatry, 4,* 2–11.

– (2003). Is the prevalence of mental disorders a good measure of the need for services? *Health Affairs, 22,* 8–27.

Melzer, D., Fryers, T., & Jenkins, R. (Eds.). (2004). *Social inequalities and the distribution of common mental disorders.* New York, NY: Psychology Press.

Michaels, W.B. (2006). *The trouble with diversity: How we learned to love identity and ignore inequality.* New York, NY: Metropolitan Books.

– (2009, August 27). Class trumps race. *London Review of Books, 31,* pp. 11–13.

Miech, R.A., Caspi, A., Moffitt, T.E., et al. (1999). Low socioeconomic status and mental disorders: A longitudinal study of selection and causation during young adulthood. *American Journal of Sociology, 104,* 1096–131.

Miller, J. (2007, September/October). Outsized offshore outsourcing. *Dollars and Sense,* pp. 30–5.

Miller, P., & Rose, N. (Eds.). (1986). *The power of psychiatry.* Cambridge, UK: Polity Press.

Mills, C.W. (2000). *The power elite.* New York, NY: Oxford University Press.

Miringoff, M., & Miringoff, M.-L. (1999). *The social health of the nation.* New York, NY: Oxford University Press.

Miringoff, M.-L., & Opdycke, S. (2008). *America's social health: Putting social issues back on the public agenda.* Armonk, NY: M.E. Sharpe.

Mirowsky, J., & Ross, C.E. (1989). *Social causes of psychological distress.* New York, NY: Aldine de Gruyter.

– (2002). Measurement for a human science. *Journal of Health and Social Behavior, 43,* 152–70.

– (2003a). *Education, social status, and health.* New York, NY: Aldine de Gruyter.

– (2003b). *Social Causes of psychological distress* (2nd ed.). Hawthorne, NY: Aldine de Gruyter.

Mirowsky, J., Ross, C.E., & Reynolds, J. (2000). Links between social status and health status. In C.E. Bird, P. Conrad, & A.M. Frement (Eds.), *Handbook of medical sociology* (pp. 47–67). Upper Saddle River, NJ: Prentice-Hall.

Mishel, L., Bernstein, J., & Allegretto, S. (2005). *The state of working America 2004/2005.* Ithaca, NY: ILR Press (of Cornell University Press).

– (2007). *The state of working America 2006/2007.* Ithaca, NY: ILR Press (of Cornell University Press).

Mishel, L., Bernstein, J., & Boushey, H. (2003*). The state of working America 2002/2003.* Ithaca, NY: ILR Press (of Cornell University Press).

Mishel, L., Bernstein, J., & Shierholz, H. (2009). *The state of working America 2008/2009.* Ithaca, NY: ILR Press (of Cornell University Press).

Morris, M., Bernhardt, A., & Handcock, M. (1994). Economic inequality: New methods for new trends. *American Sociological Review, 59,* 205–19.

Mullaly, B. (2007). *The new structural social work* (3rd ed.). Oxford: Oxford University Press.

Muntaner, C., Borrell, C., Benach, J., et al. (2003). The associations of social class and social stratification with patterns of general and mental health in a Spanish population. *International Journal of Epidemiology, 32,* 950–8.

Muntaner, C., Borrell, C., & Chung, H. (2006). Class relations, economic inequality, and mental health: Why social class matters to the sociology of mental health. In W.R. Avison, J.D. McLeod, & B.A. Pescosolido (Eds.), *Mental health, social mirror* (pp. 127–41). New York, NY: Springer.

– (2010). Class exploitation and psychiatric disorders: From status syndrome to capitalist syndrome. In C.I. Cohen & S. Timimi (Eds.), *Liberatory psychiatry: Philosophy, politics, and mental health* (pp. 105–30). New York, NY: Cambridge University Press.

Muntaner, C., Eaton, W.W., & Diala, C.C. (2000). Social inequalities in mental health: A review of concepts and underlying assumptions. *Health, 4,* 89–113.

Muntaner, C., Eaton, W.W., Diala, C.C., et al. (1998). Social class, assets, organizational control and the prevalence of common groups of mental disorders. *Social Science and Medicine, 47,* 2043–53.

Muntaner, C., Eaton, W.W., Miech, R., et al. (2004). Socioeconomic position and major mental disorders. *Epidemiologic Reviews, 26,* 53–62

Murphy, J.M., Olivier, D.C., Monson, R.R., et al. (1991). Depression and anxiety in relation to social status. *Archives of General Psychiatry, 48,* 223–9.

Murphy, R. (1985). Exploitation or exclusion? *Sociology, 19,* 225–43.

Musselman, D.L., Evans, D.L., & Nemeroff, C.B. (1998). The relationship of depression to cardiovascular disease. *Archives of General Psychiatry, 55,* 580–92.

Myers, J.K., & Bean, L.L. (1968). *A decade later: A follow-up of social class and mental illness.* New York, NY: Wiley.

Negrete, J.C. (2000). Aetiology of alcohol problems. In M.G. Gelder, J.J. Lopez-Ibor, & N.C. Andreason (Eds.), *New Oxford textbook of psychiatry* (pp. 477–82). Oxford: Oxford University Press.

Nestadt, B., Romanoski, A.J., Brown, C.H., et al. (1991). DSM-III compulsive personality disorder: An epidemiological survey. *Psychological Medicine, 21,* 461–71.

Nestadt, B., Romanoski, A.J., Chahal, R., et al. (1990). An epidemiological study of histrionic personality disorder. *Psychological Medicine, 20,* 413–22.

Netterstrom, B., Conrad, N., Bech, P., et al. (2008). The relation between work-related psychosocial factors and the development of depression. *Epidemiologic Reviews, 30,* 118–32

New Oxford Dictionary of English. (1998). Oxford: Clarendon Press.

Niedhammer, I., Goldbert, M., Leclerc, A., & David, S. (1998). Psychosocial factors at work and subsequent depressive symptoms in the Gazel cohort. *Scandinavian Journal of Work and Environmental Health, 3,* 197–205.

Nock, M.K., Hwang, I., Sampson, N.A., et al. (2009) Mental disorders, comorbidity, and suicidal behavior: Results from the National Comorbidity Survey Replication. *Molecular Psychiatry, 14,* 1–9.

Northwestern National Life Insurance Company. (1991). *Employee burnout: Causes and cures.* Minneapolis, MN: Author.

O'Connell, R.A., & Mayo, J. (1988). The role of social factors in affective disorders: A review. *Hospital & Community Psychiatry, 39,* 842–51.

Olfsun, M., & Pincus, H.A. (1994a) Outpatient psychotherapy in the United States, I: Volume, costs, and user characteristics. *American Journal of Psychiatry, 151,* 1281–8.

– (1994b) Outpatient psychotherapy in the United States, II: Patterns of utilization. *American Journal of Psychiatry, 151,* 1289–94.

Ortega, S.T. & Corzine, J. (1990). Socioeconomic status and mental disorders. In J.R. Greenley (Ed.), *Research in community and mental health: A research manual: Mental disorder in social context* (Vol. 6, pp. 149–82). Greenwich, CT.: JAI Press.

O'Toole, J., & Lawler, E.E., III. (2006). *The new American workplace.* New York, NY: Palgrave MacMillan.

Packer, G. (2003, November/December). The end of equality. *Mother Jones,* pp. 30–3.

Page, B.I., & Simmons, J.R. (2000). *What government can do: Dealing with poverty and inequality.* Chicago: University of Chicago Press.

Paglia, C. (2010, June 27). No sex please, we're middle class. *New York Times,* p. WK 12.

Pappas, G., Queen, S., Hadden, W., et al. (1993). The increasing disparity in mortality between socioeconomic groups in the United States, 1960 and 1986. *New England Journal of Medicine, 329,* 103–9.

Pardington, S. (2009, July 11). When a tuition hike feels like a win. *Oregonian,* pp. A1, A5

Paris, J. (1999). *Nature and nurture in psychiatry: A predisposition-stress model of mental disorders.* Washington, DC: American Psychiatric Press.

– (2008). *Prescriptions for the mind: A critical view of contemporary psychiatry.* New York, NY: Oxford University Press.

Parkin, F. (1979). *Marxism and class theory.* New York, NY: Columbia University Press.

Pearlin, L.I. (1982). The social contexts of stress. In L. Goldberger & S. Breznitz (Eds.), *Handbook of stress* (pp. 367–79). New York, NY: Free Press.

– (1983). Role strains and personal stress. In H.B. Kaplan (Ed.), *Psychosocial stress: Trends in theory and research* (pp. 3–32). New York, NY: Academic Press.

– (1989). The sociological study of stress. *Journal of Health and Social Behavior, 30,* 241–56

– (1999). Stress and mental health: A conceptual overview. In A.V. Horwitz & T.C. Scheid (Eds.), *A handbook for the study of mental health* (pp. 161–75). New York, NY: Cambridge University Press.

Pearlin, L.I., & Lieberman, M.A. (1979). Social sources of emotional distress. In R. Simmons (Ed.). *Research in Community & Mental Health* (pp. 217–48). Greenwich, CT: JAI Press.

Pearlin, L.I., Menaghan, E.G., Leiberman, M.A., et al. (1981). The stress process. *Journal of Health and Social Behavior, 22,* 337–56.

Pearlin, L.I., Schieman, S., Fazio, E.M., et al. (2005). Stress, health, and the life course: Some conceptual perspectives. *Journal of Health & Social Behavior, 46,* 205–19.

Pearlin, L.I., & Schooler, C. (1978). The structure of coping. *Journal of Health and Social Behavior, 19,* 2–21.

Peck, H.B. (1974). Psychiatric approaches to the impoverished and underprivileged. In G. Caplan (Ed.), *American handbook of psychiatry* (2nd ed., pp. 524–34). New York, NY: Basic Books.

Perrucci, R., & Wysong, E. (1999). *The new class society.* Lanham, MD: Rowman & Littlefield.

– (2003). *The new class society: Goodbye American dream?* (2nd ed.). Lanham, MD: Rowman & Littlefield.

Perry, M.J., & Albee, G.W. (1994). On 'The science of prevention.' *American Psychologist, 49,* 1087–8.

Phelps, E.S. (1997). *Rewarding work: How to restore participation and self-support to free enterprise.* Cambridge, MA: Harvard University Press.

Phillips, K. (2002). *Wealth and democracy: A political history of the American rich.* New York, NY: Broadway Books.

Pies, R. (2008, October 16). Redefining depression as mere sadness. *New York Times,* p. D5.

Piore, M.J. (1975). Notes for a theory of labor market stratification. In R.C. Edwards, M. Reich, & D.M. Gordon (Eds.), *Labor market segmentation* (pp. 125–50). Lexington, MA: Heath.

Power, C., & Hertzman, C. (1997). Social and biological pathways linking early life and adult disease. *British Medical Bulletin, 53,* 210–21.

Power, C., Hertzmann, C., Matthews, S., et al. (1997). Social differences in health: Life-cycle effects between ages 23 and 33 in the 1958 British birth cohort. *American Journal of Public Health, 87,* 1499–503.

Power, C., & Matthews, S. (1997). Origins of health inequalities in a national population sample. *Lancet, 350,* 1584–9.

Power, S. (2005, March 31). Chinese cars head to Europe. *Wall Street Journal,* p. A2.

Prilleltensky, I. (1989). Psychology and the status quo. *American Psychologist, 44,* 795–802.

– (1994). *The morals and politics of psychology.* Albany, NY: State University of New York Press.

– (1997). Values, assumptions, and practices: Assessing the moral implications of psychological discourse and action. *American Psychologist, 52,* 517–33.

Prilleltensky, I., & Nelson, G. (2002). *Doing psychology critically: Making a difference in diverse settings.* Basingstoke, UK: Palgrave MacMillan,

Putnam, R.D. (2000). *Bowling alone: The collapse and revival of American community.* New York, NY: Simon & Schuster.

Rabkin, J., & Struening, E. (1976). Life events, stress, and illness. *Science, 194,* 1013–20.

Rank, M.R. (2004). *One nation, underprivileged.* New York, NY: Oxford University Press.

Regier, D.A., Boyd, J.H., Burke, J.D., et al. (1988). One-month prevalence of mental disorder in the United States. *Archives of General Psychiatry, 45,* 977–86.

Regier, D.A., Narrow, W.E., Rae, D.S., et al. (1993). The de facto U.S. mental and addictive disorders service system: Epidemiologic Catchment Area prospective 1-year prevalence rates of disorders and services. *Archives of General Psychiatry, 50,* 85–94.

Reich, R. (1998, February 16). Broken faith: Why we need to renew the social contract. *Nation,* pp. 11–17.

– (2010). *Aftershock: The next economy and America's future.* New York, NY: Knopf.

Rewarding the wealthiest. (2000, October 5). *New York Times,* p. A30.

Richmond, R. (2004, January 12). It's 10 a.m. Do you know where your workers are? *Wall Street Journal,* pp. R1, R4.

Richters, J.E., & Hinshaw, S.P. (1999). The abduction of disorder in psychiatry. *Journal of Abnormal Psychology, 108,* 438–45.

Rifkin, J. (1995). *The end of work: The decline of the global labor force and the dawn of the post-market era.* New York, NY: Putnam.

Risch, N., Herrell, R., Lehner, T., et al. (2009) Interaction between the serotonin transporter gene (5-HTTLPR), stressful life events, and risk of depression. *Journal of the American Medical Association, 301,* 2462–71.

Roach, S.S. (2004, July 22). More jobs, worse work. *New York Times,* p. A23.

Roazen, P. (1974). *Freud and his followers.* New York, NY: New American Library.

Robins, L., Helzer, J.E., Weissman, M.M., et al. (1984). Lifetime prevalence of specific psychiatric disorders in three sites. *Archives of General Psychiatry, 41,* 949–58.

Rochlin, G.I. (1997). *Trapped in the net: The unanticipated consequences of computerization.* Princeton, NJ: Princeton University Press.

Rogot, E., Sorlie, P.D., & Johnson, N.J. (1992). Life expectancy by employment status, income, and education in the National Longitudinal Morbidity Study. *Public Health Reports, 107,* 457–62.

Rogow, A.A. (1970). *The psychiatrists.* New York, NY: Delta.

Roose, S.P., Glassman, A.H., & Seidman, S.N. (2001). Relationship between depression and other medical illnesses. *Journal of the American Medical Association, 286,* 1687–90.

Rosenbaum, J.F., Pollack, M.H., Otto, M.W., et al. (1997). Anxious patients. In N. Cassem (Ed.), *Massachusetts General Hospital handbook of general hospital psychiatry* (4th ed., pp. 173–210). St. Louis, MO: Mosby.

Ross, C.E., & Mirowsky. J. (2001). Neighborhood disadvantage, disorder, and health. *Journal of Health and Social Behavior, 42,* 258–76.

– (2009). Neighborhood disorder, subjective alienation, and distress. Journal of Health and Social Behavior, 50, 49–69.

Ross, C.E., & Wu, C-L. (1995). The links between education and health. *American Sociological Review, 60,* 719–45.

Ross, L. (1977). The intuitive psychologist and his shortcomings: Distortions in the attribution process. In L. Berkowitz (Ed.), *Advances in experimental social psychology* (Vol. 10, pp. 173–220). New York, NY: Academic Press.

Ross, N.A., Wolfson, M.C., Dunn, J.R., et al. (2000). Relation between income inequality and mortality in Canada and in the United States: Cross sectional assessment using census data and vital statistics. *British Medical Journal 320,* 898–902.

Russell, G. (2000). Anorexia nervosa. In M.G. Gelder, J.J. Lopez-Ibor, & N.C. Andreason (Eds.), *New Oxford textbook of psychiatry* (pp. 835–55). Oxford: Oxford University Press.

Sacks, P. (2007). *Tearing down the gates: Confronting the class divide in American education.* Berkeley, CA: University of California Press.

Sadler, J.Z. (1999). Horsefeathers: A commentary on 'Evolutionary versus prototype analyses of the concept of disorder.' *Journal of Abnormal Psychology, 108,* 433–7.

Sanger, D.E. (1990, March 19). Tokyo tries to find out if 'salarymen' are working themselves to death. *New York Times,* p. A8.

Sapolsky, R.M. (2004). *Why zebras don't get ulcers* (3rd ed.). New York, NY: Henry Holt.

Sarbin, T.R., & Allen, V.L. (1968). Role theory. In G. Lindzey & E. Aronson (Eds.), *Handbook of social psychology; Vol. 1. Historical introduction/systematic positions* (2nd ed., pp. 488–567). Reading, MA: Addison-Wesley.

Scase, R. (1992). *Class*. Minneapolis, MN: University of Minnesota Press.

Scheiber, N. (2008, July 6). What safety net? [Review of the book *High Wire: The precarious financial lives of American families*]. *New York Times Book Review*, p. 14.

Scheid, T.L., & Brown, T.N. (Eds.). (2010). *A handbook for the study of mental illness: Social contexts, theories, and systems* (2nd ed.). New York, NY: Cambridge University Press.

Schnall, P.L., Landsbergis, P.A., & Baker, D. (1994). Job strain and cardiovascular disease. *Annual Review of Public Health, 15*, 381–411.

Schofield, W. (1964). *Psychotherapy: The purchase of friendship*. Englewood Cliffs, NJ: Prentice-Hall.

Schor, J.B. (1991). *The overworked American: The unexpected decline of leisure*. New York, NY: Basic Books.

Schumpeter, J. (2010, May 22). Overstretched: Many people who kept their jobs are working too hard. What can companies do about it? *Economist*, p. 72.

Shapiro, T.M., Meschede, T., & Sullivan, L. (2010, May). *The racial wealth gap increases fourfold*. Institute on Assets and Social Policy: Research and Policy Brief.

Sharfstein, S.S. (2005). Big pharma and American psychiatry: The good, the bad, and the ugly. *Psychiatric News, 40*, 3.

Shierholz, H. (2010, July 10). Job seekers still face intolerable odds. Economic Policy Institute. Retrieved from http://www.epi.org/publications/entry/job_seekers_still_face_intolerable_odds

Shulman, B. (2003). *The betrayal of work*. New York, NY: New Press.

Siegrist, J. (1996). Adverse health effects of high effort-low reward conditions at work. *Journal of Occupational Health Psychology, 1*, 27–43.

Siegrist, J., Siegrist, K., & Weber, I. (1986). Sociological concepts in the etiology of chronic disease: The case of ischemic heart disease. *Social Science and Medicine, 22*, 247–53.

Siegrist, J., & Theorell, T. (2006). Socio-economic position and health: The role of work and employment. In J. Siegrist & M. Marmot (Eds.), *Social inequalities in health: New evidence and policy implications* (pp. 73–100). Oxford: Oxford University Press.

Silver, H., Feldman, P., Bilker, W., et al. (2003). Working memory deficit as a core neuropsychological dysfunction in schizophrenia. *American Journal of Psychiatry, 160*, 1809–16.

Simonsick, E.M., Wallace, R.B., Blazer, D.G., et al. (1995). Depressive symptomatology and hypertension-associated morbidity and mortality in older adults. *Psychosomatic Medicine, 50,* 427–35.

Singh, G.K., & Siahpush, M. (2006). Widening socioeconomic inequalities in US life expectancy, 1980–2000. *International Journal of Epidemiology, 35,* 969–79.

Smith, L. (2005). Psychotherapy, classism, and the poor: Conspicuous by their absence. *American Psychologist, 60,* 687–96.

Smith, M.J., Carayon, P., Sanders, K.J., et al. (1992). Employee stress and health complaints in jobs with and without electronic performance monitoring. *Applied Ergonomics, 23,* 17–27.

Snowdon, D.A., Ostwald, S.K., & Kane, R.L. (1989). Education, survival, and independence in elderly Catholic sisters, 1936–1988. *American Journal of Epidemiology, 130,* 999–1012.

Sorlie, P.D., Backlund, E., & Keller, J.B. (1995). US mortality by economic, demographic, and social characteristics: The National Longitudinal Mortality Study. *American Journal of Public Health, 85,* 949–56.

Spitzer, R.L. (1991). An outsider-insider's views about revising the DSMs. *Journal of Abnormal Psychology, 100,* 294–6.

Stansfeld, S.A. (1999). Social support and social cohesion. In M. Marmot & R.G. Wilkinson (Eds.), *Social determinants of health* (pp. 155–78). Oxford: Oxford University Press.

Stansfeld, S.A., Fuhrer, R., Shipley, M.J., et al. (1999). Work characteristics predict psychiatric disorder: Prospective results from the Whitehall II study. *Occupational and Environmental Medicine, 56,* 302–7.

Stansfeld, S.A., Head, J., Fuhrer, R., Wardle, J., & Cattell, V. (2003). Social inequalities in depressive symptoms and physical functioning in the Whitehall II study: Exploring a common cause explanation. *Journal of Epidemiology and Public Health 57,* 361–7.

Stansfeld, S.A., Head, J., & Marmot, M.G. (1998). Explaining social class differences in depression and well-being. *Social Psychiatry & Psychiatric Epidemiology, 33,* 1–9.

Storck, L.E. (2002).Hearing, speaking, and doing class-aware psychotherapy: A group-analytic approach. *Group Analysis, 35,* 437–46.

Streeck,W., & Heinze, R. (1999, May 10). An arbeit fehlt es nicht [There is no lack of work]. *Der Spiegel,* pp. 38–45.

Subramanian, S.V., & Kawachi, I. (2004). Income inequality and health: What have we learned so far? *Epidemiologic Reviews, 26,* 78–91.

Substance Abuse and Mental Health Services Administration (2010). *Results from the 2009 national survey on drug use and health: Mental health findings*

(Office of Applied Studies, NSDUH Series H-39, HHS Publication No. SMA 10–4609). Rockville, MD.

Swartz, M., Blazer, D., George, L., et al. (1990). Estimating the prevalence of borderline personality disorder in the community: Associations with demographic factors. *British Journal of Psychiatry, 142,* 238–46.

Syme, S.L. (1989). Control and health: A personal perspective. In A. Steptoe & A. Appels (Eds.), *Stress, personal control and health* (pp. 3–18). Chichester, UK: Wiley.

Tangri, R. (2003). *Stress costs, stress cures.* Victoria, BC: Trafford.

Tausig, M., Michello, J., & Subedi, S. (2004*). A sociology of mental illness* (2nd ed.). Saddle River, NJ: Pearson Prentice Hall.

Taylor, M. (2010, August 15). Academic bankruptcy. *New York Times,* p. WK 10.

Taylor, P., Funk, C., & Craighill, P. (2006). Labor Day 2006: Public says American work life is worsening, but most workers remain satisfied with their jobs. Pew Research Center. Retrieved from http://pewresearch.org/pubs/318/american-work-life-is-worsening-but-most-workers-still-content

Their fair share. (2008, July 21). *Wall Street Journal,* p. A12.

Thoits, P.A. (1995). Stress, coping, and social support processes: Where are we? What next? *Journal of Health and Social Behavior, Extra Issue,* 53–79.

– (2006). Personal agency in the stress process. *Journal of Health and Social Behavior, 47,* 309–23.

– (2010). Sociological approaches to mental illness. In T.L. Scheid & T.N. Brown (Eds.), *A handbook for the study of mental health: Social contexts, theories, and systems* (2nd ed., pp.106–24). New York, NY: Cambridge University Press.

Tilly, C. (1998). *Durable inequality.* Berkeley, CA: University of California Press.

Toporek, R.L., Gerstein, L.H., Fouad, N.D., et al. (2006). *Handbook for social justice in consulting psychology: Leadership, vision, and action.* Thousand Oaks, CA: Sage.

Torrey, E.F. (1999). Epidemiological comparison of schizophrenia and bipolar disorder. *Schizophrenia Research, 39,* 101–6.

Tsuang, M.T., Faraone, S.V., & Green, A.I. (1999). Schizophrenia and other psychotic disorders. In A.M. Nicholi, Jr. (Ed.), *The Harvard guide to psychiatry* (3rd ed., pp. 240–80). Cambridge, MA: Belknap.

Turner, R.J., & Avison, W.R. (2003). Status variations in stress exposure: Implications for the interpretation of research on race, socioeconomic status, and gender. *Journal of Health and Social Behavior, 44,* 488–505.

Turner, R.J., & Brown, R.L. (2010). Social support and mental health. In T.L. Scheid & T.N. Brown (Eds.), *A handbook for the study of mental health: Social contexts, theories, and systems* (2nd ed., pp. 200–12). New York, NY: Cambridge University Press.

Turner, R.J., & Lloyd, D.A. (1999). The stress process and the social distribution of depression. *Journal of Health and Social Behavior, 40,* 374–404.

Turner, R.J., Wheaton, B., & Lloyd, D.A. (1995). The epidemiology of social stress. *American Sociological Review, 60,* 104–25.

Uchitelle, L. (1993, January 31). Staunching the loss of good jobs. *New York Times,* pp. F1, F6.

– (2006). *The disposable American: Layoffs and their consequences.* New York, NY: Knopf

Umberson, D. (1987). Family status and health behaviors: Social control as a dimension of social integration. *Journal of Health and Social Behavior, 28,* 306–19.

'Upper Bound,' (2010, April 17). *Economist,* pp. 29–30.

U.S. Census Bureau (n.d.a). *Historical income tables: Households,* table H-8. Retrieved from http://www.census.gov/hhes/www/income/data/historical/household/index.html.

– (n.d.b.). *Historical income tables; Households,* Table H-3. Retrieved from http://www.census.gov/hhes/www/income/data/historical/household/index.html

U.S. Department of Education, National Center of Education Statistics. (2002). *Coming of age in the 1990s: The eighth-grade class of 1988, 12 years later* [NCES 2002–321]. Washington, DC: U.S. Government Printing Office.

U.S. Department of Health & Human Services. (2008). *The 2008 HHS poverty guidelines.* Retrieved from http://aspe.hhs.gov/POVERTY/08poverty.shtml

– (2009). *The 2009 HHS poverty guidelines* Retrieved from http://aspe.hhs.gov/poverty/09poverty.shtml

U.S. Department of Labor, Bureau of Labor Statistics (2009). *May 2009 national occupational employment and wage estimates United States.* Retrieved from http://www.bls.gov/oes/current/oes_nat.htm

U.S. Department of Labor, Bureau of Labor Statistics (2010). *Labor force statistics from the Current Population Survey.* Retrieved from http://data.bls.gov/PDQ/servlet/SurveyOutputServlet?request_action=wh&graph_name=LN_cpsbref3

U.S. minimum wage earners fall behind. (2003, October 24). *Oregonian,* p. B1.

Vaughn, C.E., & Leff, J. (1976). The influence of family and social factors on the course of psychiatric illness: A comparison of schizophrenic and depressed neurotic patients. *British Journal of Psychiatry, 129,* 125–37.

Wadsworth, M.E.J. (1991). Serious illness and childhood and its association with later-life achievement. In R.G. Wilkinson (Ed.), *Class and health* (pp. 50–74). London: Tavistock.

Waitzkin, H. (1991). *The politics of medical encounters: How patients and doctors deal with social problems.* New Haven, CT: Yale University Press.

Wakefield, J.C. (1992). The concept of mental disorder: On the boundary between biological facts and social values. *American Psychologist, 47,* 373–88.

Wakefield, J.C., Schmitz, M.F., First, M.B., et al. (2007). Extending the bereavement exclusion for major depression to other losses: Evidence from the National Comorbidity Survey. *Archives of General Psychiatry, 64,* 433–40.

Warner, R. (2004). *Recovery from schizophrenia* (3rd ed.). Hove, UK: Brunner-Routledge.

Warren, E. (2007). The vanishing middle class. In J. Edwards, M. Crain, & A.L. Kalleberg (Eds.), *Ending poverty: How to restore the American dream* (pp. 38–52). New York, NY: New Press.

Warren, E., & Tyagi, A.W. (2003). *The two income trap: Why middle-class mothers and fathers are going broke.* New York, NY: Basic Books.

Wheaton, B. (1997). The nature of chronic stress. In B.H. Gottlieb (Ed.), *Coping with chronic stress* (pp. 43–73). New York, NY: Plenum.

– (1999). The nature of stressors. In A.V. Horwitz & T.C. Scheid (Eds.), *A handbook for the study of mental health* (pp. 176–97). New York, NY: Cambridge University Press.

Wheaton, B., & Montazer, S. (2010). Stressors, stress, and distress. In T.L. Scheid & T.N. Brown (Eds.), *A handbook for the study of mental health: Social contexts, theories, and systems* (2nd ed., pp. 171–99). New York, NY: Cambridge University Press.

Where the jobs are. (2009, July 24). *New York Times,* p. A18.

White, W.A. (1924). *Outlines of psychiatry,* (10th ed.). Washington, DC: Nervous and Mental Disease Publishing.

Why business is bad for your health. (2004). *Lancet, 363,* p. 1173.

Wilkinson, R., & Pickett, K. (2009). *The spirit level: Why more equal societies almost always do better.* London: Allen Lane.

Wilkinson, R.G. (1996). *Unhealthy societies: The afflictions of inequality.* London: Routledge.

Williams, S.J. (1998). 'Capitalising' on emotions? Rethinking the inequalities in health debate. *Sociology, 32,* 121–39.

Wittchen, H.U., Zhao, S., Kessler, R.C., et al. (1994). DSM-III generalized anxiety disorder in the National Comorbidity Study. *Archives of General Psychiatry, 51,* 355–64.

Wolf, C. (2000). Globalization: Meaning and measurement. *Critical Review, 14,* 1–10.

Wood, D. (2003). Effect of child and family poverty on child health in the United States. *Pediatrics, 112 (Part 2),* 707–15.

Work rises, leisure drops. (1992, February 17). *New York Times*, p. A7.

World labour report 1993. (1993). Geneva: International Labour Office, pp. 65, 70.

Wright, E.O. (1997). *Class counts: Student edition.* Cambridge: Cambridge University Press.

– (2008). Logics of class analysis. In A. Lareau & D. Conley (Eds.), *Social Class: How does it work?* (pp. 329–49). New York, NY: Russell Sage.

– (2009). Understanding class. *New Left Review, 60,* pp. 101–16.

Wysong, E., & Perrucci, R. (2007). Organizations, resources, and class analysis: The distributional model and the US class structure. *Critical Sociology, 33,* 211–46.

Yalom, I.D. (2002). *The gift of therapy.* New York, NY: HarperCollins.

Zweig, M. (2000). *The working class majority.* Ithaca, NY: ILR Press (of Cornell University Press).

Index

Page numbers in *italics* indicate figures and tables.